13 churches will be attacked.

Today.

Last year there were over 5000 incidents* of burglary or vandalism against Anglican churches, so clearly there is a pressing need for the best insurance.

With over 100 years experience of serving the Church, Ecclesiastical offers extensive cover combined with invaluable support and advice. For instance, we sponsor regular security seminars around the country.

Our policies are competitive and flexible and our attitude, open, honest and erring on the generous. With Ecclesiastical there'll be no nasty gaps in the cover when you need to claim.

Ecclesiastical are proud to donate available profits to the Church and charities. For further information call 0345 77 33 22.

CHURCH PULPIT

YEAR BOOK

A Complete set of Expository Outlines for the Sundays of the Year, also for Saints' Days, & Special Occasions

1999

CHANSITOR PUBLICATIONS

Copyright © Chansitor Publications, 1998

Published 1998 by Chansitor Publications,
a wholly owned imprint of Hymns
Ancient and Modern Limited, St Mary's
Works, St Mary's Plain, Norwich,
Norfolk, NR3 3BH

ISBN 1-85175-166-1

Typeset by Rowland Phototypesetting Limited,
Bury St Edmunds, Suffolk
Printed in Great Britain by
St Edmundsbury Press Limited, Bury St Edmunds, Suffolk

Preface

Lambeth at Canterbury

From outside, the Lambeth Conference might well have appeared quaintly comic – all those purple cassocks and shepherds' crooks! But there was certainly lively and strong debate going on: burning issues being tackled with very real seriousness.

Priorities

Just what are the most important issues? That in itself is a controversial question. For some – mostly American or British – it was sexual morality, whether from the vociferous 'gay rights' angle or the implacably clear-cut traditional aspect. The strength of conviction on both sides indicates that a simplistic judgement either way will not do; but the right course between Bible principle and new understandings is not precisely nor definitely clear.

Meanwhile bishops from Africa, Asia and Latin America are aghast at these preoccupations, whilst they daily see the effects of poverty, disease, illiteracy, and the crippling burden of international debt crushing the lives of millions. 'Did not Christ come to bring good news to the poor?' seems their message to us. They see, too, a hunger for God, not just for food for the body.

Authority

The Archbishop of Canterbury's address made very clear that the Anglican view of authority is not 'monarchical' or hierarchical, but dispersed through the whole body of the Church. No centralized power structure has a monopoly on God's truth. But what he did say is that to cherish and celebrate our diversity and differences does not mean a vague and woolly 'anything goes' approach. 'There are boundaries to our faith and morals which we cross at our peril. We affirm that the Scriptures are uniquely inspired witness to divine revelation, and the primary norm for Christian faith and life.'

Understanding

At the same time it is important to recognize that the Scriptures must be translated, read and understood, in a continuing process of interpretation and interplay of Bible, tradition and reason. The Church must try to be obedient not just to the written letter, but to the living Word and the Spirit. Dr Carey said, 'The challenge is to bring to the world an authoritative vision of the God of love and justice.'

Our own small contribution to church life and thought, the *Church Pulpit Year Book*, is dedicated, as ever, with respect and admiration to our Parish Clergy, to Non-Stipendiary Ministers, to Deacons and Readers – all busy people with more and more demands upon their time, energy and gifts – in the hope that the material in this book will be of help, week by week. Comments and suggestions are gladly received, also possible contributions for future editions.

Francis Stephens
Editor

CHANSITOR PUBLICATIONS

Where in the World do you go for good Financial Advice?

We specialise in the Clergy Sector and understand the financial needs of Clergy men & women. We have established ourselves as the largest Independent Financial Advisers for the Clergy in England.

Travelling the length & breadth of the country, we meet with thousands of members of the clergy to discuss their financial affairs including tax efficiency, investments, mortgages, pensions & life assurance.

We have invested tens of millions of pounds for our clients using products from a wide range of top performing investment houses, including ethical investments.

If you would like a <u>free</u> consultation with one of our advisers, please telephone:-   **01476 560662**

RUSSELL PLAICE & PARTNERS - for financial peace of mind
70a Castlegate, Grantham, Lincs NG31 6SH

Regulated by the Personal Investment Authority
* Mortgages are not regulated by the Personal Investment Authority

Preliminary Note

For each Sunday of the year, *two* sermons are provided. The *first* is suggested for the 'Principal Service', assumed to be the main Eucharist, at which the readings will be from the New Lectionary (RCL, as authorized by the General Synod for use from Advent Sunday under GS 1161A). Similarly the *second* will be in most cases based upon the readings given under 'Second Service' – probably in most churches still Evensong. For Saints' Days and special occasions, one outline is provided, which can suit the Eucharist or other service as may be desired.

Please feel free to adapt or alter, to suit the needs of your particular parish or congregation; or to use the book as a quarry for themes and ideas.

Acknowledgements: The Editor gratefully acknowledges permission from the Central Board of Finance of the Church of England, to reproduce material from *The Christian Year*; *The Alternative Service Book 1980*; *Lent, Holy Week and Easter*; *The Promise of His Glory*; *Patterns for Worship*.

Thanks are also due to many other sources, individuals and schools of thought, for help and material. The Editor trusts that the use of such material will be forgivingly regarded as a small aid to the advancement of the Kingdom. Thanks are due to The Revd Tom Devonshire Jones, The Revd Dr John Thewlis, The Revd John Ovenden, The Revd Joanna Yates, The Revd Harold Stringer, The late Rt Revd Brian Masters, to The Revd Dr Joyce Critchlow for her many contributions, and to Gordon Knights of SCM-Canterbury Press.

Special thanks to my wife, Roma, for proof-reading and immense help in so many directions.

On the receiving end

The clergy are used to being on the receiving end. We take them our problems, we ask them to explain the inexplicable, we blame them for things we don't like about the church, and we expect them to behave like saints.

Small wonder that clergy sometimes wilt under the strain – a strain that can be greatly increased at times of personal crisis and financial hardship. Clergy stipends are not large and additional costs – such as education, removals, resettlement and child-minding (especially for a single person) – can be hard to afford. Without a helping hand debts may result and, although we can help with debts too, we would much rather come in before things get to that stage.

The Corporation was founded over 300 years ago to help Anglican clergy and their dependants in times of need. We offer a wide range of grants for the serving, the retired, widows and widowers, and for their dependent children. If you would like to know more, do please send for our Information Leaflet.

Our grants run at around £1,250,000 a year, and for clergy families at our 'receiving end' the benefits are beyond price. But there is always more to be done, for, sadly, the stresses under which our clergy live and work ever increase. And as their need grows, so the need grows for support from the rest of us.

Please help us to lighten their load, with a donation or covenant, or with a bequest.

Corporation of the Sons of the Clergy

Founded A.D. 1655

1 Dean Trench Street, Westminster, London SW1P 3HB. *Tel.* 0171– 799 3696. *Reg. Charity 207737*

CONTENTS

The readings are those approved in the General Synod of the Church of England, Report GS 1161A, and are those for Year A – the year of Matthew in the 3-year cycles of the Revised Common Lectionary (*RCL*), except where otherwise stated.

Ordinary time

SERMONS FOR SAINTS' DAYS and SPECIAL OCCASIONS

𝔖𝔈ℜ𝔐𝔒ℜ𝔖

FOR THE CHRISTIAN YEAR
(FOLLOWING RCL LECTIONARY)

Also sermons for special services

For full details please send a
self-addressed, stamped envelope to:

F W SERMONS,
Dept PY,
PO Box 28,
Barnstaple,
Devon,
EX31 2PU.

First Sunday of Advent *(Fourth Sunday before Christmas)* 29 November 1998 *Principal Service* **Watch!** Matthew 24:36–44

'Watch therefore, for you do not know on what day your Lord is coming.' Matthew 24:42 (RCL) or 'Now is the time to wake out of sleep: for now our salvation is nearer than when we first believed.' Romans 13:11 (ASB & RCL)

Expectancy!
The word 'Advent' means a coming, an arrival; and the theme of our Church Season of Advent is the coming of Christ into the world. All through these weeks we are in a mood of expectancy; an expectancy which has two different aspects. Firstly we think of the coming of Jesus as a babe at Christmas; then, on the other hand, we think of that mysterious event, a quite different coming, which we call the 'Second Advent'. So it is that all through the weeks of Advent we are in this special mood of expectancy. On one side of it, our expectations will be fulfilled when Christmas comes, and we are able to sing:

> *Christians awake! salute the happy morn*
> *Whereon the Saviour of the world was born.*

> *(NEH 24)*

But what can we say about that other expectation, that other Coming?

> *He will come again in glory*
> *to judge the living and the dead,*
> *and his kingdom will have no end.*

In the Nicene Creed the whole Christian world confesses its faith. These words stir our imaginations, and speak to what is very deep within us. God's victory was won upon the Cross; yet God's enemies are still strongly entrenched in their positions, and there are many battles still to fight. Our ancestors' expectation of the Lord's early return proved an illusion; from time to time events occurred which gave rise to hopes that the great day was at hand, but those hopes were always disappointed, as such hopes have been disappointed many times since.

Imagination

The promise of his coming was, for the early Christian teachers, a matter of profound conviction; but they speak variously, and sometimes obscurely, about the manner of that coming, in time and place, and of what is to follow. At first they had looked for it almost any day; but they were always disappointed. Yet, they did not give up the hope of another coming of Christ; God's victory was won, but it was yet to win. Both ideas are true – thus our Christian life becomes a tension between realization and expectation. After all, in our daily prayer we say, 'Thy kingdom come ... For thine is the kingdom, the power and the glory, for ever and ever.' The kingdom is still to come – and yet it is present, always; and so we have confidence in praying for its coming.

This may indeed be a paradox, but this tension has been, and is, a great strength to the Christian religion. For the early Church the coming of Christ was both present and future, both at once. That could not be said of any ordinary event in history; for the coming of Christ is an event that lies outside our system of time reckoning: it has no date. And so for the whole season of Advent, we can speak of the Coming of Christ, meaning both his birth as a child into the world a long time ago, the Millennium in fact, and also the unimaginable fullness of his coming again, in power and glory, in the future.

'Marana-tha' – 'Lord, come!'

There is a very simple prayer that has come down to us from the earliest days. It is in the Aramaic language, which was the native tongue of Jesus and his first disciples, and consists of two words only: *'Marana-tha!'* – 'Lord, come!' These words go back to Aramaic-speaking Jewish Christians, probably of the mother church at Jerusalem, the historians tell us, and are quoted by St Paul (in his first letter to the Corinthians, 16:22)

The first Christians met together regularly, and shared a meal together; they made their memory vivid by repeating what he had said and done on that never-to-be-forgotten last supper. So it was that the facts of his life and death were more than a memory: they were a present experience. *'Marana-tha!'* bears witness to the spirit of tense expectancy that brought them together; they knew that a

Presence was there, unseen and unheard, but real: the Lord had come to them. 'He was known to them in the breaking of bread.'

And the more deeply they – and we – appreciate what is received, the more clearly they – and we – know that nothing on earth is complete – there is always more to hope for. Here then, in our act of worship, it is that we look for a key to the paradox of a coming of Christ which is past, present and future all in one; and for which we must be ready, for the Son of Man is coming at an hour we do not expect. 'Watch therefore, and be ready.'

PRAYER FOR THE COMING OF CHRIST

Almighty God,
you sent your Son to redeem the world,
and will send him again to be our judge.
May we so imitate him
in the humility and purity of his first coming,
that, when he comes again,
we may be ready to greet him
with joyful love and firm faith;
through the same Christ our Lord.

David Silk

First Sunday of Advent *Second Service*
Tribulation Matthew: 15–28

'False Christs and false prophets will arise, and show great signs and wonders, so as to lead astray, if possible, even the elect.' Matthew 24:24

Daniel

The gospel challenge, in Matthew's account, is to stay awake, to keep our minds aware, not to be caught out by events nor led astray by false information or propaganda. The ancient prophet and leader Daniel, about whom such wonderful stories and legends were carried down by tradition and by folk tales, is seen as foretelling sacrilege in the Temple – and not only false accusations and ideas, there, but fearful changes in weather and the seasons, with earthquakes and natural disasters, and such tribulations as have never been seen before (v. 21). But we are not to be led away from the truth, and certainly not from the love and the care of our Lord. The life and faith of the early Christians was imbued with a sense of tremendous hope. The same strong, clear, voices that assert the Cross and the Empty Tomb, also assert the wonder of the Coming in Glory. We cannot, we dare not, just ignore what is clearly a part – and a vital part, let us be quite clear – of the message of the early Church.

Living now

That the Day of the Lord comes in the great crises of history, is true enough. But there is far more than this in the belief, and the conception, that prophets down the ages have proclaimed. St Matthew tells us of the return of Christ at the end. When God's purpose is fulfilled here, that purpose which we see in Christ, then will come the End, and he will be all in all. We read in the Gospel of desolation and of tribulation; our Lord speaks of mounting evil before the end. But whatever takes place, of the final victory we have no doubt, since we know of the death and the resurrection of Christ. The final victory will be with the good, a glorious climax indeed.

The upward road

For some, the bold thinking of Teilhard de Chardin may be helpful – his vision of an evolutionary growth of the spirit, the whole universe developing and reaching out to its climax, in the Christ – the Alpha and Omega of all Creation. 'In its highest and most general sense, the doctrine of the Cross is that to which all human minds adhere who believe that the vast movement and agitation of human life opens onto a road which leads somewhere, and that that road climbs *upward*. Life has a term; therefore it imposes a particular direction, orientated, in fact, towards the highest possible spiritualization by means of the greatest possible effort. To admit that group of fundamental principles is already to range ourselves among the disciples – distant, perhaps, and implicit rather than explicit, but nevertheless real – of Christ crucified.' (*Le Milieu Divin*)

Second Sunday of Advent *(Third Sunday before Christmas)* 6 December *Principal Service*
He who comes! Matthew 3:1–12 (RCL)

'The one who comes after me is mightier than I.' Matthew 3:11 (RCL))

A strange preacher

We hear today how a very strange man, called John, astonished the people by his preaching. Strange he was in dress and appearance – he wore a rough cloak of camel hair, tied around him by a leather belt; his hair was long, and his whole style marked him out as a hermit of the desert. His sermons, too, were strange. Instead of trying to attract hearers, he repeatedly warned them, ran them down by telling them they were sinners and must reform their wicked ways. Careless of his own safety, he spoke out boldly against those in positions of power who did wrong. John made little of himself, but spoke in the highest terms of a great successor, close at hand, for whose coming they must prepare themselves.

A fresh start

As a symbol that his hearers were to make a fresh start, he plunged those who declared themselves repentant under the cleansing waters of the River Jordan, and because of this he was called 'The Baptist'. In spite of the inconvenience of making the trek to the edge of the desert, and in spite of the oddity of his dress and appearance, the power of his voice and his preaching brought great crowds to listen to him, and to take in his message.

Repentance was what the crowds heard from him most often; but repentance cannot be considered the true theme of his preaching. The message he had for the nation was the nearness of the coming of a Saviour and Deliverer – the hope that the Hebrew people were always looking forward to was actually very near.

'Christ is near'

The message of John the Baptist is repeated to us in our day – 'Christ is near!' In our New Testament readings, in our Prayer Books, in our hymns, this message is clear and is especially brought to us in Advent. John's words could be used often, to

5

describe the spread of the gospel; we read in the pages of history of brave people, men and women, who have carried the gospel for the first time to countries ignorant of Christ. It was a stage in a nation's history when it could truly be said that Christ was near; for us, we remember the mission of St Augustine to England, though other missionaries had taken the Good News to Wales, Scotland and Ireland. The message, alas, could become dulled and distorted, so the Reformation brought the Bible in the native languages; John Wesley's preaching meant a new start in many people's hearts; and today our churches are striving to reach out together to bring the love, the joy and the blessings of Christ to all our peoples.

Christ's coming
The Millennium should bring us to think how wonderful it was that our Lord should come to our tiny planet, our little world, as he did two thousand years ago, and how wonderful it is that in a different, but just as real, sense, he continues to come near both individuals and nations, in our time today. His call is still the same – 'Come to me, all who labour and are heavy laden [with sin and fear] and I will give you rest. Take my yoke upon you, and learn from me' (11:22,23).

King George the Sixth visited the city of Coventry immediately after it was almost destroyed by enemy action in the Second World War. As he walked among the ruins and destruction, and spoke to some of the homeless and distraught, an old woman called out, 'Thank God, your Majesty, that we have a king who will come to a place like this!'

Christ's coming to this world at the first Christmas, and his continued spiritual presence with us, brings confidence, courage and joy of heart, to his followers.

Second Sunday of Advent *Second Service*
Who are you? John 1:19–28
'I am a voice that cries in the wilderness, "Make a straight way for the Lord," as the prophet Isaiah said.' John 1:23

Time of crisis

John made his appearance at a time when decay had firmly set in, upon both the Jewish Church and the Jewish nation. The Jewish Kingdom had gone – it had kept its unity until the death of Herod the Great, but at his death, the Romans divided it into tetrarchies, each with a governor ruling only by the grace of the Roman Emperor. The sceptre – the power – had finally departed from Israel; the ancient glory of the land of David had gone. The historic Kingdom needed resuscitation, or replacement by a new and revivified one. A national leader was looked for, and was essential for the health and glory of the nation. There was a general feeling that the fullness of time had come. Religious life was in great need of reform, for it had become corrupt in both rule and administration. So it was that John came at the psychological moment.

A pioneer

John began his career as the pioneer of the Lord. It is plain from the Gospels that his ministry was one of preparation for the advent of the Messiah. The long-expected, deeply-looked-for, Prince of Peace must soon come; John's work was to prepare a smooth path for the Lord.

But it was not by force that John's mission was to be fulfilled. His vocation was to lift up his voice in warning, and as a summons to action. Isaiah had foretold that work; John had to work in the valleys of the depressed and despairing souls, bring down the mountains of conceit and pride, the crooked ways of sin, and the rough, uncouth ways of uncivilized nature.

John's mission was one to all people, to all classes, all types. His preaching was the preaching of penitence; and his baptism was a baptism of repentance – which means 'Stop! Think! Turn around; change your ways!' – and the symbol of that repentance is baptism.

Baptism was in use in those days amongst the Jews. When a Gentile became a proselyte, a convert, it was necessary to undergo cleansing, moral and ritual. John's baptism, then, points to the need for the Jews themselves to be cleansed, especially in view of the 'wrath to come' (Matthew 3:7).

Yet John clearly sees that he himself is only the fore-runner, the pointer to the One who is to come. For a short time the Baptist is, as it were, the axis upon which the whole course of events, the

7

destiny of the world, turns. He draws all together that has gone before, and points to Jesus, saying, 'Not me – but him!'

Advent
For us then, here John personifies the message of our Advent season, looking back to all that has gone before, then turning to herald what is yet to come. He gives his unqualified witness to the fact that Jesus is the Messiah, the Christ. John is the first to recognize in Jesus the Servant-Saviour – he who came 'to serve not to be served, and to give his life a ransom for many' (Mark 10:45).

This then is the witness of John the Baptist, to his Lord and Master. What is *our* witness to Jesus, the Christ, whose advent at Christmas we look forward to celebrating – and whose advent as Judge of the world, we must expect?

THE FORERUNNER

Almighty and everlasting God,
whose servant and prophet John the Baptist
bore witness to the truth
*   as a burning and shining lamp:*
Lead us to bear witness to your Son,
who is the eternal light and truth,
and lives and reigns with you and the Holy Spirit,
now and for ever.

Promise of His Glory

St Catts · 10:15 13/12/58

Third Sunday of Advent *(Second Sunday before Christmas)* 13 December *Principal Service* **A Preacher in Prison** Matthew 11:2–11
'John, who was in prison, heard what Christ was doing, and sent his own disciples with this message – "Are you the one who is to come, or are we to expect some other?"' *Matthew 11:2–3*

8

Prisoners

There are many prisoners mentioned in the Bible. Some were prisoners of war, as we would say; some were in prison for doing wrong – criminals, we would call them; others – many – were good men who were imprisoned because they would not do what they were ordered, since they believed that that conduct or action was against God's will; or they spoke out boldly for what they thought was right, or against what was wrong or evil.

An outstanding example of a man put in prison for speaking boldly on the side of right is John the Baptist. Openly, in his sermons to the crowds who followed him, he would condemn the scandalous behaviour of no less than King Herod, and his Queen, Herodias. She was originally the wife of Herod's brother, Philip, whom she left for Herod. Angry at the criticism, Herod had John arrested, and imprisoned in a lonely fortress beside the Dead Sea. Herodias probably played a part in this arrest through her influence with the King, and her own fury at the exposure of her illegitimate sexual conduct.

Execution

It must have been a strange and unpleasant contrast for John, in his filthy cell, compared with his early years in the countryside, and later in the desert and beside Jordan, preaching in the open air by the river banks, supported by his own disciples. But his enemy Herodias was not finished with him; by a trick which has provided musicians, dramatists and artists with subject matter, she induced Herod – perhaps somewhat against his will – to have John brought from prison and summarily executed.

Parallels today

There are parallels today for John's imprisonment and tragic end, in the lives of those Christians who live where the State authorities are hostile to Christ's religion. Some are imprisoned without trial; others, like John Baptist, have been executed. Even in countries where there is no direct religious persecution, to live as a follower of Christ amongst a predominantly non-Christian population has its own difficulties. Are we not fortunate in living where our loyalty to Christ is not put to the severe tests some of our brothers and sisters have to undergo? Let us be thankful to God that, while we do have our own problems to solve and difficulties to face as Christians in our own lives and works, these are insignificant beside those of other Christians past and present. And we must do all we can to help, by making our concern vocal, and applying whatever pressures are possible.

In prison
Doubts take the place of John's certainty, expectations are disappointed, and there may well be a sense of betrayal. 'Are you he that should come? Or should we look for someone else?' The forceful preacher, who was prepared to challenge the way even royalty behaved, now begins to feel uncertain about Jesus. Was it all in vain? Is this a foolish cause? Can we be mistaken in our hopes of the Messiah? Jesus tells John's followers – and through them, John himself – that the Messianic Kingdom is indeed being inaugurated, but by doing good rather than by sudden punishments or exotic manifestations. The start of God's Kingdom is marked by miracles of healing, and the preaching of the good news to the poor. Do we suffer from a fading faith? Do we find our hopes uncertain? What a good thing it would be if our people today paid more heed to John the Baptist's warnings against our sins, against our low standards of morality and honesty, against our fears and our selfishness, and our doubts. Above all, we must place our needs and our hopes and our fears in Our Saviour's presence, and receive from him the Spirit of Hope. Let us make this Advent Season our vision of Hope.

Third Sunday of Advent   *Second Service*
Bearing Witness   John 5:31–40
'You sent to John, and he has borne witness to the truth.' John 5:33

High praise
Our Lord praises John Baptist – 'He was a burning and shining lamp, and you were willing to rejoice, for a while, in his light' (v. 35). The following of John - the listening to his preaching, the taking in of his message – these were good actions, good decisions for the crowds who followed and listened to what John had to say, and then did their best to amend their lives in the light of his teaching. This is indeed praiseworthy, but Jesus points out that

we should aspire to the higher teaching of the Lord himself. 'The testimony which I have is greater than that of John' – for the Father has sent Christ his Son, and this is borne out by the Bible itself if we will but read it (v. 39). We must read with open minds, however, not with minds already set in some particular cast or way of thinking. That way, the set mind, makes it most likely that we will not find what we are looking for (v. 39).

Refusal

Sadly, the Lord says, 'You refuse to come to me that you may have life' (v. 40). How do such people treat Jesus when he comes to them? A certain number, like the citizens of Nazareth, violently disown him. This occurs, for instance, when those who have grown up under strong Christian influence turn their backs completely upon the Christian faith.

To others Jesus is a welcome guest; they take him to their hearts, seek for ways they can perform acts of service for him, and try to make their own lives more like his.

There is also a third group, and it is a large one. As well as all the people in Nazareth who were hostile to Our Lord when he returned to his native town and spoke in the synagogue, it is probable that there were some of the folk who regarded him with indifference, and others who perhaps had memories of him in his early youth, but lacked courage to take his side against the notabilities of the town. These people also have their counterparts in our present time. They are the members of churches who should be well aware of the calls Jesus makes upon his followers, but who either fail to hear them, or make no vigorous effort to respond to them in their own lives.

A danger . . .

There is a certain danger in having had what is often called 'a Christian background' over many years. We can all too easily fall into the trap of supposing that because we have such a background, we respond keenly to Christ's claims upon us – but in reality we take all too little notice of his calls, and merely suppose that our reputation does all that is needed or required. Jesus at Nazareth was, we may assume, full of hope that he would be well received, his message understood, and his call answered. He met with disappointment. Let us see that he is not disappointed when he comes to us.

Fourth Sunday of Advent *(Sunday next before Christmas)* 20 December *Principal Service*
The Birth of Jesus Matthew 1:18–25

'The birth of Jesus Christ took place in this way.' Matthew 1:18

New things ...

One of the great watchwords of Advent is 'Change'. The times are changing, new things are happening. A new world is coming – indeed, is already started. We are called to see God's hand and God's power in changes, and we are changing ourselves in accordance with God's actions and intentions. Old ideas, the old long-existing customs, have to change.

We see this through the eyes of St Joseph. He, we are told by the evangelists, was just a man, that is, a decent, God-fearing Hebrew, a man of piety and of honour. He was going to treat his unfortunately pregnant bride-to-be with decent consideration. There would be a quiet divorce, no fuss, no publicity. Here was the response of a civilized, pious man.

Then, as the vivid Bible idiom puts it, 'an angel of the Lord appeared to him in a dream.' We would say, probably, that Joseph became aware of God's will for his wife and for himself, and for the Child to be born.

Decisions

Joseph had to make a decision, as Mary had already had to make one. She accepted the annunciation wholeheartedly, with joy and trust. Joseph accepted, but we are not told that he was particularly joyful! Indeed, in the old legends and carols Joseph is depicted as more than a little uncertain, even grudging. Perhaps this is how it was – a natural enough reaction in the circumstances, surely. But the main thing is, Joseph went along with what he knew to be God's will. Whatever his inner feelings, he did his duty.

Doing what has to be done

Our Lord, much later on, in his missionary travels, brings out more than once the parable or story of the man who seems unwilling to do what is asked of him.

He even refuses. But then he does actually perform what is required.

We might think of him as a rather grumpy person, yet in fact he is doing his particular allotted task, and that is the important thing: God's will is being carried out. And Jesus praises him, the person who gets on with the job, without any song and dance, as we might say.

Changes
It was a big change in thinking and acting, required of a devout, conventional Hebrew man. It meant, no doubt, the abandoning of his own hopes and visions of what a son could be to him – a support in his old age; the family business carried on; life and the family continued in grandsons and granddaughters – a big change.

As big a change, almost, as for Mary. She accepted, in the first place, the possibility of her husband's rejection – a social disaster. In the second place, she was abandoning the dreams and hopes of a mother for a son who would live a safe, conventional life, industrious and respected, devout and well-thought-of, with wife and family to carry on the line.

Uncertainty – yet growth
How do we face up to changes and uncertainties in our lives? Only through change – which means growth – can we develop. As Newman put it, 'To change means to grow. To change often means to grow much.'

Whether we are like Mary, ready and open, indeed eager, to place ourselves in God's hands, or like Joseph, slower and less accepting, unwilling to go the whole way unless we can see the whole plan – and that we rarely can – let us make sure that we are working along with God, in trust and in faith. As the Post Communion Collect for today puts it, 'Fill us your servants with your grace, that in all things we may embrace your holy will', like Joseph, and then with Mary we can 'rejoice in your salvation'.

Fourth Sunday of Advent   *Second Service*
Behold, I am coming soon   Revelation 22:6–21
'I am the Alpha and the Omega, the first and the last, the beginning and the end.' Revelation 22:13 or, 'Hannah conceived and bore a son, and she called his name Samuel, for she said, "I have asked him of the Lord".' 1 Samuel 26

Children in the Bible

The coming birth of Jesus has been in our thoughts for the past weeks; the Bible has stories of the birth and childhood of other children, and some at least help us to appreciate the story of Mary and her Son. One such story is that of the birth and upbringing of the boy who became in due course the Prophet Samuel. (We can read all this in the First Book of Samuel.)

A woman named Hannah, married but so far without the desired blessing of a child, prayed for a son very earnestly in the tabernacle (or shrine as we would call it) at Shiloh. She promised that if her prayer was granted, she would dedicate the boy to God, for his whole lifetime.

It was the common practice of those times to speak prayers aloud; but, perhaps because of the private nature of her request, Hannah did not do this. Instead, although her lips moved as the words of her prayers passed through her mind, no words could be heard. Also, she showed visibly the extent of her agitation and distress – so much so that Eli the priest assumed she had been drinking. He lectured her on the evils of drink; she indignantly denied this charge, and Eli, by way of a kind of apology, gave her a pious blessing and commendation of her request to the grace of God.

In due time, Hannah's prayer was answered, and a son was born to her. With considerable generosity of spirit, she fulfilled the promise made to Eli that the boy would be dedicated to the Lord, and he was brought to the tabernacle at Shiloh. He grew up to be a great and wonderful prophet indeed.

Hannah and Mary

Hannah and the Blessed Virgin Mary, who is so much in our thoughts at Christmas, have often been compared. Although we know scarcely anything about Hannah, and much less than we would wish about Mary, yet we can piece enough together to make it worthwhile placing them side by side for a brief time.

Songs of praise

What they have most closely in common, is that their stories contain lovely songs of praise and thanksgiving for the wonderful events that take place in their lives. Indeed, Hannah's song is thought to have influenced Mary's in some respects. Perhaps it was from memories of Hannah's Song that the Magnificat was composed, beautiful and devotional as both are. Hannah prayed for a son and welcomed his birth with great joy; Mary did not ask God for a son, and we may be sure that the message of his impending birth came as a complete surprise.

Hannah, of her own free will, dedicated her son to God. Did she live to see him as a man of importance, a national and religious leader? Mary was not involved in giving up her child so young. Jesus grew up in the family home at Nazareth, and no doubt was helped by her training and influence. But when he became the great Teacher everyone flocked to hear, this set him more apart from her, and even led to family dissension (Mark 3:31–35), and in the end to the dreadful sorrow of the Cross.

Dedication

A lesson we can learn from the stories of Hannah in the Old Testament, and Mary the Blessed Virgin in the New, is that of dedication. Directed in the first place by his mother, Samuel gave his life to doing God's service. In a far more wonderful way, and to a far greater extent, Jesus did so too. For us then, in our far humbler spheres and lives, according to our feebler powers, we must do what we can to emulate them.

> O Lord Jesus Christ,
> before whose judgement seat we must all appear,
> and give account of all things done in the body:
> grant that, when the books are opened on that Day,
> we may stand with confidence, through your merits,
> for you are our blessed Saviour.

PHG, 40

Christmas Day   Friday 25 December
At Midnight or Early Eucharist   **Wonder**
Luke 2:1–14 (15–20)

'They made known the saying which had been told them, concerning this child; and all who heard it wondered at what the shepherds told them.'
Luke 2:18

Meanings

What does the word 'wonder' mean to you? The Christmas hymn speaks of 'A great and mighty wonder'; we speak of the 'wonder' of Christmastide, and how 'wonderful' it is to see the faces of the children light up, when the tree lights come on and the presents are revealed. 'Delight', 'surprise', something beyond what we expected! But there is another aspect, that of 'uncertainty', or question, even 'doubt'. We wonder what is going to happen to us; we wonder whether we have passed our exam. or got our pay rise. Both senses of 'wonder' fit into the Christmas scene.

Strange events

Imagine what the parents of Jesus went through. There were the angelic messages – dreams, perhaps we would say, but dreams with very important results on the lives of Mary and Joseph. There was that long journey to Bethlehem, hard for a pregnant mother; the birth itself in far from ideal conditions – a stable, draughty, smelly – but what a delight after all! Then the visitors – shepherds, hot-foot and panting, with their stories of angels, visions, messages. 'All who heard it wondered at what the shepherds told them.'

Yes, they were astonished, and no one questioned the shepherds' account of what had happened. But also the wondering is in the other sense – what is going to happen next? What is the future for this child? What is the future for themselves? What is the future for us?

Futures

So at Christmas we rejoice with the carols, the holly and the trees, the presents and the gathering of the family, the joyful services, the happy faces of the children. Yet we must also be aware of questions for the future. Think of what is going on. Already the Wise Men are nearing Jerusalem, led by their star; soon they will be at Herod's court, and having heard them, the cruel and frightened king will be planning the massacre that he believes will make sure there is no threat to his throne and his power.

It was soon indeed after the joy of Christmas, the coming of the Child, that there was to come the brutality and sorrow of a callous act that would leave so many mothers desolate, so many families bereft. The first Christmas was to be, for many, the last Christmas.

16

Our own time

In our own time we look ahead at uncertainties. The constant violence and brutality, the killings in Serbia and Albania, the terrible violence in Africa between rival tribes, and the murder of innocent people in Algeria. All this adds up to an outlook, in so many places, which no one can say is settled or certain.

Yet there is one great certainty – it was into just the same kind of world as our own, full of crises and problems, anger and violence, that the Lord chose to be born. In full knowledge he took the step of coming to our uncertain planet, our all-too-easily-upset little earth, our tiny life-boat floating in the vastness of inter-stellar space. It was certainly not into any kind of certain future that Jesus was born, nor that he grew up in, nor in which he began his mighty work of reconciliation.

Joy

Out of sorrow comes joy: the sense of wonder at the crib contains in itself the shadow of sorrows to come. Yet out of those sorrows comes the final joy. In the Birth we see foreshadowed the Death; yet also foreshadowed is the Triumph, the New and Risen Life, the Saviour.

'Behold I bring you good news of a great joy; to you is born today the Saviour, who is Christ the Lord!' And so our wonder is swept up into joy, and with the angels we say, 'Glory to God in the highest, and on earth peace among those in whom he is well pleased!'

Christmas Day   *In the day: Principal Service*
Peace   Luke 2:1–14

'To us a child is born, to us a son is given; and his name will be called the Prince of Peace' Isaiah 9:6; 'Glory to God in the highest, and on earth peace.' Luke 2:14

The birth

Surely there is no one, even the most sceptical and hardened, who will not be moved by the tenderness and simplicity of the Christmas story? Its central point – the birth of a child.

Here we all begin, do we not – the miracle of a new life. This birth could hardly be simpler, attended by no pomp or ceremony; far from it, in fact. A last-minute refuge, more by luck than preparation, is found for the Palestinian girl, in the straw and smells of the stable; the new-born child is placed in no stable or cot, but an animal feeding trough is pushed along to hold him. The Holy Family had no welcome, no room, no one took any special notice at the time. The inn-keeper was busy with the extra crowds of visitors, come for the census, we are told; Joseph and perhaps some country kitchen-maid were all who cared for Mary and her son.

Yes, it is a human story, reflecting all too clearly the human stories of refugees, exiles, displaced persons we hear about today. And yet, it is the glorious incarnation of God's eternal Son, here on this tiny planet, away on the edge of the incredibly vast universe, so vast that we find it impossible to comprehend.

Incarnation

Our celebration today is not merely a rejoicing at the birth of a child, nor even over birth and new life, great and wonderful though these things are. No, we are rejoicing at the Incarnation of the Son of God.

To the human mother Mary the gift of a human son; but to humanity the gift of God's only-begotten Son, 'that we might live through him' (1 John 4:9). If that is not true, the Bethlehem story is nothing but a pretty tale, and we are worse off than ever. But St John tells us, 'To all who received him, who believed in his name, he gave power to become children of God' (John 1:12). Christmas tells us that God intervened in human affairs by sending his Son to live as Man, and as Man to redeem mankind.

A strange and wonderful story; yet if we believe that God is love, a story that makes sense and one that we can accept, with joy and thanksgiving.

Not very far

The shepherds came to the stable and knelt to the Mother and Child. Alas, not like their simple faith, in our times we prefer to worship and kneel at almost any other shrine, rather than at the shrine of the Saviour. Nationalism, materialism, all the other 'isms' that we are told will lead us – scientific progress, pseudo 'religions'

18

from far and near; and perhaps saddest of all, mere ignorance, blindness and inertia.

'He came to his own, and his own people received him not' (John 1:11). Yet above Bethlehem the star still shines, if we will but see it; and the voices of the angels still ring round the world, if we will but hear them. Bethlehem is not far; to advance, we must first go back to Bethlehem and kneel with the shepherds, at the manger.

Here is the start of our journey, a journey with Christ through our lives, meeting Calvary, finding the empty tomb, knowing the glories and receiving the gifts, and finally – God willing – reaching the City of God.

Christmas Day   *Second Service*   The Name of Jesus   Philippians 2:1–11

'At the name of Jesus every knee should bow – in heaven, on earth, and in the depths – and every tongue confess "Jesus Christ is Lord" to the glory of God the Father.' Philippians 2:11

The Christian year

The Christian year did not take its full shape until hundreds of years after St Paul wrote this letter to the Christians at Philippi. Yet here he gives us what might be called a thumb-nail sketch of the important points of the Christian year, directing our thoughts to the great events in the Lord's life, those we commemorate on Christmas Day, Good Friday, Easter Day, and Ascension Day.

St Paul reminds his friends and converts at Philippi how our Lord, the Son of God, of his own free will became man, which is the great event we celebrate at Christmas. In his life, Jesus strove to make God known as a God of love; day by day the Lord tried to bring the people of his time to understand the real nature of the Father. After all too short a time, his enemies dragged him before the Romans, and his life was sacrificed for our sakes. He died upon the Cross to save us from our sins. This supreme sacrifice is what we remember and think upon on Good Friday.

From Our Lord's death, St Paul passes on quickly to the

Resurrection, the victory over death; and then the final triumph of Christ: his return to his heavenly Father. These are the events we celebrate on Easter Day and Ascension Day respectively.

The incarnation

In the passage which we have heard read (Philippians 2:5–11) Paul sets before us briefly and clearly who Jesus is, and what he has done for us. A theologian sums up: 'This passage is one of the chief scriptural foundations of the doctrine of the Incarnation. It brings out the truths of the deity and the humanity of our Lord.'

Many hymns have been written about the Name of Jesus, such as 'At the Name of Jesus' and 'How sweet the Name of Jesus sounds, in a believer's ear!' In some cases the authors had this passage of St Paul's writings in mind, and we should be clear that Paul was thinking chiefly of the title 'Lord' as showing his belief in the divine nature of Christ. The first Christians used this title as proclaiming their faith in Jesus – 'Jesus is Lord'. So today we thank God the Father for what he has done, in bringing his Son to us as Lord and Redeemer. And although he is the Son of God, Jesus humbles himself to become human. 'The divine nature was his from the first, yet he did not think to snatch at equality with God, but made himself nothing, assuming the nature of a slave' (Philippians 2:6–8)

Humility

Jesus was willing to accept the limitations of our humanity 'for the sake of us and for our salvation.' The Apostle holds up this quality of the Lord's earthly life for our encouragement; indeed it is a virtue which lies at the foundation of the Christian character. We need to know not only the pattern of human life as the Creator willed it, but also of our fallen nature. This will show itself in our acknowledgement of our shortcomings and of sin, so that we will cry to God 'I am not worthy that thou shouldst come under my roof.'

A deeper dependence on God leads on to a deeper knowledge of him, and to a greater hope in him. In all this, Our Lord is our pattern. Let us take this as our rule not only at this Christmas, but in all the New Year, and indeed towards the Millennium, and in all our life ahead. We will learn how much God will help us to attain that to which he has called us.

Eternal God,
whose only Son shares your glory
and yet was born in human flesh of the Virgin Mary:
strengthen us in our proclaiming and witnessing,
that we may be unharmed in conflict
and come to everlasting joy;
through Jesus Christ our Lord.

PHG, 59

First Sunday of Christmas   27 December
Principal Service   **Bitter Sorrow**
Matthew 2:13–23

'Then was fulfilled what was spoken by the prophet Jeremiah:

> *"A voice was heard in Ramah,*
> *wailing and loud lamentation,*
> *Rachel weeping for her children."*

Matthew 2:18

Innocent suffering
Herod, a savage and morose monster of iniquity, was determined that there would be no possible rival to his dynasty. When he heard from the Wise Men about the birth of a child who would become King of the Jews, Herod ordered the massacre of all the male children in Bethlehem and that region, two years old or less. Only a cruel and perverted mind could have made such a decision – the birth of the Christ was to lead to the slaughter of the Innocents.

Here is the kind of action which happens in a world in which there is evil. We can think of the most horrible acts that history records. There is the slaughter of Jews under Hitler, when millions of Hebrews, men, women and innocent children, were thrust into the gas chambers and murdered. We can think of the murders in Africa in our own days, the mass killing of members of one tribe – Tutus – by members of another, their neighbours. There is the dreadful murder of Slovenes and Croatians in the Danubian areas.

And the most cruel and brutal orgies of throat-cutting, decapi-
tation, rape and gunning-down of Algerians, including young
girls, and babies – anyone thought to be in any way not conforming
to Islamic fundamentalism is marked for torture and death.

On all sides we see the suffering of the innocent, in this age of
violence and brutality. Even when the outward forms of government are democratic, appearances can be sometimes deceptive.

The Church and tyranny

Whenever she can do so, without failing in her responsibilities as
witness for truth and freedom and to aid the oppressed, the
Church is wise to avoid political confrontation. But when there is
injustice, brutality and cruelty, oppression of the weak, or where
national or racial hatreds are being stirred up, we must not allow
ourselves to be fobbed off by those who say 'Not the Church's
business'. The Church must devise ways to make it clear that she
– and therefore we – are on the side of the oppressed, the victims
of tyrants and tyranny.

Let us remember also that there are lesser tyrants and lesser
tyranny, all too often in our daily lives. The selfish person tyrannizes over those who have to cover his or her mistakes, give in to
whims, whether at work, at school or at home. We see too much
of bullying; all too often actual violence, sometimes damage to
property or the persons concerned. Threats of force easily make
the threatener a tyrant or worse. The lazy person, too, can make
him- or herself a tyrant or bully in the office, the workshop, the
home. The sharp-tongued gossip can be a tyrant in the village;
the petty official showing off his or her authority can be a tyrant
in the community. May the Lord deliver us from small tyrants,
and keep us from becoming such ourselves.

Tyranny of sin

The form of tyranny most easily forgotten is one that is common
to us all, the tyranny of sin. We have all experienced this tyrant's
power over us! In New Testament times, the men and women
completely in their owners' or masters' powers were the slaves.
'You were slaves,' St Paul writes to the Christians at Rome
(Romans 6:12–23). Some were freed, some were still slaves and
would remain so, others had never been slaves at all. St Paul
points to the greatest tyranny of all, the hold that sin can take

upon us – unless we seek freedom through following Jesus Christ our Lord. In him we can find true liberty.

First Sunday of Christmas   *Second Service*
The Father's House   Luke 2:41–52

'Jesus said to his parents, "How is that you sought me? Did you not know that I must be in my Father's house?"' Luke 2:49

The finding in the Temple

During our Lord's boyhood he took part in all the 'family' observances, the Sunday Sabbaths, the annual Passover Festival and all the rest of the religious calendar festivals and holy days. His first pilgrimage, however, was special. It coincided with his twelfth birthday, and it was a pilgrimage to Jerusalem. He would see and visit the holy places and in particular of course, the Temple. They did not go alone, but would have made up a family party, brothers and sisters, fathers and mothers, children of course being of age, uncles and aunts no doubt. A great and enjoyable religious outing.

Religious

Luke tells us the very first recorded words spoken by Jesus, a glimpse into the 'hidden years' of our Lord's earthly life. After this occasion the gospel story is silent about his words for another eighteen years. This incident gives us a clue to the working of Jesus' mind at this early and formative state. What a picture it gives of a devout home, a religious home, in which all was kept as demanded by the Law. Now on his first visit to Jerusalem, imagine how it would be to his alert, sensitive, enquiring and above all, devout, mind. We have to remember that he is now moving on towards manhood, and on the verge of adolescence. We can, as we read between the lines, judge where his interests were centred – his Father's House, the Temple.

Development

We are told how eagerly Christ listened to the learned rabbis of the Temple. He not only listened to their words, but asked them questions of such depth that they were surprised at his insight.

23

So eager was he in his quest for knowledge that he quite forgot the need to return home, regarding the Temple as his Father's House as naturally as he did the humble Nazareth home to which he ultimately returned. From this account, we gather that at this early stage in his development he had already concluded that he was chosen to serve in some great cause that would bring glory to God and blessings to humanity. Notice, too, how in this first recorded utterance he spoke of his Father – that word takes on a new meaning from this moment. Already the Son of the Father shines forth through the eyes and words of the Holy Child, and to the end of his days he will find nothing dearer than the Father's Name, nothing so urgent and inexorable as the Father's business.

Adolescence

Every normal and healthy adolescence has in it a resemblance to the adolescence of the Son of Man. There is an awakening and a broadening of intelligence; what was once accepted from parents is now questioned and examined. Things are looked at from new points of view; conclusions may be arrived at that differ from those of parents and teachers. There will be, as with Jesus, the hearing and asking and answering of questions. Now ideals are formed and followed with fervour. In later adolescence philosophic speculation and religious doubts appear in many minds; this may lead to cynicism or, on the other hand, may issue in a life fired by a lofty idealism and an enthusiasm to serve humanity and the world, in some far-reaching manner.

Promise

We need to receive young enquirers with sympathy and understanding. As their minds spread out and push into new fields, their idealism is not to be treated scornfully or lightly. Adolescent unsureness can easily be confused or even frustrated. Ideals and dreams should be respected, nurtured until they grow up to maturity; then they can be standards accepted as a guide for life. Christ confronted the perils that confront the life of a growing boy; yet we may be sure that in the home to which he returned with Mary and Joseph, he would be helped on his way. And he emerged from that background equipped and ready for the ministry of reconciliation, and the life of his Father's business, as the old phrase puts it. As Christians it is part of our duty to worship in our Father's house, but also, in our small way, to be about the Father's business.

Second Sunday of Christmas   3 January 1999
Principal Service   **The Word**
John 1: (1–9) 10–18

'The Word became flesh and dwelt among us, full of grace and truth; we have beheld his glory, glory as of the only Son from the Father' (John 1:14) or, 'To all who received him, who believed in his name, he gave power to become children of God' (John 1:12).

Children of God
We human beings in our time, and in our moods, are very variable creatures. The great playwright and poet, William Shakespeare, reminds us 'all the men and women . . . have their exits and their entrances . . . and one plays many parts' (*As You Like It*). We can be fierce, we can be stupid, or greedy, or obstinate – but we can also think and plan and dream. We are children of the great God, the maker of the universe; are we not made in his spiritual likeness?

Because we are God's children we ought to live like children of God in our relationships to others in the great family. How much do we care for our brothers and sisters? Do we recognize them as brothers and sisters, here in this town, this country, this continent, this little space vehicle Earth, in our tiny corner of the vast universe? Perhaps we don't like them, don't like their style, their funny languages, the way they carry on? Well, Christ thought them – and us – valuable enough to be born on earth for, worth dying for. He sought us out and set us free, as God's children, delivered from the dominion of darkness. Christ, the Word of God, the Light that cannot be overcome.

Light
God-created light, as St John the Baptist witnessed to, and which St John the Evangelist expounds as 'the true light that enlightens everyone', is the light that shines in the darkness, and darkness has not, cannot, overcome it.

We have light on our duty and upon our destiny, because Christ illuminates what life is really about, and who we really are, and what we may become. So it is that we must live a life of intelligent, not easily beaten, love and benevolence towards ourselves and towards all others.

From our recognition of Christ, the Word that became flesh, and our beliefs in his name, we are made children of God; therefore we are related as brothers and sisters to each other, all children of the light. Our life is not meaningless; we are created in love with a purpose of love. That love will, one day, show us the truth of our belief. 'All things will be reconciled through him and for him, everything in heaven and everything on earth' (Colossians 1:16)

Glory

All creations will sing together in an exultant song of joy and triumph, as the whole universe truly becomes, like the Word that created it, 'full of grace and truth'.

As Christians in a world which has become a village through technological progress, we must think of the whole world and not confine our thoughts and prayers to our own small region. As St John puts it, 'To all who received him, who believed in his name, he gave power to become children of God' (John 1:12). The whole world is now so closely linked that an event in one tiny corner can be seen and heard at once all over the globe.

Love

We need more than ever before the peace of Christ, that is, a peace founded on love for one another, on respect for one another. Love founded on the belief that we are all children of one God, respect for each other because we are all brothers and sisters of one another, through the fatherhood of that God. Only through God, with God and in God can true peace be made. As we listen to the song of the angels, God's Christmas wish for us – 'Peace on earth' – let us look into our own hearts, search our own souls, make first our peace with God. And then by word and example preach the Christmas message 'Glory to God', and, coupled with glory, 'Peace' – through forgiveness, love and goodwill.

Second Sunday of Christmas *Second Service*
Knowing God Colossians 1:1–14

'We have not ceased to pray for you, asking that you may be filled with the knowledge of his will in all spiritual wisdom and understanding, to lead a life worthy of the Lord, fully pleasing to him, bearing fruit in every good work, and increasing in the knowledge of God.' Colossians 9–11

Knowledge of God

The Apostle here used a Greek word for 'knowledge' which is intended to convey a stronger meaning than the ordinary noun, emphasizing the idea of concentration. So we may say that the knowledge of which the Apostle here writes, is a knowledge that has grasped the meaning of a word, and penetrated to the heart of it. In this case, God's Will – not with some reference to abstract ideas of truth and speculations, but referring to the moral and practical – the will of God and his desires for the behaviour and morality of our lives. We might say that there are many people who are willing to discuss God, to think and talk about him; but not many of them, we fear, are ready to try to get to know him. Yes, an interest in religion exists, often in some good measure, yet real religion is not the study of the subject, but the living of a life. There is a difference between 'knowledge of' and 'knowledge about' any thing, or any person.

Our friends

Indeed, looking at people we know or at least have an acquaintance with, we may know details such as employment, hobbies, home life, political views, interests, and so on. These are points about a person, but we do not have a knowledge of him or her in anything much of a personal or intimate way. Are they kind and considerate, what do they have going on in their minds? And so on. Yet there are others, maybe a small number only, who are indeed our friends. We know them in a manner very different from the others. We see them when they are alert and wanting to please, and we see them also when they are, as it were, 'off guard'. Some experts tell us that it is easier to read a face when the person is at rest, not thinking in particular about anything, than when that face is wreathed in smiles or with brows furrowed over some

27

problem or other. But true friends we can see and know under both circumstances; they have little to hide from us and we have a clear idea of their aims and ideals.

Our God

Similarly, we can know about God, and we can know him. There have been acute theologians who have delved deeply into theology; and there have been profound philosophers who have simply never come to any real knowledge or appreciation of God. As with our friends, it is possible to be so fascinated by studying a subject that we miss the person who is truly behind it.

Of course, it is possible that some minds have to travel to a knowledge of God by way of knowing about him. Indeed, the writer of the Epistle to the Hebrews says, 'Let us come with confidence to the throne of grace, that we may receive mercy and find grace to help in time of need' (Hebrews 4:16). To 'come with confidence' there must be One to whom it is possible to come; and if the aim of drawing near is to find 'mercy and grace', that One must be able to offer help. In another verse the writer says, 'Whoever would draw near to God must believe that God exists, and that he rewards those who seek him' (11:6).

The thought is the same – to know *about* God and also to know him as a *person*.

Knowledge

There are two points which St Paul links with the knowledge of God, and which can be taken as evidence of that knowledge: 'Leading a life worthy of the Lord, pleasing him; and bearing fruit in every good work.' And these will testify to the knowledge of God.

The Epiphany   Wednesday 6 January
Principal Service   **Worship**   Matthew 2:1–12

'Going into the house, they saw the child with Mary his mother, and fell down and worshipped him. Then opening their treasures, they offered him gifts, gold and frankincense and myrrh.' Matthew 2:11

Christmas joy

St Matthew in his Gospel is writing for Christians in Palestine, Jewish converts to Christianity. They need confirmation in their new faith; they need an assurance that they are still loyally within the promises of the ancient prophecies, that is, what we call the 'Old Testament'. Therefore the first concern of St Matthew is to show how it is that Christ's birth fits in with the Bible history of the ancient kings of Israel. Christ belongs to the dynasty of David, as Matthew's long family tree demonstrates – from the royal annals, combined with Micah 5:1 – to show that Christ will unite the divided people of Judah and Israel. Loyal to the prophecies of the Old Testament, therefore, a Jew may indeed be a Christian.

In that case, how could it be that the Jews as a whole had not become Christians? To answer this question, Matthew inserts the episode of Herod. Pagans were the first to be moved by the Messiah's birth, and it was they who came to find him. Those who, from their professions as priests and scribes, should have been ready for this birth, knew very well where the Messiah was to be born (2:5,6). Their knowledge was precise, but their faith was non-existent. They would not shift themselves to go and see. Herod thought of going, and we know with what intention. So, what characterizes Matthew's account is his contrast between Jewish unbelief and the faith of the pagans.

Indeed, it is precisely the moment when the pagans were adoring Jesus and offering their gifts, that reminds Matthew of the prophecy of Isaiah (60:6).

> *'All those from Sheba shall come.*
> *They shall bring gold and frankincense,*
> *and shall proclaim the praise of the Lord.'*

He is moved to see its fulfilment in the episode of the adoration. Thus Jews who had become Christians had a further reason to confirm their faith: their own Jewish prophecies foretold the Jewish refusal, and the entry of pagans into salvation.

Moses and Christ

We may notice that the entire gospel account of the infancy of the Lord, as told in Matthew, seems to be what the scholars call a *'midrash'* ('story' or 'commentary', a learned use of biblical material for the edification of the faithful), in this case, on the childhood of Moses as told in Exodus. The magicians tell a worried Pharaoh and his people about the birth of Moses, just as the star informed an equally worried Herod and his people. Christ escaped Herod as Moses escaped from Pharaoh. As did Pharaoh in Jewish tradition, so Herod took counsel with the wise men before decreeing the death of all the first-born. Indeed, the second chapter of Matthew seems wholly concerned with presenting Christ as the new Moses; but the effect of the Good News is as St Paul says: 'Henceforth there is no more Greek nor Jew, but all are one in Jesus Christ.'

The Kingdom
The Church is the body of Christ here on earth, the Kingdom of God 'amongst us', and not a people among the other peoples of the world. In the Church, people of every race and quality may receive and exchange the riches of God. The Church is truly universal; this nature depends, however, on the quality of our faith, of us, the members of the community of believers. Let the Epiphany tell us that the scope of Christ's mission is unlimited; he came to save men and women of every nationality and race. Let us be reminded that young and old, rich and poor, wise and simple, all can find rest, peace and joy, and salvation in him.

The Epiphany *Second Service* **The Glory of Service** John 2:1–11

'This, the first of his signs, Jesus did at Cana in Galilee, and manifested his glory; and his disciples believed in him.' John 2:11

Manifesting his glory
Manifesting his glory – by providing wine at a wedding! It does not seem a very imposing beginning, especially if we recall St John's expression of that glory, in the previous chapter of his gospel: 'We beheld his glory, the glory as of the only Son of the Father.' Not in raising the dead, not in quelling a storm, not even in a healing of the sick – but in a kindly little act at a village wedding, after the broad hint of Mother Mary – 'The wine has run out, so please do something about it right *now*, and save this nice young couple from embarrassment, with all their friends and neighbours here!'

Rendering service

He protests; what his mother expects him to do, or how far she realized his latent powers, we are not told. But plainly from his answer and her further remark, she expects that he will do something to relieve the situation. And he does what he is asked to do. Without any further fuss, he renders the service that will satisfy everyone, even the steward with his educated taste. We ought to learn that simple kindness is never thrown away. There are plenty of little services in life, which seem usually trifling and unworthy of our time, our interest and even our money, but which have results out of proportion to what they may have cost us, or the pains we have taken, or the time spent.

Life is made up of small things – a lesson to learn

There are things we call ordinary, secular, even bothersome. His loftiness of purpose brought Our Lord into special touch with the weightier matters of life; his sympathy brought him into special contact with the sick and the sorrowing. But it is ever remarkable that the first manifestation of his power and glory was in an act of comparatively small importance, and on an occasion of simple joy and truly human gaiety, which he was truly happy to encourage and enjoy.

First Sunday of Epiphany *(The Baptism of Christ)* 10 January *Principal Service* **Christ and the Spirit** Matthew 3:13–17

'This is my beloved Son, with whom I am well pleased.' Matthew 3:17

'Do you come to me?'

Crowding round John the Baptist, at the bank of the River Jordan, are those who have listened to his words of warning. To them, the call to repentance for sins has struck home. John baptizes them, symbolically washing away from their souls their sins, as the water cleans their skins from grime, sweat and dirt. Jesus has left his home at Bethlehem, has followed the Baptist, mingling with the crowds, attentive to John's preaching, no doubt coming closer at each visit. John is astonished. 'Do *you* come to *me*? Rather I should come to you and be baptized by you!' In spite of John's unwillingness, Jesus persuades him to perform the baptism.

Voice from heaven
After the baptism, as Christ walks up from the river, there comes the divine manifestation, the ecstatic experience of Jesus himself as the Holy Dove comes down from the torn clouds and alights upon him, while the Voice of God claims him as the Son of the Most High, in whom the Father is well pleased. This manifestation of the Spirit, at the beginning of Christ's public ministry, over a world that has become a wilderness through sin, indicates that, through Christ, the world will again be made rich and fertile through grace.

After his baptism, Christ is led by the Spirit into the wilderness, the desert, for a time of fasting and prayer. There he will be tested by Satan, and then emerge into his public ministry, showing by his life and teaching, and later by his passion, death and resurrection, the salvation of the human race.

Saviour
His baptism shows to us the depth of his calling – he identifies with us as sinners, he makes it possible for us to be holy by his redeeming love and forgiveness. His acts of healing love, his lessons of inspired teaching, and then at the end being the Redeemer who carried our sins and sorrows – by his wounds we are healed. He offers his life in atonement, as the Suffering Servant who is also the Saviour. United with Christ, our sinful humanity stands in the cleansing waters to be made holy by him who is all holy; and to emerge to be led as a new people of God into the promised land of his Kingdom.

> *Almighty God,*
> *who anointed Jesus at his Baptism with the Holy Spirit*
> *and revealed him as your beloved Son:*
> *give to us who are born of water and the Spirit*
> *the will to surrender ourselves to your service,*
> *that we may rejoice to be called your children;*
> *through Jesus Christ our Lord.*

PHG

First Sunday of Epiphany *Second Service*
Truth in the Son Hebrews 1:1–12

'God, who gave to our forefathers many different glimpses of the truth, in the words of the prophets, has now given us the Truth in the Son.'
Hebrews 1:1

Greater than the angels

Certainly it is true that God has revealed himself in many ways to humanity, and through many people. Indeed, he is still doing so. Yet the supreme revelation of all that he has granted to humanity, is the revelation which he gave to us in and through his Son.

What is more, because God is the God of all eternity as well as Lord of time, that revelation through his incarnate Son still lives on. Jesus *was* the living Word, and his word *is* still the living Word to humanity. Note that the text speaks of the old revelation as being given 'in the words of the prophets'. This means that it was not simply through them – using them as instruments – but it was *in them* as the quickening power of their life. Then the words 'in the Son' surely fix attention upon the nature, not the personality, of the Mediator of the new revelation. 'God spake to us in One who has this character – that he is Son.'

The old revelation

The revelation given through the prophets was given through a purely human medium. Their revelation was a series of glimpses, not an unveiled sight; it was given little by little over a very long time. It was always fragmentary and, consequently, incomplete. It was also multiform, given, that is, in manifold fashion. God spoke in dreams, visions, voices, angels, sacrifices, and through the prophets. Yet all was the revelation of parts, of portions, of sections of the one Eternal Mind.

The new revelation

There is a completeness, a finality, about the revelation in our Lord. It could not be otherwise – our Lord is the eternal Son of the Father, one with him. So it is because of the essential unity in the Godhead that the Son could perfectly reveal the mind of the Father. It has been said,

'Jesus was to God as the rays are to the sun, wherein all its splendour is apparent, and as the melted wax is to the seal, answering to it line by line ... Such is the revelation of God speaking to Jesus, in contrast with what the prophets uttered in fragments.'

The prophets were inspired men, but Christ is the eternal Son. The prophets were servants, our Lord is the Incarnate Son. He alone has showed us that God is Father, and that he is Love. Christ is the full revelation of God, he is himself the pure Light, uniting in his one Person the whole spectrum. This is why Christ could say: 'He that has seen me has seen the Father' (John 6:46).

The full revelation
The divine revelations of redemptive truth to our humanity are found in all their fullness in Christ. We must not expect any new or further revelations to be given to us. Yet to the devout and earnest student of Christ, brighter and clearer light will stream forth from the revelations already given. His words are the words of eternal life, and so are of inexhaustible significance. But those meanings and their importance will become increasingly clear to those who, with a listening ear and a seeing eye, seek to know the Father's mind.

> *Almighty God,*
> *who anointed Jesus at his Baptism with the Holy Spirit*
> *and revealed him as your beloved Son:*
> *given to us who are born of water and the Spirit,*
> *the will to surrender ourselves to your service,*
> *that we may rejoice to be called your children;*
> *through Jesus Christ our Lord. Amen.*

PHG, 215

Second Sunday of Epiphany   17 January
Principal Service   **Behold the Lamb of God**
John 1:29–42

'The next day John saw Jesus coming toward him, and said, "Behold the Lamb of God, who takes away the sins of the world. This is he of whom I said, 'After me comes a man who ranks before me, for he was before me'."' John 1:29,30

Names for Jesus

The Gospels, and particularly St John's Gospel, introduce a number of well-known words or phrases which describe Our Lord and his work, titles such as 'The Light of the world', 'The Bread of Life', 'The true Vine'. Most come from Jesus himself, for he used them first. An exception, however, is 'The Lamb of God'. This originates from what John the Baptist said to two of his disciples as Jesus passed by. We may wonder what John meant. What was in his thoughts as he spoke of Jesus in this way?

When asked by the priests and the Levites to tell them who he was, John the Baptist quoted the prophet Isaiah, who had said, 'I am a voice crying in the wilderness, "Make the Lord's highway straight!"' When he called Jesus the Lamb of God, John may have had in mind another passage from Isaiah, describing the Servant of God as being led like a lamb to the slaughter, but bearing the sins of many people.

A new leader

Something else may have been in John's thoughts. Although it seems a strange animal to choose for the purpose, it is true that among some Jewish teachers of religion the lamb symbolized a leader who would bring others to defeat the forces of evil. So it seems that John was telling his two followers that here was a new leader, far greater than himself, who would bring men to grips with the sins that John could only denounce in sermons. This is borne out by the fact that the two men seem to consider John's words as advice, or even an order, to follow Jesus – which they did at once. Andrew got hold of his brother Simon and told him, 'We have found the Messiah!', and brought him to Jesus.

Jesus looked at Simon, and in his quizzical, half-humorous way told him he would be known as 'The Rock' – a tribute to Simon's solid style, no doubt.

The Saviour
John the Baptist's words about Jesus being the Lamb of God should remind us of the Saviour's death on the cross, for us and for the world, and should also remind us of our every-day relationship with Jesus. We are to take him as leader and guide, not only in great matters but in the every-day problems and decisions of life. If we follow in his steps, and model our lives, as far as we can, on his example, we can be brought by him to the glory of eternal life.

Second Sunday of Epiphany *Second Service* Paul's Conversion Galatians 1:11–24

'He who once persecuted us is now preaching the faith he once tried to destroy. And they glorified God because of me.' Galatians 1:23,24

A restored tradition
St Peter and St Paul were the most prominent of the apostles in the founding and spread of Christianity in the early days. Of very different characters and upbringing, they were united in their zeal to bring the message of Christ; and in the end they were united also by their martyrdoms in the centre of the ancient world, the great city of Rome itself.

Paul
Paul began his life as an enemy of Christ, and ended it with love for him. 'The love of Christ urges me on,' he said. That love meant suffering. 'Who shall separate us from the love of Christ? Shall tribulation or distress, or persecution, or famine, or nakedness, or peril, or the sword?'

Paul endured all these. His path to sanctity was strewn with thorns, not least that 'thorn in my own flesh', which may well have been some form of epilepsy. At the same time he could cry out, 'Gladly will I glory in my infirmities, that the power of Christ may dwell in men.'

Peter

Peter, in the beginning, seems to have been a weak man, even a coward on occasion. He was boastful and impetuous, up on the peaks one moment, down in the depths the next, unstable, hardly to be relied upon. But under this unstable surface, Christ discerned the possibility of deep faith, and saw that Peter was fundamentally a man of goodwill and generosity. It was on this rock-like faith that Christ founded his Church, using a pun in Greek and in Aramaic. ('*Petros*' is Greek for rock, '*Cephas*' is Aramaic for the same word.)

But Peter had to suffer humiliation for the three-fold denial of the Lord Jesus he made just before the trial and crucifixion of Christ. Three times Christ asks the penitent disciple, 'Do you love me?', and Peter's repentant heart is cut to the quick, before his restoration is complete.

United

Peter and Paul, men of very different characters, capacities and styles, were yet united in their zeal to spread the message of Christ.

Paul, we are told, even attacked Peter – not out of any personal dislike, but simply because he felt Peter was wrong in not 'walking straight in accordance with the gospel' (Galatians 2:14). But this confrontation arose out of zeal, and it was soon enough healed. Perhaps such events were inevitable in the early birth-pangs of the Church of Christ, when so much was still fluid and unsettled.

Each of these great men, in his own way, built up the Church, so that when they were martyred the Church was already visible for men and women to see and to be attracted to. They are truly regarded as the twin pillars of the Church of God.

> *Lord, you have founded your Church*
> *on Peter's firmness, on Paul's understanding*
> *and clear wisdom, and on the inspired*
> *teaching and utterances of both,*
> *to combat error and ungodliness.*
> *Lord, we praise you for both,*
> *taught by them in the knowledge*
> *of you, Jesus, Saviour of our souls.*

> *Prayer of the Eastern Churches*

Third Sunday of Epiphany 24 January
Principal Service **Fishers of Men**
Matthew 4:12–23

'Jesus began to preach, saying, "Repent, for the kingdom of heaven is at hand." As he walked by the Sea of Galilee, he saw two brothers, Simon who is called Peter, and Andrew his brother ... And he said to them, "Follow me, and I will make you fishers of men."' Matthew 4:18,19

Preaching and teaching

Jesus has completed his time of preparation; he has, in the peace and quiet of the wilderness, taken for his meditation those words from Isaiah which sounded forth from heaven at his baptism: 'My Son, my chosen One, in whom I am well pleased' (Isaiah 42:1) and 'I have grasped you by the hand; I formed you, and have given you as a covenant to the people; a light for the nations' (v. 6). On the one hand, he is most truly God's Son, 'the mirror of his being' (Hebrew 1:3), and on the other, 'Lord of all' (Acts 10:36). From this time, this battle with the enemy takes place over forty days, and forty nights as Matthew adds, perhaps thinking of Exodus (34:28).

From here on, Jesus moves swiftly; on hearing of the imprisonment of John the Baptist, he begins his preaching and teaching, starting at Galilee 'of the Gentiles' as prophesied by Isaiah (9:1–2). The scope of his teaching is wide – he announces the Kingdom of Heaven (v. 23), and the impact of his ministry is widely recognized from Syria in the north down to Jerusalem and Judea.

The signs of the times

Christ's preaching is summarized in the quotation: 'Repent, for the kingdom of heaven is at hand!' (v. 17). The Greek word translated repent (lit. 'change your mind') is in New Testament times equivalent not so much 'to grieve for one's sins' but 'to turn around, return'. This 'conversion' is the radical conversion to God of an apostate nation (see Jeremiah, for example). The Kingdom of Heaven is Matthew's term for the Kingdom of God, having a Jewish flavour in avoiding mentioning 'God.' The Kingdom is the most important subject in the synoptic Gospels, while having a humbler place in John and other New Testament writings. In the New Testament the term is more than a reference to God's 'sovereignty' or 'reign'; it is a synonym for 'the Age to Come'; and this is not a new concept of Jesus but a drawing upon common Jewish expectations.

The first disciples
Simon Peter, James and John formed the group of closest followers and friends to Jesus. Matthew gives the names Simon and Peter, which indicates that Peter was a name given later (John 2:42 '*Cephas*' meaning 'stone' or 'rock' – see the Second Sunday, third paragraph of second sermon 'Peter'), as we might say, a nickname, by which Christ made it clear that he regarded Peter as a strong character in many ways. He was certainly one of the close inner circle about the Lord; a figure of power and strength, but also of weakness and impetuosity. Yet it was Peter who was the leader of the little band, under Christ of course, and he came into his own after the terrible time of Good Friday.

What was it that Christ added to their lives which makes Peter, James, John, Andrew and the rest household words throughout the world? Clearly, apart from Christ they would have done nothing special, just been unknown, respectable Galilean fishermen, as good as the rest, no doubt, but not the figures we know today. Jesus gave their lives a new value, a universal value based upon his own teaching and life. Merely honest men and women will not redeem a selfish world. Love is the secret, with the new Spirit. Jesus alone makes fishers of men. Give your life to Jesus.

Third Sunday of Epiphany *Second Service*
Cause for Great Joy 1 Peter 1:3–12
'The inheritance to which we are born is one that nothing can destroy or spoil or wither. It is kept for you in heaven – this is cause for great joy, even though now you smart for a little while, if need be, under trials of many kinds.' 1 Peter 1:4–6

Hard times
Peter has just addressed the people he is writing to as 'God's scattered people'. In his opening sentences, Peter uses Christian equivalents to the style of address which a Jewish leader would

have used in greeting his own people. Peter is writing to Christian inhabitants scattered over a large area, naming no fewer than five Roman provinces – Pontus, Galatia, Cappadocia, Asia and Bithnyia – which would cover practically the whole of Asia Minor. The Christians, unlike the Jews, would have no common nationality, but would be held together in a common loyalty to the Lord Jesus, a loyalty indeed taking the place of any national loyalty. And Peter makes this clear by using the word 'lodge', implying a temporary life in one place for a while, since beyond and above all earthly affairs they are held together by a faith far stronger than any national beliefs. As of old, they have been chosen in the purpose of God the Father; hallowed into his service by the Spirit, though not attached by any participation in the Hebrew cult centred in the Temple at Jerusalem, but only by their obedience and 'the sprinkling of the blood of Jesus Christ'. As the Old Covenant was made by the sprinkling of the blood, by Moses when he received the Law from God at Sinai and read it out to them, they replying 'We will be obedient' and he then sprinkling them, so the Christians now had a new Covenant, made by the poured-out blood of Christ.

Great joy
This encouragement is of great blessing and help to Christians – 'great joy' – even though there may be trials of many kinds to endure – and these trials will not endure for more than a little time. Compared with a Christian's faith, even gold fresh from the refiner's furnace can be considered perishable!

And, the Jesus known only by faith and longed for, will be revealed one day all his glory, so that all people will know him.

Gospel: Luke 4:14–21

Fourth Sunday of Epiphany 31 January
Principal Service **The Glory of Service** John 2:1–11 (*see* **The Epiphany,** *Second Service*, p. 30)

Fourth Sunday of Epiphany *Second Service* **A Useful Helper** Philemon 1–16

A runaway
The letter to Philemon is an unexpected small item in the midst of the letters, often long and closely argued, from Paul to the churches he has founded or is deeply concerned over. This letter concerns the future of one man only, the runaway slave, Onesimus. In prison in Rome, Paul came into contact with this man; by coincidence he already knew the slave's master, Philemon, who had been converted to Christianity by Paul himself. Philemon lived at Colosse, a well-to-do man, who was something of a patron to the Apostle.

A Christian
Paul writes to Philemon not merely as a member of the Church, but as an individual friend. Legally, a slave who ran away would be due for certain punishment, and ought to be handed over to the authorities. Onesimus, however, had come under Paul's influence while in Rome, and is now a baptized Christian. He had proved himself most helpful to the Apostle, acting as secretary as well as general factotum. There is a pun here, in that 'Onesimus' means 'useful'. Paul would not want to keep the man, however, without Philemon's consent, though he points out that Onesimus is now 'more than a slave – a beloved brother', yet at the same time offering to send him back.

What actually happened, we do not know.

Onesimus the bishop?
Some scholars put forward the theory that the bishop of Ephesus early in the second century, whose name is recorded as Onesimus, was the very same man that Paul wished to retain with him. Certainly it was chiefly this bishop who collected up as many of Paul's letters as he could, for preservation, during a period when Paul's influence had somewhat waned.

It is striking to think that this short personal letter was probably included as a kind of guarantee and token of responsibility. If this were so, it would make a fine example of what the theme of this Sunday is – God's love and care for sinners, and his loving ability to restore them to his favour and presence, on repentance.

The Presentation of Christ in the Temple (Candlemas)   Tuesday 2 February   *Principal Service*   The Light of the World   Luke 2:22–40

'The parents of Jesus took him up to Jerusalem, to present him to the Lord, observing what stands written in the Name of the Lord.' Luke 2:22

The presentation of the first-born

The ancient Jewish custom was to present the first-born male child of a family to God, and to dedicate him to God's service. This rule is to be read in Exodus 13, where all the first-born males are set aside, both animal and human; they could be 'ransomed', however, hence the presentation of the two turtle doves – the cheapest 'ransom' permitted, for a poor family. Such was the Law, and Joseph and Mary showed their reverence by their obedience to it, for their first-born, Jesus, thus fulfilling the Mosaic Law, and in the very heart of the Law, the splendid and magnificent Temple in Jerusalem, fresh from the hands of its builders, the glory of Israel.

Fulfilment

The presentation of Jesus in the Temple was the fulfilment of the words of the prophet Malachi, read as our first lesson today (Malachi 3:1–5). 'Suddenly the Lord will come to his Temple; the messenger of the Covenant in whom you delight, is here, here already . . .'

This coming was not only sudden but also unostentatious. For most families, the occasion would have been a family celebration, but here, only Mary and Joseph were present – a poor woman and her equally poor husband, unable to afford anything above the absolute minimum. And the only witnesses, apparently, were an old man, Simeon, and an old woman, Anna. Day by day, beside the throngs of visitors and pilgrims, the Temple attracted a number of older worshippers. We may think of the dutiful and regular people who come to our cathedrals and churches for weekday services. How thankful we are for their support and presence and faith!

The light of the world
Drawn by the Holy Spirit, Simeon and Anna blessed the baby, and foretold a great future for him – and a sorrowful time for his mother. Still today, in our evening prayers, 'Nunc dimittis', the Song of Simeon, is used in our churches to remind us how Jesus Christ has brought the light of goodness, and the love of God, into our lives. The task of the Church is to show that light to the world, that peoples of all nations may see and follow it.

Mary must have wondered much about the future of the child she held in her arms during the Temple ceremony. Certainly she understood that he was a very special child, for whom great things were in store in the years to come. For herself, too, the future held unknown events, but bringing her sorrow and pain. Yes, we know what was to happen – here in the Temple Mary stood, holding her Son, full of joy, but the time would come when she would stand beside him on Mount Calvary, as he suffered and died upon the Cross. Not joy, alas, but deepest agony, would then be her bitter part.

Blessed Simeon! Blessed Anna!
May we grow into an old age like yours, taking each physical diminishment as an opportunity for growth into God. So we may recognize in our situation the wonder and joy at the presence of Christ, that you acclaimed in yours.

A PRAYER FOR CANDLEMAS

God our Father,
whose Son was revealed to Simeon and Anna,
as the light of the nations and the glory of Israel:
Grant that, guided by your Holy Spirit,
we may live by the light of faith
until we come to the light of glory;
through Christ our Lord. Amen.

PHG, 78

The Presentation of Christ in the Temple *Second Service* Simeon the Prophet Luke 2:34–35

'This child is destined for the falling and the rising of many in Israel, and to be a sign that will be opposed so that the inner thoughts of many will be revealed – and a sword will pierce your own soul too.' Luke 2:34–35

Observance of the Law

Forty days after his birth, Jesus was taken by Mary and Joseph to the Temple: a formal presentation at the focus of his nation's religion. If funds permitted, a female yearling lamb was offered, but poor families brought a pair of turtle-doves. As we see, Jesus' earthly parents were not affluent. Mary and Joseph offered the doves and redeemed Jesus with the statutory five shekels. The child was blessed and restored to his mother . . . all in accordance with Jewish law regarding the first-born son. There was no special treatment even for the Son of God . . .

Simeon's prophecy

. . . Until an old man approached, took the child in his arms, and pronounced the amazing words: *'Nunc dimittis* . . . Master, now you are dismissing your servant in peace . . . for my eyes have seen . . . a light for revelation to the Gentiles . . .'

Did Mary recall her song to Elizabeth, a few months before? 'He has remembered the promise he made to our ancestors, to Abraham and to his descendants for ever . . .' (Luke 1:55).

'Abraham and . . . his descendants.' For who, in the Temple, that purification day, did not know that God had said to Abraham: 'By your offspring shall *all* nations of the earth gain blessing'? (Genesis 22:18).

Candlemas

The celebration of Candlemas has a long history. Certainly from as early as the sixth century church processions were held with lighted candles. It came to be known as ' "Candlemas, the Purification of Our Lady" ', in the Catholic West, and in the Orthodox East as ' "The Presentation of the Lord" '. Today in many churches candles will be blessed, often in two bundles – one of long, thick, decorated candles, for use at Festivals until next Candlemas; and the second of smaller candles lit and held by worshippers at today's services, and then taken home and used on special occasions, symbolizing Christ's 'light for the Gentiles'.

Old and new
The significance of Candelmas is the meeting of the old dispensation and the new: Simeon and Jesus; Judaism and the Universal Church. The little child lying in Simeon's arms is to be the watershed between innocent animals being offered for our sin, and the innocent Lamb being offered for us on Calvary.

The darkness of Calvary was there, in the Temple that day; but the Light for the Gentiles was to outshine it. Unless we take on some of this Candlemas light, its message will go out for us when we snuff out our little candles.

> *Here we have greeted the Light of the world.*
> *Help us who extinguish these candles never to forsake*
> *the light of Christ.*

> *Final Responsory, Feast of Candlemas*

Second Sunday Before Lent *(Sexagesima: Eighth before Easter)* 7 February *Principal Service* **Seek First the Kingdom** Matthew 6:25–34

'Seek first his kingdom and his righteousness, and all these things shall be yours, as well.' Matthew 6:33

Wisdom
In the Sermon on the Mount Our Lord Jesus gives words of wisdom, words of spiritual insight of enormous value, yet couched in such forms that everyone can understand. He teaches us to see the works of nature not only as products to sustain life, but also as demonstrations showing the work of a loving heavenly Father. They show, if we look, actions of divine love and wisdom; here we learn to see something of the depths of Creation, reflecting God's ways, reaching from the great swirling streams of glowing

material that make up the constellations, to the exciting problems of the distant suns. Those suns surely carry planets with them, of which we know little or nothing – yet we picture all manner of strange creatures and watch strange adventures on our TV screens, or read science fiction by Ray Bradbury or J. G. Ballard, or any of the other authors who specialize in 'other worlds'. But in our own small planet Earth, God revealed himself in a way that all of us could understand. What was this way? A book, sacred texts, like the Koran, the Vedas, the sacred words of the Buddha or Confucius? Or through an angel with a message? The angel was not enough; the book was not enough. God spoke to us in a human life – 'When the time was fully come, God sent forth his Son' (Galatians 4:4). Whatever form God's coming may take elsewhere, 'for this world the Word of God is Christ' (Colossians 3:11).

God's care
Jesus teaches us to regard the works of nature not only as products to sustain human life, but also as operations which show the activity of God's love and wisdom. The birds, Jesus tells us, along with the flowers, proclaim God's care and providence. Look at them and consider, says Jesus; we need eyes to see, and hearts to ponder over, the goodness and care of God for humanity. Surely we can see the divine hand in the rule of law throughout his world. When we learn to see something of the depths of Nature, as reflecting God's way and his intentions, so we learn more of God himself. St Paul took that attitude: 'Ever since the creation of the world, God's invisible nature, namely his eternal power and deity, has been clearly visible in what has been created, to the eye of reason' (Romans 1:20).

As we attain a spiritual outlook and knowledge, we can surely see that the changing seasons demonstrate the truth and the goodness of God; nature in all its variety helps us to learn more of God himself.

Spiritual action
Faith is the very spirit and spring of action. The Christian faith teaches God's providence as being a care and direction universal, encouraging the human soul to higher spirituality, understanding the natural world as well as things of the spirit as helpful, and indeed teaching us more of God himself. 'Seek first his kingdom' then tomorrow will not trouble you – 'all these things shall be

yours as well.' Trouble there must be in the world, but no one need have more than each day brings. If we make our duty our priority, our very first objective in life, then God will take care of our happiness. The highest wisdom is to devote our life to God now; he gives us a promise, and he will not fail to fulfil it if we do our part. 'Look at your priorities – and God will look after the rest.'

Second Sunday before Lent   *Second Service*
The Origin of Wisdom; Praise the Lord!
Proverbs 8:1,22–31; Revelation to John ch. 4

'Worthy art thou, our Lord and God, to receive glory and honour and power, for thou didst create all things.' Revelation 4:11

The ancient Hebrew writings are in the main the products not of prophets or preachers, but of serious observers of the world, sober teachers, very practical in their concerns, and rationalistic in their comments and advice. They are, in general, preoccupied with our human situation and our human destiny. Certainly, God is taken very seriously, and his meaning for human existence also; the call is for humanity to relate itself in obedience and in faith to the divine action; in particular, for Israel to be aware of the nation's inheritance of faith. The general subject of the contents of the book of Proverbs is the art of right living, looking to a background of revealed religion, and teaching its principles.

Religion
We are taught that God gave wisdom to humanity; yet wisdom is not a mere human achievement, but a universal reality, the work of God which precedes his creation of the world (Proverbs 8:22,23–31). This divine Wisdom is presented as a person who calls human beings and seeks to help them in their search for knowledge; and as such constitutes a type of divine activity on behalf of humanity. This personal divine Wisdom must probably be considered a per-sonification, rather than some metaphysical drive or concern. It is a development which is of great importance for our historical understanding of the New Testament's presentation of Our Lord.

Wisdom

As an expression of the creative action of God, Wisdom's special function is the bringing of human beings to the realization of 'noble things' – truth, righteousness, and what is upright and straight, free from anything that is twisted, wicked or perverse. Wisdom is pure light, but only those illumined by her know it. She is the first act of the Lord, the antecedent to all creatures. The identification of the Wisdom with the Word of God, the Law, the Spirit, and with Christ, always includes this element of the decisive action of God. For many theologians, teachers and scholars point to an increased awareness that the figure of primeval Wisdom represents an aspect and phase of Israel's assimilation of the mythology and patterns of worship of the ancient Near East. However, the Lord's creation of Wisdom (Genesis 14:19, Psalms 139:13) indicates that Israel's faith in a Creator was not compromised by assimilative thinking.

Revelation of St John, chapter 4

In this astonishing and powerful book, St John writes (or more probably dictated) his vision of Heaven; it was more than a vision for he is called to go 'up there', and is immediately 'in the spirit' and away in the heavens. The setting suggests something of the Most Holy Place in the Temple, no longer a bare empty space, but now a Throne Room indeed. Over the Ark – the chest in which were retained the stone tables of the Law (Exodus 25:10–22) – stood two winged cherubim, guarding 'God's Throne'; these have now become, from being statues, 'four living creatures', each with its own personality, i.e. one with a lion's appearance, one with the style of an ox, one with the face of a man, and the last the appearance of an eagle.

The Inner Room of the Temple now becomes the heavenly Throne Room, where God holds court among the angels and spirits who worship him, praising him day and night, singing,

> *'Holy, holy, holy, is the Lord God Almighty,*
> *who was and is and is to come!'*

The twenty-four families of priests who officiated in the outer rooms of the Temple are replaced by twenty-four elders; while the seven-branched candlestick of the earthly Temple is replaced by seven flaming torches, which are the seven 'spirits of God'.

Perhaps these are the traditional seven archangels, or perhaps a symbol for the Spirit of God.

Another feature of the Temple of Solomon, the great bronze basin which stood in the courtyard for the washing of the faithful, now appears transformed into a sea of glass, 'like crystal'.

In every paragraph of St John's 'Revelation', at the beginning at any rate, there is something of the ancient worship carried through at Jerusalem in the Temple, with the imagery of the Kingdom of the Spirit, now showing forth in visions and the spirit, in the hearts and minds of the Hebrew people – today without the great and marvellous Temple in Jerusalem any more. Worship is the secret of this unseen world; the keyword of John's book and of all revelations; the last word and the master word of the Bible's message to all humanity, to all peoples, to all looking for a new vision and a new way of life, with new ideals and new thinking. And at the centre, with the figure of Jesus, now in glory and in triumph over death and sin, yet accessible to his followers and to all who will recognize him, and take him as their Leader and their King.

Sunday Next Before Lent   (*Quinquagesima: Seventh before Easter*)   14 February   *Principal Service*   This is my beloved Son
Matthew 17:1–9

'He was transfigured before them, and his face shone like the sun, and his garments became white as light.' Matthew 17:3

A crisis point

When this astonishing event took place, Jesus had reached a crisis point in his earthly ministry. Indeed, the Transfiguration has been compared to a watershed in his career. The first period of novelty, of popularity, and indeed of success, had passed; now beginning was the period of suspicion, endurance, and persecution. The Saviour had warned his followers of what was coming. So it seems that this unique display of his inherent majesty, and of the Father's love and confidence, came at the very moment when it was most needed. It can be said that the close connection of the Transfiguration with the disaster, shame and woe of Calvary is clear from the story itself, and from the central position it occupies in his ministry.

The Transfiguration

The higher the three apostles climbed with Jesus, no doubt the more exhilarated by the keen mountain air they became; and there, as the sun rose in the clear sky, so the inherent glory of the Lord shone through the disguise of his human weakness and humiliation. For once, he appeared to be what he really was in himself – the Son of the Father and the Lord of the world. The moment came when they saw Jesus suddenly and gloriously changed into a Being of splendour and power; and with him were the two most venerated figures of the Old Testament, after Abraham. Moses was the giver of the Law, while Elijah was the head and leader of the Prophets. They had foretold the coming of Jesus, and they had prefigured him; now they appeared and bore witness to him, the great Lawgiver and Prophet they had foreshadowed.

Jesus the new Moses

Matthew is particularly concerned to make it clear that Jesus is the new Moses, the legislator of the new way of life. Moses is a great figure to Matthew; unlike Mark Matthew mentions him before Elijah; and it is only Matthew who speaks of Christ transfigured, shining, recalling the radiance of Moses on Sinai (Exodus 34:29–35). Similarly, the voice that speaks from the cloud corresponds with the voice from the cloud on Sinai (Exodus 19:16–24). The command 'Listen to him' is the reminder of the words spoken to Moses about the future prophet 'whom you shall heed' (Deuteronomy 18:15). Lastly, Matthew, unlike Mark and Luke, who only quote 'Behold my Son' (Psalm 2:7), adds 'in whom I am well pleased' from Isaiah 42:1, which gives an added meaning to the quotation, since it is an allusion to the servant who is 'the Light of the nations', because he does the will of God.

Acceptance

The suffering servant won his position as the light of the world through his obedience (Isaiah 42:6,7). Christ earns his title as the new leader of thought and teacher of the new law of love because he is the first to put this into practice (Matthew 17:9).

The account of the Transfiguration in Matthew is of course basically the Lord's investiture and recognition as Messiah; but it is also the introduction to chapter 18's discourse on the powers of the Church as the Lord gives admonitions, warnings and ordinances for life together, and for discipline.

Sunday Next Before Lent *Second Service* **The Vision** Matthew 17:9–23

'Tell no man the vision, until the Son of Man is raised from the dead.'
Matthew 17:9

Coming down the hill
No words can express the divine glory that belongs to Jesus Our Lord, but the disciples are allowed to glimpse something of it, and what it means. It is so rich, so wonderful, that they want to stay gazing upon it ('We will make three booths – shrines – one for you, one for Moses, and one for Elijah,' says Peter). But the full vision must await heaven, and a time when we are prepared and ready for it. So it is, then, that the disciples are to go with Jesus, down again to the crowd waiting below – down to the earthly sicknesses and sufferings, the all-too-human needs and demands – but carrying with them something of the glory glimpsed in the heights.

The vision
'Where there is no vision, the people perish' (Proverbs 29:18). We all need to have times of withdrawal, of worship, of adoration and prayer. We must gaze upon the 'glory', the dazzling beauty; but we cannot remain in contemplation. Yes indeed, our life, our spiritual life, our worship itself, without colour, music, poetry, movement and richness, would be dull and dry. Without times of vision, we grow slack and dead. But the glory and the vision must be taken into the tasks of life, our every-day life, which can then be tackled with renewed energy and effectiveness.

· As for the disciples' question, 'Why do our teachers [the scribes] say that Elijah must first come?' The scribes' teaching was that Elijah must come 'before the Day of the Lord' in accordance with the traditional interpretation of Malachi 4:5 that all would then be set right. Jesus' reply is that Elijah will not be recognized, and will suffer death – not the belief of the ordinary people – and indeed that 'the Son of Man' himself will be killed. This fore-shadowing was certainly depressing for the disciples, and they are further depressed by the very public complaints of the man whose son was an epileptic, and whom the disciples were quite unable to heal.

How long am I to be with you?
A note is struck here by the words of Jesus, suggesting that the Lord is on earth as visiting the world to start his Church; hints have already been given that Jesus' departure would involve him in 'laying down his life' for others: 'Where I am going you cannot come' (John 13:34). Peter said, 'Lord, I will lay down my life for you' (John 13:37). But the disciples were not ready, nor had they the faith required (v. 20). 'Because of your little faith,' says the Lord; and if they had faith 'nothing would be impossible'. And here is given (v. 23) the second prediction of the death and resurrection of Jesus, but with no further questions, only a great sorrow . . . 'They were greatly distressed.'

In His service
If the radiance of the glory of Jesus surrounds our life, if we follow his way, we must learn to give ourselves in his service, to 'lose our life' in order to find a richer and fuller life. The Christian has to die to self, abandon self-centredness, and live for Christ. Here is the way to achieve abundant life, a fullness of life, which satisfies and fulfils.

Ash Wednesday 17 February *Principal Service* Sackcloth and Ashes Matthew 6:1–6, 16–21; Joel 2:12–17

'Beware of practising your piety before men in order to be seen by them; for then you will have no reward from your Father who is in heaven.' Matthew 6 or Isaiah 58:5

Ashes

If we read the passages in the Bible where marking ourselves with ashes is mentioned, the meaning of doing so is very clear. People did this very seriously indeed; it was a sign of sorrow and distress. Maybe they were sorrowful about personal troubles (Job 2:8). Sometimes they were sorrowing for some national disaster (Jeremiah 6:26). Or their sorrow was for their own sins, or for the sins of the nation – and then the ashes were a mark of repentance (Matthew 11:21). How did people first arrive at the idea that ashes were a sign of trouble, or of sin, or of sorrow?

Destruction

Ashes are a mark of destruction. We may have a bright fire burning on the hearth giving warmth to the house, or it may be in the kitchen cooking food. But all the time the fire is destroying the wood, coal or gas used to provide fuel; and when we stop feeding the fire with fuel it goes out, leaving behind merely some ash. It is not only in the home that we may be reminded how apt a symbol of destruction ash can be – photographs or TV pictures show us houses, farms, homes, villages, offices, factories burnt by the enemy after being plundered, ruined, destroyed, with nothing left behind but shattered ruins and piles of ash and rubble. It is dreadful to consider the fate or the future of the inhabitants.

Sin

At work in the world, and in the individual lives of people, is the destructive force of sin. Sin destroys in men and women many good plans, good ideas, hopes and thoughts, acts of love and service and help – and destroys them completely. If sin is allowed to work its will, it can destroy whole lives, making them barren and useless, cutting them off from God.

While we must be on our guard against the destructive power of evil, we should remember that evil itself is not untouchable – we ourselves can strive to make an end to wrong impulses, sinful desires, foolish actions, bad intentions, and whatever in us is evil.

Purifying

Scripture often speaks of fire as a purifying force. The prophet Malachi compares God at work in human lives to the hot furnaces used by goldsmiths and silversmiths to rid precious metals of impurities (Malachi 3:2,3).

Let the ashes in our lives be those of evil things, bad thoughts and actions, but never of what is good, of what is helpful to other humans in trouble or need, or of something that could, and should, develop into what is useful and for the help or benefit of good causes of every kind. Let the ashes in our lives be those of evil things, never of good.

Ash Wednesday

On Ash Wednesday it is good to remember how this day got its name, from the marking of our foreheads with ash as a sign of repentance. It tells us that today our thoughts should be not only about self-denial and self-discipline, but about our own guilt in God's sight, our need to repent of our sins, our need to lead a new life, and above all, our need to seek God's mercy and forgiveness.

Ash Wednesday *Second Service* Father, I have sinned Luke 15:11-32

'I will arise and go to my father, and I will say to him, "Father, I have sinned against heaven and before you; I am no longer worthy to be called your son; treat me as one of your hired servants." And he arose and came to his father.' Luke 15:18-20

Happy ending

The story of the prodigal son ends with a surprise party. When the prodigal's elder brother was returning from a hard day's work, he could scarcely believe his ears. There was the sound of music and dancing coming from the father's house!

Life had been pretty quiet since that disreputable jackanapes had left home. 'What can my father be up to?' the elder brother asked himself – then questioning the servants, he found out! That wretched brother had returned, rags and dirt, and to welcome him – Welcome him! – this party was in full swing. Well, no wonder the elder brother was furious. Here he was, slaving away doing at least two men's jobs, and *he* never gets a party. But let this wasteful, dissolute fellow come back penniless and filthy, and a party is laid on at once.

Unfair!

Yes, unfair indeed – yet how unfavourably the elder brother's rankling grievance compares with the striking love and generosity of the father. Not only had he gone out to meet the returning prodigal – instead of holding back, as would befit his dignity – he had not waited to hear his son's repentance and accept his submission, but straightway led him to the farmhouse, clothed him, and set in train the feast.

What joy! Here we can read off a general lesson from Jesus, about the nature of God's forgiveness, compared with the rules and regulations laid down by scribes and Pharisees. No conditions, no reparations, no testing for genuineness – the son simply returns to his father's arms. 'What joy in heaven over one sinner who repents!'

Grim and gruff

The elder son can't see it this way at all, however. The awards given to the younger son are inappropriate indeed and completely unfair. *He*, on the other hand, has gone on working the estate for his father's benefit – even though it was technically his *own* property – while his brother, by squandering his inheritance, had deprived both the father *and* the elder son. We sense something of the elder brother's nature.

While the prodigal is certainly easy-going – probably foolishly so – he has an engaging personality, while the elder seems a sourpuss at best. His years of 'slaving' have turned him in on himself, and he is now embittered, a prisoner of his own restrictions. We should feel sorry for such people, unable to loosen up, to enjoy the ordinary pleasures of life, shut up behind a wall of their own making.

The critics

Jesus' critics – from whose opposition this and the preceding parables stem – unite in condemning the Lord because 'he welcomes sinners and eats with them'. In orthodox Hebrew religious thought penitence was valued, and a truly repentant sinner would be welcomed back into the company of the faithful. But first he must properly repent, work off his debts, and only then can be taken back by God and his fellow Hebrews.

Jesus' offence, then, in the eyes of the religious, consisted in not waiting for signs of repentance, and the renouncing of bad ways, by the younger son. But for Jesus, repentance is not simply a way of making amends so as to rejoin the ranks of the pious, and take a front pew in the synagogue again. Repentance belongs to a different order of things altogether; it is a complete change, and it is a complete joy, on earth and in heaven.

Under Jewish law the father was not free to leave his property as he liked. The elder son was entitled to two thirds; the younger one third. It was not unusual for a father, before he died, to give his sons their shares.

First Sunday of Lent *(Sixth before Easter)*
21 February   *Principal Service*
Temptation   Matthew 4:1–11
'Jesus was led up by the Spirit into the wilderness to be tempted by the devil.' Matthew 4:1

Exalted
Our Lord was tempted almost immediately after he had under-gone a great spiritual experience – his baptism by John the Baptist, together with the coming of the Holy Spirit – one of the greatest happenings of his early life. The time also was just when Jesus was about to begin his mission of preaching, teaching and healing. He would have been planning for the future and full of hope for the success of his ministry.

Both these reasons would make it a time when he felt elated and exalted. How often this is the kind of time when we may be sorely tempted too. We also may have undergone some experience which has deepened our spiritual life, and made us keen to serve God – and this is the very moment when Satan strikes, because we are over-confident and over-sure of ourselves. Or we have done well at our business or profession or work – and then some weakness or indulgence takes over, and our future is destroyed.

The place
Our Lord was tempted while spending a long time alone, in an uninhabited piece of desert. Often we hear people talk of the temptations offered by big cities – and it is true that there are

many places in towns to attract people into sin. On the other hand, do not plenty of ways of doing wrong exist in the depths of the country? The truth is that there are temptations in every kind of surroundings – some are obvious, others less apparent but more subtle.

Jesus conquered temptation when he was without human aid in the desert. He did not despise the help of friends when it was available. For instance, he sought support and companionship from three of his apostles in the Garden of Gethsemane, when he was tempted to turn back from the suffering that lay ahead, although on that sad occasion he did not receive the help he sought.

The help

In our temptations, we may be able to get help from friends and loved ones; and we too may sometimes be able to give strength and support to others in their struggle with evil.

But remember Our Lord, isolated in the desert, fighting against temptation. The help he had there came from the Holy Spirit; and by the Holy Spirit's power and by his own strength of will, Jesus conquered.

Whether we have to do so alone, or have helpers at our side, we will seek to fight the evil around us and within us in the same way that Jesus did, by resisting it with all our human powers – and, far more important still, by seeking the Holy Spirit and using his help against our enemy, to support our own all-too-human efforts.

> *God of compassion,*
> *through your Son Jesus Christ,*
> *you have reconciled your people to yourself.*
> *As we follow his example of prayer and fasting,*
> *may we obey you with willing hearts*
> *and serve one another in holy love:*
> *through Jesus Christ our Lord.*

> *Patterns for Worship, 52.11*

First Sunday of Lent *Second Service*
The Joy of Finding Luke 15:1–10
'Rejoice with me, for I have found that which was lost.' Luke 15:6

Seeking
This parable was spoken to those of the Pharisees and scribes who complained: 'This man receives sinners – and eats with them!'

Luke sets three parables in the context of the grumbling objections set off by the leaders of Israel to Christ's human treatment of the outcasts – the tax collectors and other sinners who broke the Law, thereby separating themselves from the chosen people, and of course foreshadowing the Gentiles. The parables suggest something of the hopelessness and helplessness of the sheep that had strayed. So wayward people cannot return to God in their own strength, or even defend themselves unaided under the attacks of the Evil One, exactly as lost sheep are scattered. Repentance is indeed important – the repentance of the sinner is contrasted with the 'righteous', who are really self-righteous.

Again, neither the sheep nor the coin can repent; the sinners' repentance may be a gift of God, consequent upon being found – 'I have found the sheep that was lost', 'Rejoice with me, for I have found the coin which I had lost.'

Joy
The shepherd's joy in finding and recovering his sheep is shown in the parable by his calling his friends and neighbours together, to share in his joy. Similarly, the housewife, having swept and sought diligently, finds the lost coin and calls her friends and neighbours to rejoice together. This pictures for us the Saviour's joy when a soul is redeemed from sin and enters into the life which is eternal; the very angels in heaven share in the rejoicing over the return of what was thought to be lost.

Lost and found
Though the wandering sheep was merely one in a hundred, the shepherd did not despise it, but sought it out and brought it home. Moses the great Lawgiver learnt his first lessons in the care of sheep; the great King David had the same training. They were taught to care for their flocks; to care for each silly member of the

58

flocks. They were taught to feel for their flocks, to feel for each foolish dim-headed sheep. So they came to understand something of the love and care felt by the Lord for the nation of Israel, and for each member of that nation. The relation of the shepherd to his sheep was not calculated in money; they were each dear to him, he knew each one, any straggler would be missed, and searched for. The shepherd would go any distance and into any danger to bring back the sheep that had strayed.

The Good Shepherd
Christ, the Good Shepherd, came to save the lost sheep of God. He came to lay his hand upon us, lift us up on to his shoulder, and take us back to the fold.

Whether the sheep is fallen into some morass of vice and crime, or upon the dark and desolate moor of doubt, or upon the steep hillsides of error, the wandering charge is found by the persevering Lord – the shepherd who 'leaves the ninety-nine and goes after the one that is lost', or the woman who has lost a coin and 'seeks diligently, sweeping the house' until it is found. And over the lost when found, there is joy among the angels, and in the shepherd's heart, and indeed in the very heart of God himself.

Second Sunday of Lent (Fifth before Easter)
Principal Service   The Kingdom of God
John 3:1–17
'Truly, truly, I say to you, unless one is born anew, he cannot see the kingdom of God.' John 3:5

A seeker
Nicodemus was a learned man; he had been impressed by all he had heard about Jesus, and was deeply interested. As a leading and representative Jew, he is in a position of some authority; he is, however, not yet prepared to commit himself – hence the visit 'by night' – though he is ready to accept the view that Jesus 'comes from God' and calls him 'Rabbi'. Their conversation at first is diplomatic enough, but the Lord sweeps away everything, to

confront his visitor with his real need – entrance into the Kingdom of God.

Nicodemus is aware of rebirth by water, from John's preaching and career; and he has ideas of God's Kingdom, too, although birth of the Spirit was new to him, or so it seems. Yet this birth of water and the Spirit is alone able to give the privilege of entrance into the Kingdom. It is not enough to *know of* the Kingdom; it is more important to know it from within, by personal experience of it. After all, the Kingdom of God is a spiritual reality, experienced within the soul, but showing itself outwardly in the life that is lived. It has been said, 'the Kingdom is the world of invisible laws by which God is ruling and blessing his creation' (Hort).

Mere waiting for the Kingdom does not suffice; already, through Jesus, the Spirit is available as an agency of the new creation – 'You must be born anew,' and we must accept by faith that which is offered to us here and now, if we are indeed to have a new existence, whose origin is in God, and is on God to be centred.

Puzzled

By all this Nicodemus is frankly puzzled. He, of all people, a professional and learned teacher of the Old Testament, asks, 'How can this be?' Can he not understand that human existence is meaningless apart from God? Jesus tells him frankly that, among human beings, only one, the Son of Man, has direct knowledge of the heavenly world (v. 13). The 'lifting up' has a double meaning, pointing to both exaltation in glory, and the lifting up on the Cross. In John's thinking these are two aspects of the same thing – the crucifixion of Jesus *is* his glory. The Son of man is lifted up in this way in order that those who believe in him may be saved, just as those bitten by serpents were cured when they looked at the brazen serpent (Numbers 21:7–9). It was God's intention that the world should be saved, and for that reason he sent his Son to act as revealer – not as judge, but as saviour (vv. 16 and 17). The world is loved by God, and those who believe receive eternal life.

Our response

God has a right to expect our obedience to his will and way, so to know God's will should be to obey – 'Blessed are they who keep his commandments.' Because we are in Christ, we are members of the Kingdom of Heaven; this is assured to us by the indwelling presence of the Holy Spirit, who is also the pledge that we shall reach the fullness of the Kingdom in the life of the world to come.

Second Sunday of Lent *Second Service* **The Cost of Discipleship** Luke 14:27–33

'Whoever of you does not renounce all that he has, cannot be my disciple.'
Luke 14:33 'Bear your own cross and come after me.' v. 27

Difficulties

The Lord's audience has just heard the parable of the Great Banquet (14:15–24). The theme is the arrogance of those who will have nothing to do with the poverty-stricken, the maimed, the lame, the blind, and other outcasts, and certainly will never allow such creatures to share in the good things – their banquets and dinners, for example, where the poor and the others have no way by which they can repay, in any manner, the rich meals of the better-off (v. 14).

The multitudes (v. 27)

The Lord now turns to the crowds who accompany him, attempting to be counted as disciples, yet not wanting to leave behind comfortable family ties, or to abandon their paid occupations (their own life). No, sacrifice indeed is demanded, the Lord bluntly tells them, and the pains will be like carrying a cross – the all-too-well-known brutal and long-drawn-out trail to execution.

Have you, he says, decided that you will follow me on my rough, brutal and in the end, fatal, track? Or put it another way – count the cost. Suppose you were hoping to build your family a tower, for safety and protection? We can see, even today, in some Italian cities, family towers, places of refuge and safety. (San Gimignano in Tuscany retains no fewer than thirteen fortress-houses which give a fascinating medieval aspect to this pictur-esque hill city.) But if you ran out of money, and were not able to finish your tower, everyone would laugh at you; equally foolish would be a king who wanted to start a war against another ruler, but never checked that his army would be big enough to win – he would do better to beg for peace, would he not? So, do not consider becoming my disciple, unless you have decided to renounce all your possessions, and to accept a life of pain and suffering.

Way of life
The Christian way of life has much indeed to attract people. Some children are lucky enough to be brought up in good homes with Christian training. Whether they actually build upon it or not, they have been given a good foundation. In our adult years, we are more responsible for our foundations. Do we trust in Christ and try to follow his example? Do we keep in touch with the Church, and spend time in the company of good-living people? Do we read our Bibles, come to Communion, try to build up a Christian life, helping others, doing what we can to spread the gospel message? The Christian way of life has much about it which attracts men and women, but the high demands drive some away before long. Are we capable of being finishing Christians, not merely beginners? Lent is a time to consider more than small pieces of self-denial; it reminds us of the need to put the things of God before the things of this world; and to seek for the heavenly treasure, the riches we find in serving and loving God.

Third Sunday of Lent (*Fourth before Easter*)
7 March   *Principal Service*   **Living Water**
John 4:5–42

'Jesus, wearied as he was with his journey, sat down beside the well.'
John 4:6

Water and women
Jesus is sitting, tired and thirsty, at the side of the road on which he has been walking from Judea to Galilee. He is in Samaria, beside a well, 'Jacob's Well', very ancient and very deep. He has no means of drawing even a little water, but then a woman approaches with bucket. Another difficulty presents itself – the ancient antipathy between Jew and Samaritan. So close, with such similar roots, yet they are bitterly opposed to each other – indeed, to use the same drinking vessel would be forbidden. Again, while it was not for-

bidden for a man to converse with a female stranger, it was against all custom for a rabbi to do so. Today, how much fuss there is about 'Women's Lib' – yet without fuss or talk Christ simply accepted women as equal and rightful members of the human race, and treated them as such.

Fresh water

What a dream come true it must have seemed to the woman at the well, to have fresh clean water available all the time at her home. No trudging up and down the dusty road to the well, no more heaving and hauling; no more worry as to whether there was enough in the house for the needs of the day. And – living water! fresh, cool, not stale and flat and dull.

Don't we know the difference between city water, processed and treated with chemicals (for our good, of course, but . . . !) and country water, fresh from the stream or spring? Difficult for us to share the thoughts of those people, when we have our taps and showers, basins and toilets, and for most of the year at least, unlimited water, all we need, at the turn of a tap. Thank God for the benefits of science and engineering, and let us do all we can to help less fortunate folk.

Worship

But all this is leading up to Jesus' comments on worship. The bitterness between Samaritan and Jew was exemplified by the two different centres of worship – the Samaritans turned to pray towards their sacred Mount Gerizim, where the ruins of their ancient sanctuary still remained, the very mountain, in fact, at the foot of which Jesus and the woman were talking! The Jews, of course, turned towards Jerusalem. And Christ makes it clear that both these conceptions are outdated now – no longer do we need a *localized* worship, orientating ourselves towards that place on earth which God had made particularly his own. Exactly the same idea gives the Muslims today their need to find the precise bearing of the sacred city of Mecca, as they prepare to perform their daily worship.

'In truth'

Jesus opposes this concept with a new idea, that of 'worship in spirit and in truth'. God is not tied to any place – or time – and similarly his worship must be detached from dependence on any particular place.

But more than this – Christ was giving spiritual significance to the natural realities of life, in this case, to water. He tells the woman that we all need 'living water', that is, spiritual refreshment, keeping us spiritually alive and giving value to all that we do. Yes, we may need water physically, but we also need a divine spring of spiritual water within us, which will be life from God issuing in eternal life for us.

The woman does not yet understand what Jesus is telling her; but his statement concerning her irregular married life shocks her into recognition that he has indeed the powers of a prophet – and may well be the promised Messiah. Jesus tells her she is right – in him all the promises of God are brought to fulfilment. She glimpses the wonder of the moment, and leaving her water jar, goes off to tell the people of the town what has happened, and encourages them to come and see.

The disciples

The disciples are surprised to find Jesus talking to a woman, but are more concerned for him to eat. He has no need, he says, for his food is to do the will of God, and accomplish God's demands. The disciples are to be sowers and reapers, working together to bring in the harvest of the Kingdom, he reminds them. The Samaritans of the town are captivated by the account from the woman, and persuade Jesus to stay on for two days; they are so far convinced by what he says that they entitle him 'Saviour of the world' – not of Jews only, be it noted. A great step forward, indeed. Our Eucharist is the new worship, not of one or another sect, separated from each other like the bitter Jews and Samaritans, but bringing together in the feast of unity all who believe in Christ as the Saviour of the world (v. 43).

Third Sunday of Lent *Second Service* **The Whole Armour of God** Ephesians 6:10–20

'Put on the whole armour of God, that you may be able to stand against the wiles of the devil.' Ephesians 6:11

The wiles of the devil

We think of the allurements which come to us from 'the world, the flesh, and the devil'. This continuous reckoning with temptation has led people to speak of 'the battle of life'. In every-day matters we have to struggle against indolence, lust, dishonest tendencies, and many other things in ourselves. We also have to contend with opposition, bad treatment, temptation on the part of others, and the depressing effects of trials and disappointment. 'We tried hard but something went wrong,' we say; or, 'Life is a struggle!' All hard work is a struggle, is it not? It is the same for the physical worker, straining muscles, the brain worker coping with difficult computations, and the busy housewife – of whom it is truly said 'her work is never done'. All these are the spheres in which we encounter 'the temptations of the world, the flesh and the devil' as the Collect has it.

Weakness

The temptations of the world and the flesh attack us through our appetites, our wish for the 'easy way', and our vain self-esteem. Yes, these all have what we might call a 'wily approach', getting us on their side by making it all seem so pleasant and easy. We need to exert ourselves and take a piece of real self-examination, which will tell us what they are. Look back at our experiences and we will all too often be told how they achieved their successes. Then there are the 'wiles of the devil', as our text puts it. These allurements to evil are in a different category from the others. They appeal to what we call 'our lower nature', sensuality, that is. But there are the wiles that appeal to what we may call our 'higher nature'. This 'higher nature' is ours because we are spiritual beings. Because we are self-conscious, aware of ourselves as thoughtful beings, we can set ideas before us with hopes to reach them, for our own benefit for sure, or perhaps even for the benefit of others. But often these aims mean, in some way or other, the putting forward of dubious ideas, clever plans, quick changes, which may produce what we are after. Yet we are using methods, suggestions, to achieve our aims, which are a betrayal of our higher nature. They may mean taking advantage of the weaknesses of others, or using methods which are not truly genuine and even untruthful. We betray our own higher nature, and allow our spirits to consider debased and even destructive ideas for our benefit.

Peril

Pride has been described as 'the inordinate love of one's own excellence.' Pride may be like vanity, but it is not the same thing. Pride is inwardly satisfied in its own self-importance, and is indifferent to the opinions of others. Indeed, the height of pride may be seen in a scorn for the admiration of others, even a dislike or hatred of other people's opinions, and a contempt for the 'dim mob, the ideas of the crowd'. We make idols of ourselves, of our own merits and our capacities. No, we are not licentious, nor worldly 'climbers'. Yet we have a demand for the subservience of others, especially those in the same firm or company or business. Pride leads us on; demands the subservience of others, calls for the acceptance of our own opinions and makes our dictates the rule of the occupation. We may of course fall victim to an over-confident belief in ourselves. This is folly, however clever or competent we may be; such thoughts too often presage disaster. Again and again we are urged to 'keep up with the times', or perhaps more often, 'to move with the times'. Merely moving with the times may lead to faulty decisions and mistaken judgements. Of course we need to be aware of what people are thinking and saying – we need to 'be aware of the times' – but we must be able to weigh and examine both thought and action to see if they express, and allow for, the mind of God.

Fourth Sunday of Lent *(Third before Easter)*
14 March *Principal Service* **The Light of the World** John 9:1–41

'We must work the works of him who sent me, while it is day; night comes, when no one can work. As long as I am in the world, I am the light of the world.' John 9:4,5

A blind man

The spectacle of human suffering put an acute question to religious believers, in those days as indeed now. If God is just and good, how can he allow this? Jesus' reply does not deny the possibility of a general relation between sin and suffering, but does deny any specific and personal relation, and points to the use that God has presented for the display of the power of healing that Jesus has been given. This power will, however, only be available as long as Jesus is in the world, offering life and light. The man, eyes anointed with clay, goes to the pool of Siloam and comes back seeing.

The Pharisees take umbrage at the making of paste and the anointing with it upon the Sabbath, thus breaking the Sabbath rule of 'doing work' (v. 6). Others say, 'How can a man who is a sinner do such signs?' and again, 'Give God the praise; we know that this man [Jesus] is a sinner' (v. 24). The blind man says bluntly, 'Whether he is a sinner, I do not know; one thing I know, though I was blind, now I see' (v. 25). The Pharisees want him to go over the treatment, but he refuses – 'I have told you already, and you would not listen . . .' Quite clearly he is getting somewhat cross – and how natural! To ordinary people it was quite clear where Jesus 'came from' – from God; and some Pharisees at least might take the same view. Others cannot join in the popular acclamation: 'This fellow is no man of God; he does not keep the Sabbath!' (v. 17). Yet others try to cast doubt on what had actually happened, and when this fails, they resort to angry talk: 'Who are you to teach us?' and cast the man out (v. 34).

The moral of the episode may be said to be that the man's acceptance of Jesus is as definite as the Pharisees' rejection. Jesus brought into the world of the present the Divine Judgement, which is usually thought of as something in the far distant future. The response of the 'blind' man in declaring his belief in the 'Son of Man', and his worship of Jesus, is symbolic indeed; while the final response to the Pharisees, who refuse to 'see', is the placing of guilt upon them, due to their own ignorance and lack of vision.

> *Grant us your light, O Lord,*
> *that the darkness of our hearts being done away,*
> *we may be brought at the last*
> *to that light which is Christ. Amen.*

PHG, 47

Fourth Sunday of Lent *Second Service* **From Darkness to Light** Micah 7 and James 4

'When I fall, I shall arise; when I sit in darkness the Lord shall be a light unto me.' Micah 7:8. 'Draw near to God, and he will draw near to you.' James 4:8

The Lord called me

Micah was a shepherd and dresser of trees; in the long watches of the night, he must have felt 'The heavens declare the glory of God', and meditated. He was no professional prophet, but felt called to denounce the evils of the sophisticated people of Samaria. He preached against greed, oppression, iniquity, and other evil-doings which certainly shocked a simple, godly, countryman. He said: 'Assemble on the hills; look at the seething and tumult among your people, and the oppressors in your midst. They grind down the faces of the poor. You have built new houses, vulgar and ostentatious – you shall not live in them.' They were looking, Micah says, for the Day of the Lord, but in terms of triumph for themselves. 'It will be darkness, a day of gloom, with no dawn.'

Penitence

In true penitence we have to say, 'I will bear the indignation of the Lord, as I have sinned against him.' We have to suffer for our sins, and make amends. True penitence will, above all else, trust in God and in his mercy. 'He retaineth not his anger for ever' (v. 18). We can learn too, for instance, from the parable of the Prodigal Son, that God is always ready to meet us halfway – or more! He is ever merciful, let us remember. After all, there is no failure except that of stopping trying. God is a God of hope – 'He retaineth not his anger for ever' (v. 18). From time to time a deep tenderness of heart shows itself in the prophet, and his pleading is as urgent as anywhere.

Sacrifice

If we now turn to St James the Apostle, we remember that he and John – 'Sons of Thunder' as the Lord nicknamed them – were rebuked gently when their mother tried to get special favour for them. To share his glory they have to share his sufferings. His main theme in his letter is in v. 22: 'Be doers of the word, not hearers only', but much good advice is to be read also – v. 27 is most touching as defining 'pure religion', and giving the advice to keep oneself 'unspotted from the world'.

James is one of the three favoured apostles, an 'inner circle' who were with Jesus on important occasions. They were witnesses to the Transfiguration, to the raising of Jairus' daughter, and to the heart-breaking events of the Agony in the Garden of Gethsemane. James' expressed willingness to 'drink the cup' was realized all too soon, in his being the first of the Apostles to die for the Lord (Acts 12:1–2). James shows us that the way to peace is through repentance and self-sacrifice. Jesus reminds us that there is no short cut to greatness – only those willing to suffer and pay the price can be great.

Fifth Sunday of Lent *(Second before Easter): (Passiontide begins)* 21 March *Principal Service* I am the Resurrection and the Life
John 11:1–45

'Jesus said, "I am the resurrection and the life; he who believes in me, though he die, yet shall he live; and whosoever lives and believes in me shall never die."' John 11:25–26

The valley of dry bones
In our Old Testament lesson (Ezekiel 37:1–14), in a vision the prophet Ezekiel sees a vast plain upon which is strewn a myriad of dry bones. To the question posed by God, 'Can these bones live?' the prophet has no answer; such an idea seems utterly impossible. But the Lord tells him to prophesy over the bones, that they shall live – and the bones then become alive and move together and rise up. 'I will open your graves, and cause you to come up out of your graves, O my people. And you shall know that I am the Lord, when I open your graves, and raise you from your graves' (Ezekiel 37:3,13).

This is brought to our minds when we hear the reading today from St John's Gospel, and how Jesus raises from the dead Lazarus, brother of Mary of Bethany, in Judaea.

The miracle

We are told at the beginning (John 11) of a message sent to the Lord from Mary and Martha, concerning the illness of Lazarus. Jesus makes (we might say) little of the message, but suggests the dangerous move back to Judaea. This horrifies the disciples, since it would mean going back into very definite danger (see 10:31, 39). One disciple, however, Thomas – he whom we find much later absenting himself from the fellowship of the sorrowing apostles, refusing to accept the Resurrection without incontrovertible evidence (John 20:25) – bursts out with complete loyalty, 'Let us go also, that we may die with the Lord!' (11:16).

At Bethany

Lazarus had indeed died, soon after Mary's message was received; now Jesus talks of 'wakening' him (v. 11), and they set off to Bethany. Martha comes to meet him, and is given the assurance, 'Your brother will rise again.' She thinks that Jesus is referring to the Resurrection on the Last Day: but Jesus reminds her, 'He who has faith in me, though he die, shall come to life; and no one who is alive and has faith shall ever die.' Has she the faith to believe? 'Yes, Lord, I believe you are the Messiah, the Son of God.'

Jesus shows tender sympathy with the sisters, as he sees their grief. He sighs heavily, deeply moved by their weeping; and when they come to where Lazarus has been buried, Jesus weeps himself. At the tomb, he orders the removal of the grave-stone. 'Four days dead,' says Martha. In Jewish folk lore, the soul haunted the body for three days, and so it was just possible that a return to life might be made in that time. But after that, death was irrevocable; the body was decomposing, and the smell of death lay heavy in the air.

The raising

Jesus utters the prayer, 'Father, I thank you; you have heard me . . .' Then comes the awe-inspiring call, a great cry: 'Lazarus, come out!' And the order, 'Loose him, and let him go.'

Lazarus hears the voice of Christ, and lives.

This is what Jesus promised should happen: it is the time 'When the dead shall hear the voice of the Son of God, and all who hear shall come to life' (John 5:25).

It is the abiding 'in Christ' by a living faith that ensures immortality; it is the believer who keeps Christ's saying, 'He that abides in me, and my words abide in him, he shall ask what he will, and it shall be done' (John 15:7).

Fifth Sunday of Lent *Second Service*
Ambition Matthew 20:17–34

'We are able.' Matthew 20:22

Going up to Jerusalem

As they are starting the journey to Jerusalem, Jesus warns his disciples, in the bluntest way, that the future is to be condemnation, cruelty and death for him, and perhaps for them also. In spite of this warning, James and John decide that they should make an attempt to reserve important and rewarding positions for themselves in the Kingdom to come. Matthew makes it clear that the mother of the two disciples is persuaded to take their hopes to the Lord (vv. 20–22). He sees through the attempt, and speaks directly and forcibly to the pair. Did they imagine that in Jerusalem Jesus would become a real king, and they would be his chief courtiers? Jesus' reply insists on the trials and tribulations that would come before any future glory. 'Can you drink the cup that I am to drink?' Suffering and afflictions must be the destiny of his followers; but precedence is the gift of the Father. More, in the new Kingdom a radical change will obtain – unlike the courts of the heathen rulers, where the important men lord it over the others – in Christ's Kingdom 'whoever wants to be great must be your servant', exactly following the example of Jesus himself.

The point of the Lord's answer

There is no short cut, no easy way, to the Christian triumph. In our smaller way, we are to be like the Lord himself, for whom the path of glory and victory, was the laborious and painful one of trial and suffering, of toil and sacrifice and even of death itself, 'a ransom for many' indeed.

For James, for John and for Peter, this was brought home to them after the Resurrection – 'Lovest thou me? Feed my lambs! Follow me.' For us, who are also, let us never forget, called to be martyrs – 'witnesses' is what that word means – the message is

71

the same. Jesus says to us, just as surely as he said it to his disciples – 'Do you love me? Follow me! Feed my lambs!'

Palm Sunday   28 March   *Principal Service*
The Passion   Matthew 26:14–27:66
or Matthew 27:11-54

'He humbled himself, and in obedience accepted even death – death on a cross.' Philippians 2:8

The Green Hill

> *There is a green hill far away*
> *Without a city wall,*
> *Where the dear Lord was crucified*
> *Who died to save us all.*

NEH 92

Jerusalem

We commemorate today the entrance of Our Lord Jesus Christ into Jerusalem, the Holy City, whose name means no less than 'Place of Peace'. Into the city of peace comes the king of peace.

How fearfully ironic that sounds, when we recall what a disputed prize of battle this city has been down the ages – Assyria, Egypt, Philistinia, the Romans, the Muslims, the Crusaders, the Turks, the Arabs, the British, the Israelis . . . All have fought over this little city; its streets have run with blood again and again, and still do even in our own day; its houses have been burnt, its walls have been razed to the ground, and the very site sown with salt. And yet, and yet – it is still a world city, it is still a symbol of immense importance to three major religions. It is still a city for which men will kill and die.

Christ's coming

The palms were waving, the children singing, the disciples and the crowds singing and shouting; the Leader was jostled and mobbed by the enthusiasts, but still by some miracle he remained upon his mount. The conqueror enters in triumph; the Christ comes in peace. He rides an ass, not a war-horse; he carries no weapon. And yet the moment of entry is itself a moment of judgement. Against Christ and his standards as he appears, we are inevitably measured; and inevitably we fall short. And his entry *into* the city is equally a moment of judgement *for* the city. A change takes place as Christ enters. It is like that moment when a strong solution of some chemical reaches saturation point – suddenly, a mere tap on the side of the container, and everything alters, the solution crystallizes. A deep change takes place.

The city

And so it is with the city as Christ enters it. Matthew takes a phrase from Zechariah (vv. 4,5) even including 'the colt, the foal of an ass'; so anxious is he to be faithful to the Old Testament, he also puts in from Psalm 8 the verse about 'babes and sucklings'. It is the theme of the fulfilment of the Scriptures that stands out prominently in Matthew; he is speaking, as explained before, to Jewish Christians who had expected a triumphant and glorious Messiah. Matthew shows them, with telling quotations, that the prophecies had foretold down the ages a suffering Messiah, and had depicted the Passion even to the minor details of actual events. We must remember he is writing for the use of the converts from Judaism to Christianity. The setting is comparable to that of the Feast of Tents; the Messiah hoped for in that feast has in fact arrived.

Hostility

Note how quickly the welcome of the city to its king changes to bitter hostility. The same crowds who welcome Jesus today, will in a few more days be howling for his death. Even the Twelve, his closest friends, will have deserted him.

We may well ask ourselves: how would we, in our cities, react to the Coming of Christ? What would our cities do to Our Lord? Our great cities, under enormous strains and stresses – faced with the problems of immigrants and refugees from war and persecution; the different cultures; the sheer physical problems and expenses of services, transport, housing, fire, police, hospitals, care. The moral problems of drug abuse, sexual abuse, violence and theft. How do we deal with these seething cauldrons of apparently hopeless difficulties and intractable problems?

73

Judgement

The coming of Christ to Jerusalem was a coming in judgement; and the result of that coming was his death. The seeming triumph of his enemies would be changed to dust and ashes in only a few hours, when Jerusalem was utterly destroyed by the Romans. Do we refuse to accept Christ? Or do we accept him at first, and then turn and reject him? The kingship of Christ can only be understood and accepted by those who are willing to suffer with him. His kingship was proclaimed from that Cross where he reigned 'from the Tree', on that green hill outside the city wall.

Each Palm Sunday and each Holy Week is a chance for us to deepen our sharing of the Cross, that we may be made ready to share in the joy of the resurrection triumph, and in the hope of being with the Lord in glory, in that New Jerusalem that we are promised.

Palm Sunday *Second Service* Two Vineyards
Isaiah 5:1–7 and Matthew 21:33–46

A song of harvest ...

The prophet Isaiah adopts, in our first reading, an unusual approach to put over his message. He speaks – or rather, sings – in the guise of a strolling minstrel at a harvest. He rejoices at the riches of the earth and at the goodness of God. The vineyard he describes is a goodly place indeed – well planned, carefully hedged and ditched, with a tower and a press built at hand – a good place for his dear friend.

But alas, the grapes prove to be of very poor quality. Instead of good, sweet succulent grapes, the fruit is *wild* grapes, sour, small and useless. What can be done with such a disappointing plot? Cut it down, lay it waste, let it lie fallow ... Then comes the moment of revelation: the vineyard is the nation of Israel! God has bestowed upon Israel his grace and loving care, and he has expected the fruit of justice and of righteousness – only to get the foul fruit of injustice and oppression. It is therefore Israel that is to be given over to destruction. God's defence of her is removed.

Jesus, entering into Jerusalem, encounters hostility and distrust
from the authorities; he tells *his* parable of the vineyard, obviously
based very closely on Isaiah. His hearers would at once recognize
the setting and the theme, and be prepared for the same kind of
allegory.

If the vineyard is Israel, then the other features of the story must
be equally symbolic. So, the owner of the vineyard is God, his
servants are the prophets, and the only son is Jesus himself. The
question, 'Whom do the vine-growers stand for?' is answered by
Matthew – the chief priests and elders (v. 23), who had in fact
provoked this parable from Jesus and now see that it is aimed at
them. One further point: Who were the 'others' to whom the vineyard would be given – the other tenants who will give the Owner
the fruits in their seasons? (v. 41). Reading the story after the
events, we answer, 'The Christian Church'.

Foresight

Did Jesus foresee his own condemnation by the Sanhedrin, and
his following death, so clearly that he was able to work it into this
allegory? Did he actually refer to himself as the 'only Son' of God
– and what would this have meant to a Jewish audience of that
time?

These are difficult questions; the scholars tell us that it is most
probable that the story, as told by Jesus originally, was concerned
more with the need to recognize *now* the messengers of God; *now*
is the time to repent, before inevitable fate overcomes you. For us,
there is the clear meaning to be understood in the story, of the
need to recognize that *now* is the time to repent; *now* is the hour
of the Lord; and also that through Christ and his sacrifice upon
the Cross we are offered a way of reconciliation and renewal. Let
us take these messages to heart.

Maundy Thursday 1 April Our Example
John 13:1–17, 31b–35
*'I have set you an example; you are to do as I have done for you.' John
13:15*

The Lord's Supper

This night, we celebrate the establishing of the Eucharist, the Christian Passover, the Supper of the Lord.

In how many places, in how many different times, in how many different ways, has this Sacrament been celebrated, after its solemn institution by Christ himself this night? And yet, remember, it is always the same Eucharist; it is the People of God coming together to remember, to re-present, the Lord's death 'until he come'; to share in the mystical Body and Blood, the Bread of Life and the Cup of Salvation.

Very moving, the service tonight, with the sudden glory of rich vestments in the drabness of Lent, with the Gloria heard again after so long a time, with the symbolic footwashing, with the procession to the place of repose, and the Watch – like the watch at Gethsemane . . .

Different

The same Eucharist . . . yet tonight is different.

Our Sunday Eucharist is celebrated in the light and the joy of the Resurrection; tonight the backcloth is very much impending doom, and destruction, and death . . . That same Jesus with whom we walked the dusty roads, paraded into Jerusalem only five short days ago, with palms and crowds and singing, we now know all too well is liable to arrest, to be dragged off and subjected to all the brutal third-degree cruelties that are the usual treatment for common criminals.

Frightened

The apostles are frightened, their nerve has gone; forces too big for them to cope with have taken over their lives. Distracted – at one moment so worn out with worry and fear that they drop asleep; at the next, up and running – they are to watch, from a safe distance, unlike the women at the Cross, their leader, the Messiah as they had hoped, being stretched out, nailed down and left to die miserably as a failed political force, like a robber or thief, with the insurgents and rioters.

For the apostles, despite the promises made to them on the way to Jerusalem, there is no hope – worse, they are, until the last bitter moments, unable to believe what is happening.

Commandment

It is only later, much later, that what has been said and done this evening, over the common meal, comes back to them, and they are able to see its true meaning. Today's title comes from the Latin *Mandatum*, commandment, 'a new commandment I give to you, that you love one another' (John 13:34). So today is really 'Commandment Thursday', the day when the Lord made quite plain what he wants from us.

Not a request – a command. First, that we love one another, as he has loved us. Second, that we serve one another, as he washed our feet, like a servant does. Third, that we 'Do this . . . for my memorial.'

There is no *request* about all this. No 'do you mind . . .', 'would you please . . .', 'if you feel like it . . .', 'perhaps now and then . . .' Oh no; *do* this, here and now, every time you gather to eat the bread and drink the cup. Love one another, serve one another – or you have no part in me, no fellowship, no life in me at all.

Tonight

Our service is much more than a mere ceremonial event. Elaborate or simple, we are making our re-commitment to service, our re-dedication to mutual love, our challenge to live out the eucharistic life, day by day, in the world as we know it and as we meet it. 'Do this in remembrance of me; do this as my memorial.'

Good Friday 2 April *Principal Service* The King of the Jews John 18:1–19:42

'Jesus, knowing all that was to befall him, came forward and said, "Whom do you seek?" They answered him, "Jesus of Nazareth". Jesus said to them, "I am he". (John 18:4;5) or, 'Pilate wrote a title and put it on the cross; it read "Jesus of Nazareth, the King of the Jews." ' (John 19:19)

Our thoughts on Calvary

During this service let us centre our thoughts on something very far off in time – the execution of Jesus of Nazareth. It happened very nearly two thousand years ago, in the country of Israel, or Palestine, which was then an unimportant little part of the great

Roman Empire, on the little hill called Calvary. Today it is not only we who are thinking of this brutal event of long ago; many, many people throughout the world are doing so too. We are not alone; it is in the minds of millions of people every Holy Week and every Good Friday.

The fact that this day has attracted, and has retained, the attention of men and women in such vast numbers, and down through so many centuries, must help to bring home to us what an all-important occurrence this brutal happening, this cruel execution, truly was.

Unnoticed at the time

It did not arouse much interest when it took place. It certainly stirred the Jews considerably for a short time. It seemed to the ordinary Jew in the street that a great Teacher – some called him a Prophet – had arisen. He preached in both town and country and made a considerable impression, though he also aroused considerable opposition from both the Church and the State. In fact, his career was cut short tragically and suddenly, when he was put to death by judicial execution. That was all that our Lord's crucifixion meant to most of them. To the world at large, it did not mean even that; the citizens of other countries knew nothing of a petty disturbance in Jerusalem and the execution there of a religious leader. Even if they knew more, they would not have been interested; such things happened all too often. When Pilate ordered that the title 'King of the Jews' be placed above the Cross, he probably meant to show the Jews how little it mattered to non-Jews who that 'king' was, and that he was a condemned criminal anyway.

Vital to us

This event that aroused no interest, except purely locally, when it took place, now draws Christians, men and women all over the world, to Jesus, for without the happenings of Good Friday, and the suffering and final brutal death that Jesus endured for our sakes, we would not be calling Jesus our King or our Saviour.

If Jesus had lived among us human people, had set us a supreme example of goodness, had taught us, healed us, and then made a quiet return to his Heavenly Father, he would have won respect; he might even have been given the title 'King' on our lips, but he would never have become King in our hearts. It required the Cross

78

to earn him that. What was to be seen on Calvary was a divine Act, which however immersed and displayed in the outward, brutal and sordid circumstances in which it took place, has its origin and cause in the Mind and Will of the eternal God, Creator of all things. A divine, yet no less truly a human act, embraced by the human mind of Jesus, accepted, freely chosen and carried out. 'Lo, I come to do thy will, O God ... a body hast thou prepared for me' (Hebrews 10:5–7).

Sacrifice

What Christ did was to offer himself, wholly and entirely, as a sacrifice expressive of the worship, praise, honour, thanksgiving, love, obedience and service that we owe to our Creator and Lord.

Further, because Christ is acting as High Priest and representative of humanity, not only as created but also as humanity really is, sinful and separated from God, so his sacrifice becomes one of propitiation, reparation, intercession, atonement and reconciliation. The Resurrection is the sign that the Sacrifice has been accepted, and the promise that its effects are within the reach of all humanity who shall desire to receive them.

And let us be clear, both act and effects are due to the fact that it was not 'a man' who suffered and died upon the Cross, but the God-Man Jesus Christ, whose divinity gives an infinite value both to the act itself and to its effects, which enable us to do what we had no power of ourselves to do

In Christ

The full meaning of the Cross, on which hung the human body of Jesus, is not really disclosed until what he began there, and consummated in the fullest manner, is seen to be carried on in his mystical body, the Church. St Augustine writes, 'Christ continues still to suffer in his members, that is – in us. The full measure of the Passion will not be complete until the end of the world.' So we may rightly say, that what Christ did for humanity is done in, and by, humanity itself united to its Head.

Good Friday   *Second Service*
Sacrifice   Genesis 22:1–18

'Take your son Isaac, your only son, whom you love, and offer him as a sacrifice.' Genesis 22:2

An almost fatal error
One of the most dramatic stories in the Old Testament is about human sacrifice. Influenced by the way in which the people of the tribes, amongst whom he lived, offered their own children as sacrifices to their heathen gods, Abraham mistakenly decided that it was his duty to show as much devotion to the true God, whom he worshipped, and therefore to offer up his son, his only son, Isaac. He and the boy made their pilgrimage to the hill in the land of Moriah, where Abraham tied the boy to a wooden altar, and was on the point of killing him when he felt that God was telling him not to do so. 'Now I know you fear God, seeing that you have not withheld your son, your only son.' Abraham realized that human sacrifice was contrary to God's will. So, he looked, and found a ram instead.

Sacrifices in the Temple
Throughout most of the Bible we regularly read of bird and animal sacrifices being offered, usually in the Temple, by the Jews. Joseph and Mary did just so, when they brought the baby Jesus to the Temple for the first time; under the later laws promulgated by Moses, the sad and cruel demand for the killing of the 'first-born' was translated into an offering of some other living creature – lamb, pigeon, donkey or ox. Joseph and Mary, being poor, gave two doves (Luke 2:22–24). Jesus drove cattle out of the Temple courts because of the disturbance which they caused, being there to be made sacrifices (see John 2:13–24). However, this form of worship only ended amongst the Jews when the Temple was destroyed.

Christian sacrifice
The Christian Church does not sacrifice animals in the way in which the Jews once did, but it would be wrong to say that 'We have done away with sacrifice.' In the first place, our whole Christian faith is based upon sacrifice – the greatest sacrifice of all, when

Jesus laid down his life upon the Cross. Again and again in the course of our worship, that act of sacrifice is mentioned, and especially in the Eucharist, when the words of our Lord are used – 'Take, eat; this is my body,' over the bread; and 'Drink of this, all of you; for this is my blood of the covenant, poured out for many for the remission of sins' (Matthew 26:26–28). Indeed, if we are genuine followers of Jesus Christ, our whole life should be one of sacrifice. We should be ready to give up what we value, and to endure inconvenience and hardship to advance his Kingdom, or for the welfare of others.

Our motives
There are very different reasons for actions of sacrifice on our part, and whether we are conscious of it or not, in doing them the Christian is following the Saviour, to some extent, and treading in his footsteps. He set us the supreme example of sacrifice, when he died for us on the Cross.

Easter Day   4 April   *Principal Service*
He has risen!   Matthew 28:1–10
'The angel said to the women, "Do not be afraid; for I know that you seek Jesus who was crucified. He is not here, for he has risen, as he said."' Matthew 28:5

Daybreak
The dreadful night of the Passion and the Death of Jesus is ended. 'Towards the dawn,' St Matthew tells us – it was to be the most wonderful dawn, the fairest morning the world had known, the morning of his Resurrection. It began to dawn: the words have a mystical as well as literal meaning. They express in a poetic symbol everything that Easter meant to Mary Madgalene and to the other Mary when they went to see the sepulchre; all that it meant to the disciples; all that it means to us. The Resurrection of Jesus was indeed the dawn, pouring light upon a shadowed world; like the dawn of day, it changed the aspect of everything. Doubt and sorrow were scattered in a moment; faith, hope and love were

re-animated within human hearts. It is indeed the Lord's Day, it is so magnificently triumphant.

Towards the dawn
'Towards the dawn of the first day of the week' – such words symbolize not only the triumph of joy over sorrow, but the triumph of good over evil. 'The angel of the Lord descended from heaven and came and rolled back the stone, and sat upon it.' He proclaimed that righteousness had triumphed, that the real law which rules the world is moral and not material, and that in the long run spirit is always stronger than mere force.

The greatest proof ever given that the world is indeed ruled by a righteous God, was given when Jesus, the sinless Victim of triumphant evil, was raised by the Resurrection from the clutches of death.

Pessimism
We need assurance today, as much as it was ever needed. Pessimism is telling you that the idea of progress is an exploded fallacy – oh yes, we constantly see or hear new aircraft, larger and faster and more magnificent; we see new cars of more and more fanciful and streamlined design; our television becomes more varied and of greater range, with news from country after country. Marvellous! But what does our TV show us – misery in country after country, hate and violence let loose, starvation of vast numbers of suffering humans, men, women and children, the old and the young, reduced to shrunken, pathetic creatures. The nuclear weapon takes precedence over care for the people of the nations – in India, Pakistan, China, Islam, Israel perhaps also. Russian nuclear material is sold off or stolen. And the people starve, sink into apathy and misery; progress is an exploded fallacy.

Encouragement
Yet it is for hours of doubt and darkness like our examples, that Easter provides a glorious message of encouragement. Through darkness of despair came the Easter dawn. It is impossible to believe in the Resurrection and at the same time believe that the spirit of this world will eventually conquer the spirit of Christ. At the empty tomb, we know that right is might, and that evil in the long run will succeed only in its own destruction. Let us, in the light of the Easter revelation, do our part and lend our help in the

slow fulfilment of God's divine purpose. The Risen Jesus shows the triumph of life over death; the complete and final triumph gives us more than hope. In the Living Lord we have the eternal guarantee that in the end, always and everywhere, Life wins.

Easter Day *Second Service* The Empty Tomb John 20:11–18

'They have taken away my Lord, and I do not know where they have laid him!' John 20:13

Where . . . ?

When Mary Magdalene went through the garden to the tomb on that first Easter morning, she expected to find the body of the Lord just where he had been laid by loving hands, loving but sorrowful, so short a time before. She came to perform the last sad offices for the dead, to wash, to wipe, and to anoint.

But the body had gone. It was not there. Where could it be? Where had it been taken? No thought of resurrection entered her mind; naturally she assumed that someone – officials perhaps? the Roman authorities? the Temple police? or maybe a group of the disciples? – had taken the body away.

Who . . . ?

Then who were these young men in white? Had they taken the Lord's body away? And if so, where had they placed him?

What a vivid and poignant dialogue we have recorded in St John's account – the bewilderment in the early morning, still dark, or maybe the sun was just sending its first beams over the horizon.

The theatre

Is there something almost theatrical about the scene? Well might we think so, for from this episode, surprising though it may seem, grew and developed all the vast tree of the English theatre, which we see and admire today. What happened was, that in the early Middle Ages, the events of Holy Week were represented – or rather, re-presented – in the churches. Christ on the donkey on

Palm Sunday, with the crowds bearing palms or green branches; the sorrowful singing of the Passion, with different voices taking the various parts; the Maundy Thursday ceremonies; the Good Friday Veneration of the Cross – and on Easter Sunday a version of the Resurrection story acted out.

One of the clergy took the part of Mary, probably in dark blue or purple robe, and mournfully came towards the Easter Sepulchre – examples of which, carved in stone, can still be seen in the chancels of our older churches. Two other clerics acted the parts of the angels, in white.

'Mary . . .'
'What seekest thou, Mary?' 'Whom seekest thou, Mary?'

And so, before the principal Eucharist of the morning, the Easter Story was acted out. Here was the germ, the first small shoot, of what was later to grow and develop a life of its own, independent of the Church where it all began – the theatre. When today plays are put on in church, it really is a return to origins. The first actors were the clergy; the first stage manager an unknown monk, the sacristan; the first costumes, the church vestments; and the stage, the sanctuary.

Aims for today
The aims of the first actors were to bring before the people the facts of the Easter story; to make real to their audience of simple and unlettered folk the Bible narrative, and the truths of the gospel. Surprising and effective it must have been. Sophisticated we are in our time, but surely we can take a lesson from those far-off days!

It should be our aim to tell others convincingly about the Easter joy, about the Resurrection story, and help them to find him who is their Lord as well as ours, using all our means and all our God-given talents in his service.

Second Sunday of Easter   11 April   *Principal Service*   **My Lord and my God!**   John 20:19–31

'On the evening of that day, the first day of the week, the doors being shut where the disciples were, for fear of the Jews, Jesus came and stood among them and said, "Peace be with you!"'

Success

The events of the week just passed, had been – from the point of view of Caiaphas, the chief priests, and the scribes and Pharisees – a considerable success. The blasphemous false prophet from Nazareth had been put down with a minimum of fuss, once the foolish mob of ordinary and ignorant people had been convinced that he was not, after all, the Leader and Messiah they supposed. The actual bloody work had been performed by the Army of Occupation – neatly trapped, with the Governor mightily anxious to quash any hints about disloyalty before the stories got started on the road to Rome and the Emperor.

A good Passover festival was over; the followers of the Nazarene had proved a pretty gutless crew, when confronted with the power of the Law. Even the second-in-command – the brawny fisherman from Galilee – had collapsed in panic and frantic denials. Let the police keep an eye on them, but otherwise the episode was over, much to the relief of the authorities. A neat clear-up, in fact.

The disciples

The followers of Jesus, bitterly ashamed, distressed by the collapse of all their hopes, and frightened of reprisals, simply hid themselves behind locked doors. In a while it should be possible to slip away, mingling with the last of the Passover pilgrims returning to the countryside from the city; and then to try to resume their ordinary lives. It had all been a terrible mistake and disaster.

Jesus!

Then, suddenly, their grief, their anger, their frustration – are shattered! All is blown away by the amazing and unexpected re-appearance of Jesus amidst them.

Could this vision be real? Was it a ghost? Was he come to haunt them? Was it a hallucination?

Rapidly he speaks to them – the same familiar tones! He shows them his hands and his side – this is no ghost, no hallucination, this is for real! Surely to report that the disciples 'were glad to see the Lord' is the understatement of the year!

Here is Christ triumphant; here is the victory that sets our gospel apart from anything else, and apart from any other religion in the world. Christ is risen from the dead, Christ has trampled down death – our death, even at the hands of the Romans, our fears, our terrors – and through this action God's own great act of judgement over the powers of evil, is proclaimed!

Thomas!
When we remember the state of mind of the disciples before the appearance of the Lord, surely we can perfectly understand the scepticism of Thomas. He is quite right to tell them that he can't believe them and has no intention of so doing – unless . . . Unless what? He can hardly bring himself to form the words, we may well think . . .

Unless he sees and touches for himself. Nothing else will convince.

And is he not right? He is the one who, for whatever reason, missed out on the astounding events that have turned the others from frightened, nervous wrecks to jubilant, joyful, ecstatic new men.

Ourselves
Jesus does not intend his final comments, as reported in our gospel today, to be taken as a slap in the face for Thomas. They are an encouragement to the post-Ascension Church, and to those millions upon millions of the faithful, who, from the earliest days until our own celebrations now, have kept the feast and proclaimed the Resurrection.

No, Thomas is afforded a unique opportunity to make his own act of witness, his unique proclamation, a proclamation without parallel or equal, 'My Lord – and my God!' Let us be sure that we not only acknowledge the Resurrection and proclaim it in our lives and in our worship, but acknowledge Jesus himself as our Lord and our God.

St Cuths 6.00pm 11/4/99

Second Sunday of Easter *Second Service* **The Women and the Angels** Mark 15:46–16:8
'Go tell his disciples and Peter that he is going before you to Galilee; there you will see him, as he told you.' Mark 16:7

Mary Magdalene

Mary Magdalene comes over as a courageous woman indeed. A follower of Jesus, she was one of the small group of women 'looking on from afar' at the dreadful scene of the crucifixion (Mark 15:40,41), and who followed Joseph of Arimathea, watching as he had the body of Jesus taken down from the Cross, and wrapped in a newly-bought linen shroud, then carried away and placed in a tomb hewn from the rock (vv. 45–47).

We do not know a great deal about Mary of Magdala (hence the name Magdalene) apart from Luke 8:1–3, where she is mentioned as one of the women who accompanied Jesus and the Twelve on their preaching journeys, and ministered to them. We need not think of Christ and his apostles as living too much in any sort of hand-to-mouth existence; from time to time we read of appointments being made and arrangements settled in a business-like way (like the donkey on which Jesus was to enter into Jerusalem, Matthew 21:1–3). Perhaps a better picture would be something like the crowds and helpers who accompanied Gandhi, as we saw on our screens some time ago.

At the tomb

The women (Mary Magdalene, the other Mary, and Salome) take the opportunity of the ending of the Sabbath to go and buy aromatic spices, suitable for anointing the dead. There had been no time to anoint the Lord's body before the Sabbath rest.

How would they get in, though? Someone would have to roll away the large stone slab which had been put in place to protect against wild beasts and thieves. To their surprise, they see that the stone has already been rolled away. With considerable courage, they enter the tomb – and there, sitting inside, is a young man in white, who greets them with an astonishing story of the resurrection of the Lord, and an instruction to go, contact the disciples – especially Peter – and tell them that the Lord is on his way to Galilee, and will see them there, as he had told them.

Mysterious!

The scholars tell us that verses 9 to 20 are not an original part of Mark's Gospel. They are not found in the earliest manuscripts, and indeed apparently were not in the copies used by Matthew and Luke, according to Peake's Commentary. Some scholars maintain that Mark intended to end his work at 16:8, but most find it incredible that no appearance of the Risen Christ is recorded. Yet it seems certain that Mark's Gospel was intended to end with the appearance of the Risen Lord to Peter, to whom, according to St Paul, he did first appear.

Was the manuscript mutilated? Was St Mark surprised by the authorities in the act of finishing his work? Or did he deliberately stop at the empty tomb, as though to say, 'There is no need to tell *you* about the companionship of the Risen Lord!'

On the whole, expert opinion seems to be that the ending *was* lost, to our great regret, due to dangerous conditions for Christians in Rome, where, it is usually believed, St Mark composed his work. If, as is generally supposed, he was the first to think of writing a life of Jesus, our debt is immense.

(Further discussion can be found about St Mark and his Gospel on pp. 200f)

St. Cuthbt 10. 15Pm 11/4/99

Third Sunday of Easter   18 April   *Principal Service*   New Life   Luke 24:13–35
'Was it not ordained that the Christ should suffer, and so enter into his glory?' Luke 24:26

Symbol
When we see a rainbow shining with the lovely spectrum of its colours, gleaming in the sunlight, we know that it is a symbol of hope, as it is the refraction of the light against the falling rain. The rainbow is built on the preceding storm. It is a symbol of hope arising out of the darkness; it is a Bible symbol, since we can remember how, long ago, God himself appointed the rainbow as a sign that the great disaster of the Flood was ended.

The two disciples who made their way to their home in the village of Emmaus were enveloped in gloom. Their leader, upon whom they had set all their hopes for a transformed and revitalized religion, was dead – brutally executed, as if he were a common criminal. Even though some strange and exciting stories had begun to circulate amongst their friends, their own minds were too numbed with the pain of the collapse of their hopes, to take in new ideas.

The stranger
Just talking to someone with no axe to grind, as they say, can be a great help to seeing our problems in a different light. It may get us out of our self-centred view, may put our troubles in their proper place, help us to stand back and give proper weight to various considerations, which may each have seemed overwhelming. There can be real value in being a thoughtful listener; how much help we can get by just listening.

So it seems to have been with the two disciples and Jesus. He listened to their worries, let them pour out their problems. Then, and not till then, he interpreted their difficulties, put them into proper scale and made the two worried people see clearly in the clear light of truth.

'Yes, yes – now we do begin to understand! How clear you make it all seem; how foolish we were to have been troubled so, and to have been slow to understand!'

Follow his example
What a help we may be, by following Jesus' example and allowing other people to bring to us their worries and problems. Let them spread out their troubles – 'unpack their luggage' – as a first and important step in clearing their minds for action. How important it is to be receptive, to be prepared to listen – just listen – to others; not always to be pouring out *our* worries and *our* troubles. Then, and only then, can we gently begin to assist another human soul to sort out his or her life, in the light available in the Word of God.

Bearing one another's burdens
Let us try to cultivate the habit of listening; try also to cultivate that inner peace and security and calm, which makes other people think, 'There's someone I can talk to; someone I can share my worries with . . .'

Bearing one another's burdens is an essential part of our following of Christ; and what simpler form can it take than allowing another person to meet you along life's path, and as you follow the road together, gently and sympathetically listen.

Third Sunday of Easter   *Second Service*
My Father's House   John 2:13–22

*'Jesus went up to Jerusalem. There he found in the Temple the dealers
in cattle, sheep and pigeons, and the money-changers seated at their
tables. Jesus made a whip of cords and drove them out of the Temple.'
John 2:14,15*

The coming of the Saviour
In New Testament times many of the Jews were hopefully looking
for the coming of the Saviour, whom the Old Testament declared
God would send to them. They made frequent guesses as to how
this coming would take place, and often these guesses were not
based on the Bible, but were strange ideas of their own invention.
One of these ideas was that the Saviour would suddenly descend
from heaven in a miraculous way; some added that he would
make this descent into the courtyard of the Temple itself, since
this seemed a very appropriate spot for the happening.

Temptation
One of our Lord's temptations in the wilderness seems to be based
upon this popular superstition. If he had gone to one of the pinnacles of the Temple, thrown himself down, and miraculously
been unhurt, the crowds who were always moving about in the
Temple precincts would unquestionably have hailed him as the
Messiah. It would have been an imposing shortcut to winning
the hearts of the people, and spreading his message to them.

Jesus, however, did not obey the tempting voice which whis-
pered how easy it would be to take this short-cut. Several times
he visited the Temple, but he never did anything to gain favour
and publicity by sensational means.

An opposite course
Instead, the lectures he delivered in the Temple were of a kind to
arouse the hostility of the priesthood and the authorities, and
sometimes of the common people as well. On one occasion he
went further, and did something which made him many enemies,
as he knew it would.

Pilgrims who came to the Temple from any considerable distance would wish to offer a sacrifice there. It would be impossible

to bring an animal from home, and local residents would often find it troublesome; so they would all buy their sacrificial animals and birds on the spot. Also, many visitors came from outside Palestine, from Egypt, Greece, Rome and elsewhere. They would want to change their money into Jewish currency, as gifts for Temple funds had to be in Jewish coinage, hence the money-changers' stalls. The trading carried on in the Temple was in principle convenient rather than blameworthy, but no doubt there was considerable abuse, and instead of pious calm an unseemly uproar, very disturbing.

Jesus is not only angry because of the noisy commerce being conducted in the Temple. Something more important is happening: he is bringing to an end the goings-on because the Temple is no longer 'a house of trade' (v. 16) but 'my Father's house'. This makes the disciples remember the words of the Psalmist, 'Zeal for thy house will consume me' (Psalm 2:17). The Jews throw his words back at him: 'Will you raise it up in three days?' when he says to them, 'Destroy this temple and in three days I will raise it up.' The disciples, of course, remember this saying, although they only fully understand it after the resurrection, when they have his presence among them, and comprehend that the reference is to the body of Jesus, where God and man meet in the incarnate Person. And the Church is the Body of Christ, hence the New Temple.

Fourth Sunday of Easter 25 April *Principal Service* The Good Shepherd John 10:1–10

'I am the good shepherd; the good shepherd lays down his life for the sheep.' John 10:11

Familiarity

Our parable today – of Christ as the Good Shepherd – is almost too well known, is it not? Victorian stained glass images of 'The Good Shepherd' look down upon us from a hundred windows; an illustration of the same theme forms the frontispiece to dozens of well-intentioned prayer books. Usually the pictures, although we may not realize it perhaps, are sadly out of touch with the facts of a shepherd's life, and especially the shepherd of the time of Our Lord.

Reality?
Christ is depicted in a long robe with an even longer cloak over it; his hair is well-combed and neatly parted, his beard trim, his face pale and aesthetic; he will have a long-staffed crook in his elbow, and a well-behaved lamb will be over his shoulders, well-groomed and neat also . . . How unlike the reality! Let us look at some of the early Christian mosaics, or wall paintings, or sculptures, to see how the Good Shepherd was regarded in those primitive days. No illusions of neatness or trimness – the shepherd is a rougher character altogether, with tunic and cloak thick enough to protect him from the cold of the night, but short enough to enable him to run easily, heavy boots and thick leggings to keep out the briars and thorns – and the bites of animals . . .

Christ was a realist, never a sentimentalist. Let us always try to see through his eyes, the eyes of a lad brought up in a small village, close to life with its needs and its harshnesses, knowing well the realities and blunt truths of an ordinary peasant existence.

His parable
Perhaps the truth of his parable escapes us, as the truth of the primitive shepherd's life escapes the studio artist who made the windows or painted the pictures. What does Jesus really say?

He tells us that a man cares naturally for his own things. He does not need to *make* himself care. The shepherd who has bought the ground, fenced the fold, and tended the lambs, whose own the sheep are, to keep or to sell – this man cares for them, knows them, understands them.

Protection
This shepherd will run risks, rather than see his precious animals mauled, bitten, and dragged away. If he sees the wolf, the shepherd will carry a heavy stick in his hand, and do his best to beat off the raider. Yes, he may be bitten himself; yes, he may even lose his own life defending his flock – but he is prepared to take the chance. If his sheep go, he is lost himself – he has nothing else to live by.

Christ the shepherd

Christ does not boast, as a man among men, that he loves humanity more than any other man, through some higher refinement or virtue. He simply says the truth.

He cares for us as no one else can, because we are his. We do not belong to anyone else; we belong to him. His dying for us in this world is the natural effect and result of his unique care, interest, love. It is the supreme act of the One who is our Creator.

> *Almighty God,*
> *as your blessed Son Jesus Christ*
>   *first came to seek and to save the lost;*
> *so may he come again to find in us*
>   *the completion of his redeeming work;*
> *for he is now alive and reigns*
>   *with you and the Holy Spirit,*
> *God for ever and ever.*

PHG, 38

The Fourth Sunday of Easter *Second Service* **Time to Speak Out** Luke 19:37–48

As Jesus approached the descent from the Mount of Olives, the whole company of his disciples in their joy began to sing aloud the praises of God, for all the great things they had seen: 'Blessings on him who comes asking in the name of the Lord!'

Public processions

On our TVs we may watch processions of protesters moving through our city streets with their accompanying escort of police. Those taking part are protesting about some real or imagined grievance, or showing their support for some cause, good or bad as we may think ourselves; but remember, these people are giving up time and effort and may have travelled a long way, or spent time in a crowded bus or train, to put their point of view in London, or in the chief city of their part of the world.

Violent endings

A number of such processions have ended in scenes of disorder or violence; abroad, things have been much worse, with serious injuries and, alas, deaths. Whether or not the demonstrations have their desired effect, at least those who take part in them do feel, at the least, that their point of view has been put over in public places and in view of many, many people. Television does bring such affairs right into our homes, and such publicity may indeed have a desired effect, here or abroad.

Palm Sunday

The first incident of Holy Week, on Palm Sunday, was a procession which had some things in common with our modern processions. Jesus rode into Jerusalem attended by his apostles and other followers. The crowds from Galilee who were flocking into the city for the Passover gave Jesus a rousing welcome, and the majority of the people of Jerusalem joined in, with cheering and singing. To compare the procession described for us in the Gospels (Luke today) with demonstrations in modern cities may sound somewhat irreverent, since some are marred by violence, and some may be held in support of wrong objects.

Yet all these marches, good or bad, are alike in one respect. They are held to draw the attention of the public or the authorities to some important matter which those taking part feel is not being properly considered.

The challenge of Jesus

This was the case with the Palm Sunday procession. Jesus had preached, and taught, and healed, and travelled for the past three years. Although he had many admirers, he had few real followers – men and women who were prepared to change their way of life in response to his appeal to them. So he forced himself on the attention of the Jewish people by an action which he knew would bring together a big crowd, and bring matters quickly to a head: the triumphal ride into the city. This indeed occurred, but his words and actions of the next few days changed initial success on Palm Sunday to apparent failure on Good Friday.

His teaching

Not merely his final entry into Jerusalem, but Our Lord's whole life, was a protest, a protest against sin. The protest in his teaching seem directed especially against certain kinds of sin – hypocrisy, conceit about our own goodness, selfishness, unwillingness to forgive those who hurt us. We must be specially on our guard about such sins; but to the Lord Jesus all wrongdoing was a matter about which he must protest.

Then we learn that Our Lord's challenge to accept or reject him, although delivered first to the people of Jerusalem and their visitors, is a challenge to us all. It is too easy to fail to understand that this challenge is indeed to each of us, or to understand the challenge but shirk making a response.

Christ calls us, and we must not close our ears to his voice, but answer his call.

Fifth Sunday of Easter 2 May *Principal Service* **Looking Forward** John 14:1–14
'I am the Way, and the Truth, and the Life.' John 14:6

A time for parting
The joy and the new life of the Easter message is still burning in the hearts and minds of the disciples; now they have to understand that the Risen Lord cannot remain physically with them. The great saga of our redemption is completed by the Ascension of Christ, that mysterious event by which the risen humanity, the living Christ, is identified and united with God the Father and Creator. The vivid actuality of the Risen Christ is taken away from his followers, once they have indeed been convinced that he is the victor over death, that he has indeed been raised by the Father to new life – to eternal life – and to glory.

A waiting time
The interval between the Resurrection and the Ascension, although a thrilling time of joy and of astonishing relief, seems to be marked by a kind of lassitude. It was a waiting time, a pause for breath, an interval to rediscover the landmarks along the road, and make clear the next step.

And the next step, after the Ascension, is the Coming of the Holy Spirit. The coming of the power of God, to transform these bewildered, delighted, anxious, joyful, uncertain yet radiant men and women, into an instrument in God's hand for the changing of the world.

The Church's role

For this is what the Christian Church is, or should be, an instrument in God's hand for changing the world. Karl Marx wrote: 'The philosophers have discussed the world, but our task is to *change* it.' Long before Marx, Christ was a revolutionary and was setting his followers a revolutionary task. Not by power politics, not by political or military force, not by physical conquest, but by the individual example of Faith, and Hope, and Love.

Today's world

The state of the world today is a bitter comment on the effects of our Christian example, and the extent of the influence of the Christian Churches – divided and confused, bitter and even distrustful as they all too clearly appear (and, alas, that includes us in our small part of the Christian body, dare we say, the Lambeth Conference?).

How far it all seems from the glory, and the power, and the burning intensity of the early Christian communities, as seen and mirrored in the New Testament.

Christ's promise

And yet, and yet, there is still the promise of Christ himself. 'The Spirit of Truth will lead you into all truth' and, 'He will glorify me.' The work of the Church, filled with the power and life of the Spirit, is to glorify Christ, to persuade and convict the world, through the living members of the Body of Christ here on earth. Here is our task.

And whatever the failings of the Church, whatever our lack of comprehension of the ideals of the Lord, there are from time to time shining examples of men and women who have indeed taken to heart the words and the commands of Christ, and have lived and died by them. Some of them, known to the world at large, are recognized, and we call them saints. Others are never recognized, by human knowledge that is, and are known only to God. So at our Eucharists we can indeed truly join ourselves with the great company of saints of all ages and all countries, known and unknown, living and departed.

Eternal God, giver of love and power,
your Son Jesus Christ has sent us into all the world
to preach the gospel of his Kingdom:
confirm us in this mission,
and help us to live the good news we proclaim;
through Jesus Christ, Our Lord.

The Christian Year, 232

Fifth Sunday of Easter   *Second Service*
The Holy City   Revelation 21:1–14

'I [John] saw the holy city, new Jerusalem, coming down from God out
of heaven, prepared as a bride.' Revelation 21:2

God enthroned

In wonderful, vivid and pictorial terms, the Holy Seer of Patmos
tells of the vision of heaven which was granted to him. We know
that the song of heaven, the *Trisagion* (title of a Greek hymn calling
upon God with triple invocation) as it is called, speaks of the
triune God whom we seek to worship. But the story of this vision
bids us remember that the confession of faith implied in that glorious song is a solemn thing, and full of awe. If our confession of
faith is real and true it will take us into the aura, the very presence,
of the Holiest – and will send us to our knees in worship and
adoration. Let us dismiss the selfishness that goes all too often by
the name of worship. 'True worship,' it has been well said, 'is
impersonal, for in it the world recedes out of sight, and the details
of our clogging material life disappear. We lose ourselves in the
Presence of God in glorifying God, simply for being what he is.'

So, the call of the day is to worship the Almighty, and to humble
our hearts in true worship, and to understand what will be the
new world.

The promise

As the Holy Seer, St John, now tells us, God promises to extinguish
death, the great enemy, and with that dismissal shall also go sorrows and tears, crying and any more pain, for 'the former things

97

are passed away' (v. 4), and God is saying to us, 'Behold, I make all things new.' And in particular, as we might say, the Holy City is renewed. We are shown (v. 9) the City descending out of heaven having the glory of God (v. 11) and light clear as crystal. This is part of God's plan, now that all evil is destroyed, and a new heaven and earth created. The transformed City is the eternal dwelling place of God and his people. The Jerusalem in the vision is that of the millennial period, where Christ will dwell and which will be the centre of evangelistic activity among the nations for a thousand years.

The spiritual citizen

St Paul gives us a picture of the life of the spiritual citizen of the New Jerusalem. 'My present life is not that of the old "I", but the living Christ within me. The bodily life I now live, I live believing in the Son of God, who loved me and sacrificed himself for me' (Galatians 2:20). However, until we reach that lofty state to which we are called, most of us will need whatever help God offers to us. The means of grace are proffered, but we have to choose to use them if they are to be effective. Then, we have to accept rules of our own desiring to guide and help us; after all, most of us are so weak that we are needing help to aid us on our way. The Lord is not yet living completely in us.

Striving

If we are striving to live the believer's life, our faces are set towards the Heavenly City, and its paths are open before us, into which we can direct our feet. Something of its joy and gladness and freedom is already ours, and its fullness is to be enjoyed unhindered in the life of the world to come.

Sixth Sunday of Easter 9 May *Principal Service* The Comforter John 14:15–21

'If you love me, keep my commandments; and I will pray the Father, and he shall give you another Comforter, even the Spirit of truth.' John 14:15–17

The guide
In today's Gospel we hear Christ telling his disciples that the Comforter, the Spirit of truth, will be sent by the Father, to abide with them for ever. The Spirit is sent to those who love Christ.

We are at our best when we love, because love is a purifying and a uniting force. True love, in other words, makes for the perfecting of the individual soul. It is, after all, common knowledge, that 'love of country' brings the needed courage to defend our land; or that the mutual love of husband and wife shows itself in unselfishness and gives the power to face life together, in spite of all its difficulties and problems. We know also that love of our fellow human beings results in the urge to help, in all kinds of manifestations, organizations, and bands of brothers and sisters. We can think of such well-known names as Oxfam, Christian Aid, Interchurch Families, Feed the Minds, Leprosy Mission, Salvation Army and many, many more.

The spirit of Love
All true love results from the coming of Christ's Spirit, he who is the Spirit of Love. And the power of the Spirit does not cease at the limits of the human heart, within a human being. No, for it radiates outwards, it transforms our every-day activities and our ordinary human relationships, at our work or occupation, all enriched by the Spirit's presence.

Indeed, the presence of the Holy Spirit enables us not only to face up to the harsh realities of life – those bonds and demands that press upon us all the time but also to understand their true needs and worth, purpose and opportunity.

The Spirit of Truth
Christ tells us that the Holy Spirit is also the Spirit of Truth (14:17). It is the Spirit that gives life – true life, the life of which Christ so often spoke. Worldly lives have been described as looking at things and seeing them, but only recognizing their market value. The spiritually-minded looks also, but sees not only the material but also the eternal values.

'Two people looked into a pool in the roadway – one saw mud, the other stars . . .'

A little while ...
Jesus said, 'Yet a little while, and the world will see me no more, but you will see me; because I live, you will live also. In that day, you will know that I am in my Father, and you in me and I in you' (14:18–20).

The disciples were to see him, but the world was not. We, like the disciples of those days, can see Christ because within us we have the Spirit who inspires us with the vision of faith.

Sixth Sunday of Easter *Second Service*
Christ's Work   John 21:1–14

'Some time later, Jesus showed himself to his disciples once again, by the sea of Tiberias.' John 21:1

This last chapter of the Fourth Gospel is often regarded by scholars as an appendix, perhaps written at a later date. The last verse of chapter 20 plainly forms a natural ending to the Gospel of John. However, this last chapter, whether considered as an appendix or a completion, is in line with the Gospel in both thought and content, and forms a most suitable close to the Gospel narrative.

Balance
The term *logos* or 'Word' was a term common to both Jews and Greeks. To the Greeks it meant 'Divine Reason', to the Jews the uttered 'Word of God' to humanity, to the Evangelist, Logos was both the Divine Reason and the creative instrument of God's purpose. As such, the Word existed before Creation; his pre-incarnate life is thus indicated to the reader. The Gospel itself is the record of the work and witness of the Incarnate Word.

It would seem, therefore, that we should regard this closing chapter of the Gospel as a record of part of the life of the post-Resurrection Christ; we learn from it something of the Saviour's conduct and power before his Ascension. There is a wonderful understanding and sympathy in the story. 'Children,' the Lord calls; he has lit a fire, put fresh fish on it, provided bread, 'Come and have breakfast.' How human, how loving the simple words and actions are.

Understanding

There is a wonderful understanding and sympathy in the story; we cannot but feel that the Lord is correcting mistakes in his gentlest way. The great catch of fish is an acted parable; the frail and erring Rock-man, Peter, is restored to his Apostleship.

Seven disciples in Galilee – where are the others? Four remained in Jerusalem, perhaps occupied with their daily work. The others – sheep without a shepherd – probably did the natural thing also and returned to their old occupation. 'I am going out fishing,' is a lead for the others from Peter. 'We will go with you,' is the response. But a night of fishing produced nothing of a catch.

The lesson

Here was work for seven men to do, and Peter led them. Do the 'seven' disciples represent the Church? – seven is the perfect number, after all. The seven set out to follow their own plan – *their* plan, even if Peter was their leader in the venture. Probably it was his own boat they used. The result – failure: 'that night they caught nothing.' Was it against the Lord's will that they returned to fishing? They had to learn to obey their Lord and Master if their labour was to be rewarded. Peter had been told that his work would be to catch men alive for God, not merely dead fish for food. Later, when they worked at the Lord's direction, they made a magnificent haul. Work for God must always be stamped with his seal and authority, with faithfulness to his direction. When we carry out his directions, we shall find him by and by on the eternal shore preparing us a welcome.

Learn from this episode that the Lord's work must be directed by the Lord, and carried out in his way. His blessing will then be upon it, and he will use it to his glory.

Ascension Day   13 May   Triumph
Luke 24:44–53

'He led them out, as far as Bethany, and lifting up his hands he blessed them.' Luke 24:50

Test case?

For a modern Christian the Ascension story must be something of a test case; a test case for our ability to cope with the antique outlook, the ancient view of the universe, which we find in the Bible. It is difficult to understand the story of the Ascension in our modern, space-age time. The Bible uses the language of 'up there'; it assumes the antique view of the world as a kind of three-decker sandwich: heaven above, earth here in the middle, and hell down below, all within easy reach of each other, a cosy universe, man-centred.

The vast universe

We in our day of space travel, men on the moon, telescopes and radio telescopes probing away into the vastness of the universe, have a very different world picture. We know that our earth is simply a tiny speck in an immense vastness; we know it is not the centre of the universe, but the third planet of an insignificant fourth-rate star on one of the remote fringes of a great galaxy – itself only one of a huge army of galaxies that extends away and away into infinity ... No longer can we believe comfortingly in the earth as the mid-point around which all else revolves; nor are the stars bright pinholes in the floor of heaven above, any more.

Question

We are forced, then, to ask what can we make, today, of the Ascension story. What is it really about? What was, or is, the Ascension? First, the Ascension is not an account of a movement in space. The difference between an astronaut and Jesus Christ is not that the astronaut came back to earth, while Jesus went on. Secondly, the Ascension story is not describing a moment in time. Probably we have been brought up on the idea that the Ascension was a specific event which happened at a specific moment of time on the fortieth day after the Resurrection. This is certainly how the Church Calendar still represents it.

The New Testament story

Our knowledge that the earth is round, is only a small speck in the vast universe, and that God is a spiritual Being, means that we do not see Christ's ascent as the start of a journey in the physical sense, as our ancestors did. Yet, this does not lessen our belief that he was rejoining his Heavenly Father. There can be no doubt that the first disciples thought that Christ's return would be soon, and it was very natural that they should do so, with the limited knowledge of the universe that they had. Some of them were affected in their attitude to daily life, and they neglected routine duties. In others, feelings of disappointment – and even of doubt – arose when they waited in vain. We should accept the fact that the time of Our Lord's return is something God does not mean us to know, and may be long delayed. Has not this resulted in our putting it out of our minds, or at best assuming that it is not likely to be in our earthly lifetime? Some of the expectations of the Millennium are tainted by foolish visionary ideas which have little to commend them.

Victory!
Where we are surely in closest accord with Christian thinkers of long ago is in our feeling that the Ascension of Our Lord is a sign to all that he had won a great victory, and this is a fact to give us courage and confidence. Let us look back on Christ's life upon earth with thanksgiving, and forward to our own future life with trust and hope.

Seventh Sunday of Easter *(Sunday after Ascension Day)*   16 May   *Principal Service*
Unity   John 17:1–11
'Holy Father, keep them in thy name, which thou hast given me, that they may be one, even as we are one.' John 17:11

Unity
This is the great high-priestly prayer of Jesus, which he made on the eve of the day in which he was arrested in the valley of the Kidron river; and we recall his words on this Sunday between Ascension and Pentecost. The deepest wish of the Lord is for unity amongst his followers, that the work of conversion to the faith of Christ should continue and should spread. 'I am praying for them,' the Lord says, 'they have believed that I came from thee, and they have believed that thou didst send me' (v. 8). The wish and the

prayer of Jesus is that all his followers should be united; a unity of all Christians.

There are more divisions than unities in our world today, alas. Rich and poor, white and black, North and South, Jew and Arab, Catholic and Protestant, Christian and Muslim; and yet there are signs and examples, if we will only look, of how the different faiths and religious outlooks are able to come together in the understanding of their common humanity. A common humanity which in so many places is under attack, defaced by sin, distorted by self-interest, that our human inter-relatedness is not sufficiently realized, or if realized, is still controversial and not fruitful for peace, insight and mutual help.

Power and glory

From the beginning, the Word, the cosmic Christ, has been there; that power of which St John tells us, 'In the beginning was the Word, and the Word was with God, and the Word was God.' The world has always had a meaning; from the beginning there has been sense and purpose in the universe. The world is no accidental or meaningless happening. To believe in God is to believe in this fundamental logic in, and of, all things, from the tiniest scrap of life or the smallest molecule of sand or rock, to the greatest galaxy or cosmic structure in the universe.

And from the beginning, the Word, the cosmic Christ, having abdicated that power when he came to earth, God restored it to him at the Resurrection and confirmed it at the Ascension (Ephesians 1:22).

Mutual love

One of the characteristics of the early Christians, which was noted by their enemies, was their love for one another. This love was a vital principle in their lives, grounded in their faith in Christ. As St John puts it: 'We love because he first loved us' (1 John 4:19). Their love was, and our love must be, a true reflection of Christ's love. Christian love may be, indeed is, the means of leading others to the redeeming, the saving, and the uplifting love of the Lord. Those who do not love have no experience of God; for God is love (1 John 1:5). It is this love that brings our love; having its roots in God, it rises spontaneous and unbidden.

Everlasting love
William Law was surely right when he wrote: 'No creature can suffer from any evil from which infinite goodness can deliver it.' God's love is a love which aims at our highest good, for it evoked the gift of himself for our salvation.

Seventh Sunday of Easter   *Second Service*
Go ... preach   Mark 16:14–20
'Go into all the world and preach the gospel to the whole creation.' Mark 16:15

Words that give life
If we look back at some of our disappointments in life there will be those that still remain sad memories, but in the case of others things have turned out much better than we feared at the time. A most striking instance of this – no doubt, *the* most striking instance of this which has ever taken place – is the experience of Our Lord's followers when he was arrested, taken to trial, and crucified. On Good Friday they were heartbroken; then on the Sunday there were these stories of him being alive, stories reported by Mary Magdalene (vv. 10, 11). But the disciples did not, could not, believe what she told them; nor did they give any credence to the two travellers who had been met on the road to Emmaus by the Lord himself (vv. 12, 13).

The Lord
Suddenly, to these heartbroken, desperately sad, completely lost followers of the Lord, sitting round a table, miserable and sunk into despair – who appears? Who but Jesus himself (v. 14) – alive, speaking to them, reproaching them for their lack of faith, giving them their orders for the future, and promising the power needed to give them success. And then, having given them his instructions, the Lord leaves them and is 'taken up into heaven'.

No doubt it took some time to assimilate the full implications of all that had happened; at first it was enough for them to rejoice because Jesus *was* alive – then as his commands sank in – they saw that there was a twofold reason to be joyful. Our Lord's death on the Cross had opened up the way to salvation, to them, to us, and to all humanity; and a great but temporary sorrow had been turned into a cause for joy, a joy which was sealed and given expression by the Lord's resurrection and triumph on Easter Day.

Jesus brings joy
The visit of Jesus put joy and strength into their hearts, pulled them out of their despair and gloom and sorrow. He came to them with that object in mind, and he has the same purpose for each of us, too. There are moments in everybody's life when sorrow is uppermost; we feel defeated, lost, unable to see beyond the misery of the moment. Then it is that the words of Christ will comfort us, will strengthen us, and will give us the joy and thanksgiving in our hearts and minds that is needed to go ahead and spread the good news of the gospel, while rejoicing in the power of the Spirit.

Day of Pentecost *(Whit Sunday)*   *Principal Service*   23 May   **The Pentecostal Gift**
Acts 2:1–21

'There appeared to them tongues like flames of fire, dispersed among them and resting on each one. And they were all filled with the Holy Spirit.' Acts 2:3

The Church
The events which are commemorated today tell us how the Church became an organized Body-corporate, with a sense of the Divine indwelling of God. The promised gift of the Holy Spirit was bestowed on the first Whit Sunday: Christ had promised the gift, and had revealed its nature as the Holy Spirit sent to dwell in the Christian soul. Of this it has been well said, 'The Spirit's full mission will lie in the future, after Jesus has been glorified'; it was after the Resurrection that the promised gift was bestowed upon the Church.

We recall how the Apostle Peter declared in his exhortation, on that very first Whit Sunday, that the ancient prophet Joel's words had been fulfilled that very day. God had promised that men and women would be Spirit-filled. The Lord Christ promised his own indwelling in the hearts of his faithful followers, through the gift of the Holy Spirit. In his great discourses before his Passion, Jesus said that this gift, or endowment, to humanity, would be the outcome of his own ministry in heaven; he spoke of his own intercession with the Father as the source of all spiritual blessing. And we know that he is able to save to the uttermost, because of his presence at the Father's right hand, which is indeed his own all-availing intercession.

We would do well to remember, far more often than we do, that our Christian life is supernatural in both origin and nature; it is a life that can be lived only by the upholding power of the Holy Spirit. Our Lord's ministry in heaven makes all his power and life available to us and applicable for our needs through the Holy Spirit.

The gift
The whole company of the believers became aware that the promised gift had been bestowed, when those astounding manifestations occurred on that first Whit Sunday. The promised state was to be, 'He dwells with you, and will be in you' (John 14:17). The Lord made it plain that the Spirit would have direct relationship with individual souls; we who are Christians know that the Spirit is the Paraclete who abides *with* us for fellowship; and he who remains *at our side* to defend us, and is *in* us as the strength and stay of our spiritual life. Yet, he is the guide, inspirer and instructor of the Church as well, as any reading of Acts shows, and as experience of the Christian life shows us today.

The wind of love
So let the wind of Pentecost blow itself through us, and blow away old dust and cobwebs, making us see things in a new light, a new clearer and fresher light; and as a wind of love, encouraging our growth in love, and a deeper and stronger union and commitment to the Lord Jesus.

Day of Pentecost *Second Service*
Witnesses Luke 24:44–53

'While he blessed them, he parted from them, and was carried up into heaven.' Luke 24:51

To convert the world
The aspostles, we are told, were startled and frightened at first, when they saw the Risen Lord (v. 37).

Going away
The effect upon the disciples of the going away of Jesus, is not part of the record, yet we cannot doubt that they were stunned by the sudden loss. The promise of Jesus 'to be with them always, even to the end of time,' must have been confusing – how could he promise to be with them and then leave them? Suddenly they seem unsure, even disorientated.

We are told that they fell down before him, 'but some hesitated' (Matthew 28:17). 'You are witnesses . . .' says the Lord (v. 48). God's power is upon us (v. 49), not to be employed tyrannically or selfishly, but to win men and women to the Kingdom of God.

Here, then, is a power we have only to draw upon (v. 46), and the promise is that we shall receive power, as the Holy Spirit comes upon us, indeed, we shall become Christ's witnesses, and truly sharers in the mission of the Saviour.

As surely as the Spirit transformed the Apostles, so he transforms the Church, the people of God, ourselves that is, if we will only let him. Our belief is that the Holy Spirit is still working with and in us, here and now, today.

The Church is the community of the Spirit; we respond to the Spirit in unity, in certainty, and in trust. Simply put, this means that the Holy Spirit helps us to love God, and to love one another. Notice the kind of power we are to receive – 'You shall receive the power of the Holy Spirit, coming upon you in strength and in unity and in trust' – coming to the aid of our weakness, as St Paul tells us.

> Holy Spirit, come, renew us,
>   Come yourself to make us live,
> Holy through your loving presence,
>   Holy through the gifts you give.
>
> Holy Spirit, come, possess us,
>   You the love of Three in One,
> Holy Spirit of the Father,
>   Holy Spirit of the Son.

NEH, 140

Witnesses

Finally, what is the power given to us *for*? 'You shall be my witnesses,' Jesus tells us. God's power is to be used for God's purposes. It is not to be employed tyrannically or selfishly; it is a sacred trust to be used and devoted only to the carrying on of the mission of Christ, to win men and women to the Kingdom of God.

Trinity Sunday   30 May   *Principal Service*
In the Name   Matthew 28:16–20

'Jesus came and said to them, "Make disciples of all nations, baptizing them in the name of the Father, and of the Son, and of the Holy Spirit."'
Matthew 28:19

Mystery of God

We may well say that Trinity Sunday calls us to the contemplation of the mystery of God's being. God is not a glorified man, He is Spirit, and when Our Lord said 'God is Spirit' he pronounced the most fundamental and stupendous proposition in all theology. God is supra-personal; while personal attributes belong to him, we must be clear in our minds that God is not 'man magnified'. Like the prophets of old, and like St John the Evangelist, the Seer of Patmos, when we think about God, it is inadequate simply to write about him. We ought to shout and sing and dance, we ought to join together in declaiming great poetry, or pouring out the loveliest music ever dreamed of. God is so great, so wonderful, so loving. The feeling of exaltation is one that comes to us on Trinity Sunday, when we think about the mystery of the eternal Trinity. It is expressed in the hymns we sing, in the glorious passages from the Scriptures that can be read today. And it is summed up in Isaiah's great vision, when we hear the cry of the angels before the throne of God: 'Holy, holy, holy is the Lord of Hosts: the whole earth is full of His Glory' (Isaiah 6:3–4).

Humility

We need the spirit of humility when we think about God. The Spirit of God is at work in the scientists, as they seek to learn more and more about the universe. The more we learn, the more amazing it all is. We know now that our sun is only one of millions of suns in millions of other galaxies, and the vastness of space and the complexity of the ultimate design is impossible to contemplate, in spite of the amazing modern telescopes, the delicacy of radio search mechanisms, and so on. And yet the scientist does not know the ultimate secret of life, or of the universe itself; but we can say that it is all of God, and God's intention is rational, is based upon love. It is the knowledge of the love of God which enables us to open our hearts to Christ, to face the painful things in our lives, and to be able to get them into proportion.

Glory

Isaiah again speaks to us, when in his glorious vision the prophet sees the angels round the throne cover their faces with their wings; the glory of God is so wonderful that they cannot gaze with unveiled faces. God is a God who hides himself, and in this life he can only be known to the eye of faith. We must await heaven for the full vision; if God's full glory appeared here and now, we should be overwhelmed by it and compelled to believe. But what God wants is the free offering of our hearts – for, because he is love, all our relationships with him must be of love.

Christ

If we are to know God, it can only be as he makes himself known to us, and this is what he has done in Christ. The claims that Christ made, the authority that he exercised, could only be made by One who was God. There was no other conclusion that could be made but that he was the Divine Son. The whole conception of God was widened from the more primitive outlook of the Old

Testament; and at Pentecost the Holy Spirit made the followers of Christ new men, filled with God, the Lord and Giver of Life.

Trinity Sunday *Second Service* **The spirit of Truth** John 16:5–15

'When the Spirit of truth comes, he will guide you into all the truth . . . He will glorify me, for he will take what is mine and declare it to you . . . All that the Father has is mine; therefore I said that he will take what is mine and declare it to you.' John 16:13–15

Jesus tells his disciples that he is going away (v. 6) and immediately the hearts of the disciples are full of grief; but if they had considered for a moment *where* he was going, they would have understood that his departure was for their advantage. He was going to the Father, and only so could he send them the Paraclete, the Holy Spirit. And the Paraclete will convince the world of sin, righteousness, and judgement; in other words, that the followers of Christ, the Christians, will be shown to have been right, and on the side of right. He promises that the Holy Spirit – 'the Spirit of Truth' – will enlighten them; the Spirit-inspired preaching of the Church will bring the world to the feet of the Lord. The departure of Jesus to the Father means his crucifixion and his resurrection, events which involve the offering of the perfectly obedient life, and the ratification of that life by God the Father's acceptance of the offering. What appeared to be the condemnation of Jesus was, by God's action in the resurrection, turned into the condemnation of the accusers, and the defeat of Satan.

Love and truth

Each and every Christian is required by God to 'love our neighbour'; that is, to exercise our wills, but only in a limited extent our feelings. This love is indeed something of a reflection of God's attitude to humanity – 'God so loved the world that he gave his only-begotten Son, to the end that all who believe in him should not perish, but have everlasting life.'

Jesus taught that God is loving, as a Father; that God is our Creator, aware of each of us and our needs; that he has compassion for us; that he is just and even-handed; and that no matter how

111

far wrong we go, he would still be showing his love and his mercy. Jesus spoke of the Father and of the Spirit; and he spoke of himself as united with both Father and Spirit.

The Trinity
Here is the basis of the Church's doctrine of the Trinity: a Unity of Love in a Trinity of Persons, the Father seeing himself in the Son, the Son seeing himself in the Father, and both united in the Spirit. The bond between the Three Persons is of course Love; a love as eternal, as infinite, and yet as personal as themselves. That love for one another that we speak of as Christian Charity is, in fact, a pale reflection of the Divine Love within the Godhead – the Divine Nature, that is. So, when we try to learn to love as God loves, our love widens and a current of Life passes through us to those near us; here then is our witness to our Lord and Master.

Day of Thanksgiving for Holy Communion
(Corpus Christi)   Thursday 3 June   *Principal Service*   **The living bread**   John 6:51–58
'He who eats my flesh and drinks my blood has eternal life, and I will raise him up at the last day. For my flesh is food indeed, and my blood is drink indeed.' John 6:54–55

The joyful feast
Our Eucharists should always be joyful, even on occasions which we would count as sad; the Church celebrates the sacrifice of Christ with joy and not with sorrow. It is true that Maundy Thursday is so under the threatening shadow of the Cross that joy cannot be displayed. Hence today is traditionally chosen as the occasion for an unclouded festival, being the first free Thursday after the great pageant of the re-enacting of the events of the life, death, and triumph of the Lord is completed in our church calendar.

Bread and wine
Here on the table is spread a fair white linen cloth. On the cloth will be placed, shortly, some bread and some wine.

Bread and wine – simple, every-day things – common, ordinary, well-nigh universal wherever humanity is dispersed over our planet. Yet also things that are full of ancient symbolism, evocative, mysterious.

The bread: the staff of life. The miracle of growth – grain from seed; farmer's care, nature's bounty, our daily bread. We break bread together, a staple part of our food, to give energy and strength to rebuild and re-create our bodies. And wine: the careful cultivation of the vineyard, the sun, the rain, the picking and the pressing. To take wine, to have a drink together, to drink a toast – joy and refreshment, uniting us in fellowship together.

Bread and wine. They stand for substance and spirit, the tangible fact and the invisible reality – for body and soul.

The life of the Church

Make no doubt about it, it is this sacrament that always has and always will be the centre of the Church's life and worship. From the earliest days, as we read in Acts, 'they devoted themselves to the apostles' teaching and fellowship, to the breaking of bread and the prayers.'

'Was ever another command so obeyed? For century after century, spreading slowly to every continent and country, and among every race on earth, this action has been done, in every conceivable human circumstance, for every conceivable human need, from infancy and before to extreme old age and after, from the pinnacles of earthly greatness to the refuge of fugitives in caves and dens of the earth ... One could fill many pages with the reasons why we have done this, and not tell a hundredth part of them. Best of all, week by week and month by month, on a hundred thousand successive Sundays, faithfully, unfailingly, across all the parishes of Christendom, the pastors have done this just to *make* the holy common people of God.'

Worship

So wrote Dom Gregory Dix in his great book *The Shape of the Liturgy* – and how well he said it. For in the Eucharist is the life of the Church, and we who join together in the worship and in the receiving of the Sacrament, we are indeed united into the Body of Christ, the Church, the People of God.

The heavenly worship

And as we worship here on earth, so we are joined in the worship of heaven. We have the Bible witness that here and now on earth we have an echo, a reflection, a model, of the perfect worship of heaven. Read the fourth and fifth chapters of St John's Revelation, his vision of the heavenly worship, and you will see that it is a *eucharistic* celebration: the throne, the priests, the choir, and the entire community surrounding the altar and joining in worship of the Lamb 'as it had been slain' upon the altar.

To the Lamb, with them, let us address the great hymn of praise:

> *Worthy art thou, for thou wast slain, and by thy blood*
> *   didst ransom us for God*
> *from every tribe and tongue and people and nation,*
> *and hast made us a kingdom and priests to our God*
> *   for ever and ever.*

Corpus Christi *Evening Prayer* **Feeding the five thousand** Luke 9:11–17

Food for many

There is no hint, in our reading from St Luke, of the effect of the miracle upon the disciples or upon the people. We are not told that they were astonished or that they suddenly believed. The effect of the miracle is not St Luke's point. Most probably he tells of it because it foreshadows the Christian Eucharist, and it is surely as a commentary on the Eucharist that we should read it.

The Gospels often relate how Jesus dealt with the needs of individuals, or of a small group like the Twelve. But this miracle is performed for the actual physical needs of the vast crowd who have been listening to the Lord for so long. When the apostles propose that the hungry and tired people should be sent off – there is nothing for them, or at least merely five loaves and two fish, there in the wilderness – Jesus takes control. He tells the disciples to settle the people down into small parties, then takes the bread and the fishes, raises his eyes to heaven, says the blessing over the food, breaks it up and hands the fragments to the disciples to distribute among the crowd. There is enough to

114

feed them all, and more – twelve baskets of scraps are left over.

However much the Lord has talked to the people about the Kingdom, at the very least he acts and deals with their hunger. The Holy Communion, however much it concerns human souls, concerns their bodies as well. Jesus still has compassion on the multitudes today. Through the Church the compassion of Jesus has to be revealed, and not merely to individuals. We cannot receive the Bread and the Wine yet be uninterested in the needs of the world, especially the people who are undernourished, starving, kept from receiving help and food because of religious or racial hatreds. 'Give them something to eat' is the Lord's command to the Twelve, and to us.

> 'My flesh is food indeed, and my blood is drink indeed.'
>
> John 6:55

Ordinary Time
First Sunday after Trinity *(Proper 5)*
6 June   *Principal Service*   The
Evangelist   Matthew 9:9–13, 18–26

'I came not to call the righteous, but sinners.' Matthew 9:13

The Evangelist

St Matthew's Gospel, more than any other, is the link between the Old Testament and the New, between the old Israel and the new worldwide Church of the People of God. Matthew's motivation was to demonstrate Jesus at the Messiah, primarily by showing how Jesus, in his life and in his ministry, fulfilled the Old Testament Scriptures. Matthew's speciality lies in relating the gospel to the Jewish Law, with his stress on Christianity as the 'New Law'. Remember that Matthew was a Jew, and the early evangelizing was carried out among Jews; as Jesus himself preached in the synagogues, so his early followers tried to do the same.

Hence we see Matthew as a Jewish writer writing for Jews; his Gospel is the product of a community and for a community. It has been called the handbook for teaching and administration within the Church, and has been compared with the *Manual of Discipline* of the Qumran.

'The First Gospel'
At least from the time of Irenaeus and early canonical witnesses, Matthew was for seventeen centuries 'the First Gospel' in a very real sense. Matthew supplied both the frame and the basic shape and colour to the Church's image of Jesus Christ. His Gospel outweighed not only that of Mark, but also those of Luke and John. On Sundays and Holy Days of the liturgical year, other Gospels filled in only where Matthew's picture was felt to be incomplete.

The Kingdom
Matthew does not think in terms of ideas or doctrines. To him the question is: Who will inherit the Kingdom? The answer is clear: The Church, or in other words, those who recognize Jesus as Messiah.

We should pay a tribute to the Jewish faith: at its best it was thoughtful, always searching for the truth about God; latterly it failed because it became too highly structured and too inflexible for its own development and good. It was becoming untenable with its emphasis upon Laws – so many that the six hundred and thirteen regulations in the Torah had to be graded into 'light' and 'heavy', otherwise life would have become impossible.

The world needed Jesus to show us how to regulate ourselves within ourselves, outside any man-made laws, however inspired they may have been.

The Gospel
Matthew's Gospel is related to Judaism in two ways: it understands the Christian faith and life not as a new religion, but as a new constituency of Israel, where the last have become the first, a messianic community which is the true heir of the Old Testament, and which, after the exaltation of Jesus, contains also Gentiles. It also argues for the right to understand itself as such, over against the Synagogue, with which it is still in constant discussion. The suggestion is made that the Gospel 'grew out of' a school led by a converted rabbi, where Jewish methods of teaching and studying were applied to the new cause. Matthew applies rules for interpretation similar to those used at Qumran, and is able to show that

the Church is right in hailing Jesus of Nazareth as the Christ, and his followers as true believers and heirs to the promises in the Scriptures – the Old Testament.

Matthew

Matthew was called early in the ministry of Jesus (Matthew 9:9), but there is no mention of any previous meeting or discussion, and the scholars think it unlikely that the writer of this Gospel, with its strongly Hebrew atmosphere, would have chosen employment in the despised outskirts of Jewish religious life. Instead, his rootage in Judaism has suggested that the Gospel grew out of a 'school' led by a converted rabbi (see 13:15, 52). Matthew's ideal was that the learned Jews should become the disciples of Jesus, and thus add the riches of the New Covenant to those already possessed of the Old.

First Sunday after Trinity   *Second Service*
Healing   Luke 8:41–56
'Who was it that touched me?' Luke 8:45

The touch of faith

'Who was it that touched me?' asked Jesus. What a strange question! Crowds were pushing up against him from all directions; he was in a mob – people had heard the astonishing story of the healing of the man possessed with demons, when Jesus had let the demons take refuge in a nearby herd of swine, which then rushed downhill into a lake and were drowned. Everyone who heard about this was, naturally, astonished; and as Jesus made his way to another call for help – this time from a very respectable character, no less than a ruler of the synagogue – the people pressed and shoved around him. How often do we see TV pictures of the crowds around some famous or notorious figure, pushing and shoving, so anxious to be near.

Power

But the Lord had a particular touch in mind. The touch of faith, a touch that drew power out of him and brought healing. The gospel story gives the impression that for a moment the Lord was

117

somehow drained of energy. We may here be given a glimpse of how much of a strain his daily life must have been; the constant demands, the constant psychic force – if we may use such a term – being used up.

No wonder he needed to get away alone, to meet his Father, to re-charge. We too, in our small way, can do something similar if we go away for a 'quiet day', or go 'on retreat', or just in the midst of our busy, busy lives, drop into a quiet church for a brief service or for just a short time of peace and silence.

Faith
The power of Christ was released by faith. A power strong enough to cure a longstanding illness; strong enough to raise a man from the grave; a power to raise a little girl from her deathbed.

On another occasion we are told that Christ could work no miracle because of the lack of the *father's* faith. Faith creates an opening for the power of God to enter. It opens the door that seems to have been shut fast; it may be another who opens *our* door – *we* may open another's.

Refusal
There are those who, like the mourners in the room with the dead child, refuse to believe Christ's words, and laugh at them. There are those who refuse to accept that our life here – compared with the future that is promised – is only like a sleep, a dream, from which we will be awakened by the touch of Christ. Death, they think, is a dead end; but we are to be like Peter and John and James. They stayed to witness the power of Christ, and rejoiced to see it.

Second Sunday after Trinity *(Proper 6)*
13 June   *Principal Service*   The Harvest is Plentiful   Matthew 9:35–10:8

'Preach as you go, saying "The kingdom of heaven is at hand."' Matthew 10:7

Chosen and sent

The Twelve have been chosen and sent out on their first evangelistic mission; they have been named in the verses immediately
before our text: 'first, Simon, who is called Peter, the Rock, and
Andrew his brother; James the son of Zebedee, and John *his*
brother; Philip and Bartholomew; Thomas and Matthew the tax
collector; James the son of Alphaeus, and Thaddaeus; Simon the
Cananean [the Zealot], and Judas Iscariot, who betrayed him,'
and our text is part of their charge. We have to recall the fact,
however, that those who go out on such work are never charged
only with a message. They have also to live the life of that message,
for our Christianity is not a system, nor even a cultus, but above
all a life.

We who are followers of Our Lord and seek to be much in his
Presence, are to become mirrors of his life. We are to reflect his
image more and more clearly as life goes on. So our duty is plain
– if we would be transformed into Christ's image we must be with
him at all times in spirit.

Association

We must continually associate with Christ, making him our constant companion. We must not reflect him in an occasional, inter-
mittent way, but steadily and continually. To do this, we must
live with him, and be careful to give a full and fair reflection of
him. We must not be half-hearted, since if we are we shall not
fully reflect the Lord; other images may well conflict or hide the
strength, the mercy, the love of the Lord

Reception

We must stand in his presence with open face, nothing hidden
nor distorted. St Paul tells us, 'We all, with unveiled face reflecting
as a mirror the glory of the Lord, are transformed into the same
image from glory to glory, even as from the Lord the Spirit'
(1 Corinthians 13:12). We may wear in the world a veil, as it were,
refusing to reflect Christ's image. This will mean that when we
return to the Lord we must uncover our face; and he will see there
the world's reflection and not his own. A covered mirror reflects
nothing; it may even hide a reflection we would not care to see.

Reflection

To state briefly Christian thinking: We must be much in the Lord's presence. We must be so fully and honestly filled with love for him that we can find him everywhere we go, and in all those we meet. Here then is something we can do for the Lord, and our mission: reflect Jesus continuously in our lives. By reflecting him we shall certainly extend the knowledge of him; let us remember that many who do not look for him, *will* look at us. We have to preach Christ by both word and life.

Second Sunday after Trinity   *Second Service*   **The Devil**   Luke 11:14–28

'Every kingdom divided against itself is laid waste, and house falls upon house.' Luke 11:14

Past ideas

In the past, many people would think of the devil as a figure of fun, or as a bogey to frighten the children. Others thought of him as a fallen angel, a very dignified Being, who perhaps deserved pity as well as blame. This concept of the devil came largely from the magnificent poetry of John Milton. The devil appeared in people's thoughts and on their lips, in a number of ways or disguises, and with a variety of names.

The great majority of people today realize how absurd many of these ideas of the devil were, and have largely rejected them. Unfortunately they do not remember that much of what they consider absurd never was the teaching of Scripture, nor of the Church. More serious still, from this rejection of common mistakes it is all too easy a step to deciding that no such person as the devil exists at all – which by no means follows!

What is the devil like?

So what is the devil like? This is much harder to answer. From very early days, and indeed to our own times, many people have personified the cumulative amount of evil in the world by thinking of a supreme evil being, and calling him 'The Devil', but we cannot be sure that this idea of a personal devil is correct. Yet when we are puzzled about this, we should remember that it is Satan's business to prevent us from knowing how he works, in order that he may lead us astray more easily, and if possible prevent us from believing in him at all!

Jesus and the devil
Our Lord spoke of the devil on several occasions. Accused of casting out demons by Be-elze-bul, the king of devils, he refuted the charge by exposing its fundamental absurdity, but he did not attempt to correct popular conceptions – or misconceptions – about the devil in any way. Rather he spoke bluntly about the reality of life's struggle, where brute force could all too easily be set to steal (Luke 11:21–22). All still far too true of our own times, and our nations of the earth. Rather bitterly, the Lord points out that those who do nothing to help are in reality working against him, and equally if a follower will not make the efforts to follow him, and do what is wanted, he is destroying what has been accomplished. Neutrality is impossible in the conflicts; either we receive the Kingdom or we are repossessed by the evil spirit, returning to its house and bringing in seven other spirits.

Finally . . . (vv. 27, 28)
A woman gives praise to Jesus by honouring him on the purely human level, it seems without accepting the Kingdom as it comes; but he points out that a disciple who hears God's Word and keeps it is more blessed than anyone with a mere physical relationship, however close.

Third Sunday after Trinity *(Proper 7)*
20 June *Principal Service*
Responsibilities   Matthew 10:24–39
'I came not to bring peace, but a sword.' Matthew 10:34

Principles
Our Lord has made it clear that the principles on which he insists must be upheld, even if the upholding of them turns out to be painful, or worse, severing the tenderest and most intimate

relations of human friendship and love. If the peace of the family can only be maintained by the sacrifice of principles, it is the peace that must go, not the principles. If the head of the household is given a bad name, even worse will come upon his family. John gives a similar reference to the fate of master and pupil (13:16) and master and servant (16:20). The atmosphere is one of a future of hardships and brutality (Matthew 10:28).

In his prediction of the strife that will be stirred up as a result of his teaching, Our Lord shows, in the most unmistakable way, that the responsibility of individuals in matters of right and wrong is displayed.

Suffering

And what suffering may be, has been, and will be inflicted on believers who try to follow the example and teaching of the Lord? How do we react to the starving of Christians in the Sudan, for instance? 'He who does not take his cross and follow me is not worthy of me' (Matthew 10:37). 'He who loses his life for my sake will find it' (10:39). What our Saviour preached he practised. He did not tone down any aspect of his gospel because his followers did not believe in him; nor when his friends were so indignant at his conduct that they sought to restrain him by force, saying that he was 'beside himself'. He was willing to incur the opposition of James and Jude, even of his mother herself, rather than that one of God's children should be deprived of the Word of Life (Matthew 12:46–50): 'Whoever does the will of my Father in heaven is my brother, and sister, and mother.'

Responsibility in public life

Christians should insist on the responsibility of each individual in matters connected not only with faith, but also in the normality of daily life. People, both men and women, are too ready to surrender their consciences to the political party, or union or organization, to which they belong. Those who in private life would be careful in all that concerns truth and honesty, can acquiesce in every detail of the policy of their political party or union – even when they know such a policy or arrangement to be morally indefensible. Then such thinking can, it seems, all too easily move over to private life; we have seen and heard of all too many men and women, engaged in politics, who have become disloyal to their wife or husband, and transferred their affections to some other person, perhaps to whom their energies and time are devoted in the service of the party. Such action is bound to result in pain and grief to the injured party, to say nothing of any children who are suddenly deprived of the presence and love of their father or mother. Also, such behaviour cannot be a good example to other members of the party; and all too easily becomes taken for granted as 'just the usual thing' in the public mind. How damaging this can be, and dangerous to our standards of life and living.

Third Sunday after Trinity *Second Service* **The Banquet** Luke 14:12–24

'Sir, what you commanded has been done, and still there is room.' Luke 14:22

Dining out

It is very clear that Jesus valued social contacts, and made the most of invitations for dining out. Food taken in common has a unifying force; friendliness may lead to friendship. He turned every occasion into one of teaching and friendliness, and was particularly anxious that the poor, the neglected, the maimed, should have their proper place at the table of good things, even if they could not repay the hospitality.

In the Kingdom to come, there would be a great and festive banquet, over which God himself would preside eternally; and it is about this banquet that the Lord gives a parable. A man of wealth and importance sends out invitations to a feast, to the notable citizens of the town. When all is ready, they begin to excuse themselves; naturally the host is angry at what are, in fact, insults, and he wants nothing further to do with them. Instead, he sends his servants out to fill up the vacant places with anybody they can find, however poor and feeble.

The leaders of Israel refused Christ's call for invitations to the poor and down-trodden, and the Gentiles; the parable is an echo of Christ's words, 'Blessed are the poor in spirit, for theirs is the Kingdom of heaven.' All are invited to the heavenly banquet, the good as well as the evil – but the latter must repent. As always in the teaching of the Lord Jesus, only those who love can enter the Kingdom.

Fourth Sunday after Trinity *(Proper 8)*
27 June *Principal Service* He who receives you receives me Matthew 10:40–42
'He who receives me, receives him who sent me.' Matthew 10:40

These little ones
The end of the discourse returns to the task of the disciples, as missionaries who travel through the country. Being disciples of the Lord, they are to be received as the Lord himself would be. An emissary is like the man himself, as an old saying has it; and in this sense the disciples are identified with Christ. There is a promise that those who serve their master well will indeed be rewarded suitably, as will those who receive the disciples, seeing their mission and their character – as prophets and as righteous men – and recognizing Jesus Christ in the activities and the agents of the Church.

Charity and charitable gifts, however small and simple, will carry with them their own rewards – 'even a cup of cold water' – when the donors recognize those who are disciples and followers of the Lord.

After the end of this exhortation, and the gifts of healing and preaching have been reviewed, with the duty to preach openly what they have been told privately, let them go onward, fearing not the opposition of Satan (v. 28) nor the quarrels of a family (v. 37). But at all costs taking up their cross and following the Lord (v. 38), when he who loses his life for the Master's sake will find it, being worthy of him.

Fourth Sunday after Trinity *Second Service*
The Kingdom of God Luke 17:20–37
'Behold, the kingdom of God is in the midst of you.' Luke 17:21

The kingdom

Jesus makes it very clear to those who are questioning him about the actual date and time of the coming of the Kingdom of God, that it is pointless to ask such things, for when the Kingdom comes, it will have been already known and familiar to those who have accepted it as here, 'the Kingdom of God is in the midst of you' (v. 21), probably better translated as 'within your power to reach out and take'. The fundamental message of Jesus is the good news that God is setting about the task of putting the world straight, getting it out of the evil plight into which it has fallen – bringing to its fulfilment his original intention in Creation. The reign of God is manifest in the deeds of Jesus as something which God gives, not as something which men 'build'. It is an act of God himself; it is his initiative in breaking the power of evil.

Suffering

The prelude to the manifestation of the Lord in glory must be his suffering and his rejection (v. 25). Noah typifies believers who are prepared and ready for the revelation of the Son of Man; those who did not recognize what was happening were destroyed in the Flood (v. 27). Similarly, Lot is linked by Luke as a parallel to Noah (vv. 28–30), and the unknowing and ignorant, carrying on with their ordinary lives, will be destroyed. Remember Lot's wife (v. 32). Matthew's account (24:40) has a saying similar to this, when one is taken and the other left (v. 35 in Luke). The disciples are still baffled by the questions of the place of the arrival of the Kingdom (v. 37). 'They said to him, "Where, Lord?"' And according to a proverb telling how, when the corpse is available it will attract the vultures, the Lord makes it clear that when judgement is appropriate and the time is right, the Kingdom will indeed arrive. The ministry of Jesus must be recognized as corresponding to the sowing time, rather than the harvest. All the same, the harvest – the Kingdom – will indeed come; and it will be seen as the Kingdom of God, God's Kingdom and not ours. We are to be prepared.

Fifth Sunday after Trinity *(Proper 9)*
4 July   *Principal Service*   **Come to me**
Matthew 11:16–19, 25–30

'But to what shall I compare this generation? It is like children sitting in the market-place and calling to their playmates . . .' Matthew 11:16

Unfair

John the Baptist came neither eating ordinary bread like ordinary people, 'his food was locusts and wild honey' (3:4), nor touching any drop of wine – so what did the Pharisees say? He is possessed! Jesus eats and drinks quite normally – then the scribes say he must be a greedy fellow and a boozer! And besides, he talks and eats with the lowest people – tax collectors (who work for the occupying power) and sinners of all sorts. Jesus compared the 'learned and expert' to children sitting in the market places, saying, 'We played the flute but you didn't dance; we sang a funeral hymn, but you didn't cry!' Those who have heard his message and seen his miracles have rejected him, or worse, ignored him (11:20–24).

Praise God!

Quite suddenly, Jesus is giving thanks to the Father (v. 25), who has hidden the truths he has been proclaiming from the wise and learned, but made them clear to mere children. What truths? That the Kingdom of God is at hand, indeed is already in their midst. Children know this, but not the experts in matters of the Law and the Faith. Jesus offers his yoke, which is easy, and his burden, which is light; all as compared with the rules and demands made by the religious leaders of the day. We must have faith: 'Trust in God and all will be well', or as the Bible puts it, 'All things work together for good for those who love God' (1 John 5:2).

Fifth Sunday after Trinity *Second Service*
Up to Jerusalem Luke 18:31–19:10

'Jesus, thou Son of David, have mercy upon me.' Luke 18:38

The cry of faith

St Mark tells us that this blind beggar was 'Bartimaeus, son of Timaeus', implying that this man was well-known in that area; day by day he would be there, asking for alms. Passers by might be generous or not, as to their cash, but no doubt would exchange a few words of gossip or news; evidently Bartimaeus had heard plenty about this preacher and holy man – enough to make him think of him as Messiah. When he heard from the crowd, 'Jesus of Nazareth passes by', Bartimaeus at once sought his mercy – naming him not as a teacher or rabbi, but as 'Son of David', which indicates a belief in Christ's divine mission, and with that went the power to help. The Lord did not seem to be taking any notice, however, and the crowd wanted Bartimaeus to stop his noise, but he became even louder. Eventually the Lord asked that he should be brought to him, and Bartimaeus found himself in the very presence of the Preacher.

Healing

The beggar's request was granted, and with his new sight the first person he could see was the Lord; in joy he followed him, glorifying God. Faith which firmly trusts in Christ's power and love will, in the end, sooner or later, gain its request. It was not the clamour of a beggar to anyone who might help him; he appealed to the 'Son of David'. We must go on praying to him, until he graciously answers our prayers and enables us to feel and know the truth of things. Yes, he was listening to the cry of blind Bartimaeus all the time, and at last he called to him and gave what he asked. It is vital for us to get into direct contact with the Lord, through faith and earnest prayer, first asking for God's mercy and later for the grace of his healing touch. Let us follow the example of Bartimaeus, the way of faith and obedience that leads to healing and life.

Sixth Sunday after Trinity *(Proper 10)*
11 July *Principal Service* **Parables**
Matthew 13:1–9,18–23

'Jesus went out of the house and sat beside the sea.' Matthew 13:1

A peaceful seaside scene; and Jesus, like any hard-working person, is glad to take a brief breather, sitting beside the water, alone and in peace and quiet. However, word gets round rapidly amongst the folk of the place, and at first in twos and threes, then by dozens, and all too soon in twenties and thirties, they come. The whole foreshore is packed; the call is for a talk, an address, please! Those at the back cannot hear, so Jesus gets into a small boat and is rowed a little way out, able to be heard now by most, if not all.

What is Jesus saying?
He gives them a series of short stories, each with a message. All are set in the countryside they all know so well – the farmer sowing his seed, hoping for a good harvest, but the birds gobbled up the seed that fell on the pathway; other seed fell on stony ground, where there was little soil, and though they shot up, the plants were soon scorched by the sun, and having little root, withered. Others were growing well but were choked by thorns. However, more fell on good soil and grew up well, giving an excellent return, or a good return, or at least a fair crop, after all.

What did he mean? the disciples ask
Jesus explains the parable in terms of the response of people to the gospel. If the message of the gospel is given to someone who doesn't understand, and makes no attempt to have it explained, the devil will sweep it away very soon, leaving the soul bare and desolate. Another hearer will receive the message of the gospel joyfully; but all too rapidly his enthusiasm fades. The gospel has not become rooted, and criticism and worldly cares, or the call of money-making, are too strong, so the gospel is choked and the hearer is useless for God's purposes, however well he may do in the business world.

Last there is the person who takes the gospel message to heart and mind, studies the words of Jesus, and with every effort spreads the message among those he or she meets with, and can bring the words of Christ to their minds and hearts. Here indeed is the fruitful believer.

Sixth Sunday after Trinity   *Second Service*
Jesus Wept   Luke 19:41–20:8

'When he came in sight of the city, he wept over it, and said, "If only you had known, on this great day, the way that leads to peace."' Luke 19:41

Tears over Jerusalem

The tears of Jesus were not for himself, although the shadow of the Cross was indeed falling over him more strongly now, but for others, the people and the city, and the destruction that was inevitably to fall upon them both. It would be a very unemotional person who could look upon Jerusalem unmoved. There would be a feeling of despair for the character of a city of such antiquity and history. There would be the religious feeling for a sacred place, the cradle of our faith – the feeling that the Jews expressed in their pilgrim psalms – 'O pray for the peace of Jerusalem!' Sadly, things have not changed that much; the Holy Land and the Holy City are still scenes of carnage, bloodshed, anger and hatred, bitterness in all directions. We today must feel a concern for the fate of Jerusalem and the Holy Land, and continue – as for centuries – to pray for peace.

Cleansing the Temple

After the rejoicing as Jesus rode on the ass (or colt, as Luke tells us) and entered the city, enthusiastically welcomed by the ever-fickle crowd, he went up into the Temple and began to cast out the dealers in animals for sacrifice. Perhaps surprisingly, Luke omits from his quotation of Isaiah the phrase 'a house of prayer for all people' (56:7). This omission may well be because Luke is writing *after* the destruction of the Temple, when it is all too obvious that the whole Temple and its system has been destroyed.

More serious, however, is the approach of the authorities – the priests and scribes, with the elders – who challenge the authority of Jesus, both as to his casting out of the sellers of animals and the changers of money, in spite of the doubtfulness of their trade, as shown up by the words from the Psalms and from Isaiah quoted by Jesus. The authorities would be glad to destroy Jesus (v. 47), but the attachment of the ordinary people made any such attempt far too dangerous.

The question of John

However, an opportunity does arise as Jesus continues to preach and teach. 'By what authority do you proclaim your views? By what power do you cleanse the Temple?' Their questioning is answered by just the one question from the Lord – 'Is the baptism of John from heaven, or from a purely human authority?'

The authorities are baffled, because the ordinary folk are convinced that John's power and authority come from God; denying this would cause a riot, and the stoning, at least, of the Temple clique. So they dare not deny that John *is* a prophet, but take refuge in saying that they do not know the source of his power. Jesus, therefore, refuses to make any direct statement about his own authority.

God's will

Going up to Jerusalem was a fundamental ritual act in the life of a Jew. Every thoughtful Jew wanted to make this journey, and receive the divine blessings bestowed in Jerusalem; and the visit would mean a true conversion to the Law, whose centre is in Sion.

Notice how on each occasion when Jesus says he is going up to Jerusalem, he adds that he is resolved to fulfil God's Will – 'I *must* go up' – to offer in Jerusalem, the centre of worship, the unique sacrifice of heart and will. The way therefore is marked out for Christians to 'follow Christ', carrying the Cross in their turn (John 14:4–6; Luke 9:51–62). We might well notice that Christ asks us to follow him precisely on those occasions when he declared that he was going up to Jerusalem (Mark 10:32–44; John 12:12–26; Luke 9:51–62).

Seventh Sunday after Trinity *(Proper 11)*
18 July *Principal Service* The Kingdom of Heaven Matthew 13:24–30, 36–43

'The Kingdom of heaven may be compared to a man who sowed good seed in his field; but . . . his enemy came and sowed weeds among the wheat . . .' Matthew 13:24

The presence of evil in the world
The presence of evil in the world is always a problem; and down the ages no one seems to have reached any satisfactory answer. A particular lesson of this parable deserves our attention. Our human minds are receptive to both good and evil seed, and it is up to us to determine which will be the encouraged growth. We can do a great deal to encourage and foster, or to check and cut back. Our daily life may be considered as the 'battle of life', since in every-day matters we have to struggle against temptation – indolence, lust, dishonest tendencies, and many other doubtful things in ourselves. No one seems to have reached an altogether satisfactory solution. In this parable we are taught something of God's way in dealing with evil.

Patient
Our Lord teaches us that his Father, who is essentially opposed to anything that is evil, is yet patient with the wicked, and spares them long, in the hope that there may be a real turning away from evil. God cannot be indifferent to evil and sin, nor can he be indifferent to those whom he has made for himself, and made, indeed, in his own image. God would have all people, all human beings, saved.

Consequently, he is long-suffering, so that the wicked may be converted and the righteous perfected, through the discipline of life, with its trials, its tests, its tribulations, and its sufferings. But there is a definite term to God's mercy, known to himself as an appointed day in which he will judge the world in righteousness.

The human way
People are often mistaken, or judge badly, and much harm has been done in the past by mistaken policies pursued by well-meaning but limited Christians. We have tried, a wise man said,

to drive out – in the wrong way – infidels and heretics; to drive out 'Iscariot from the Church'. Remember that, in this parable, the field is the world, not the Church. There is indeed a real danger of uprooting the wheat together with the weeds. When this has happened, thinking that by so doing God's work would be done, it has been a horrible and fatal blunder. The proper treatment is to let both grow together until the harvest.

A warning
Christ tells us that it is not for God's servants to anticipate what he will do on his Day. We are not to judge anything prematurely, for in God's Day the secrets of all hearts will be revealed. God has ordained the time and the season; and he will give charge to the angels, who are the reapers who will gather all in for judgement. We may recall that while the truth 'that the bad may become good, is not taught by the parable … it is provided for in the absolute prohibition to root up any,' at least until the appointed Day. God and his angels will search into all souls, and the result will be the right decision – for we know that God, as judge of all the earth, will do right.

Seventh Sunday after Trinity *Second Service* **Christ and the People** Mark 6:30–34, 53–56
'Many were coming and going.' Mark 6:31

Peace and quiet?
Jesus heard the stories of the disciples, who had been sent out 'two by two' (Mark 6:7) with his express instructions on how to travel, and what preparations to make. They were not to take any provision of food, clothes and money, not even a bag to act as a purse for any coins that might be given them. They could each have a staff, they should wear sandals, but have only one tunic each. If no hospitality was offered, they were to 'shake the dust of the place off their feet'. When they came back they must have been fairly tired. After they had told Jesus how it had been, he obviously thought they needed a decent rest in a lonely (quiet)

place. Where they were inordinately busy – 'many coming and going, and no leisure even to eat' (v. 31).

Incidentally, v. 30 is the only place in Mark's Gospel where the disciples are given the name of 'apostles'. In the early Church this title had a special significance: it meant the particular group of disciples who had witnessed the Resurrection and were given the vital task of founding the Church. Perhaps this title is given since they had just performed, for the first time, that task which was to be that of the Apostles.

Met by the crowd

Jesus had intended to get away with the disciples to some lonely place, but the crowds defeated this by getting ahead; so there was a considerable lot of people waiting at just the place intended for 'a bit of peace and quiet'. His reaction to what was a complete frustration of his intentions, was to express his concern and compassion for all these lost souls – 'sheep without a shepherd'. So he began to instruct them. (That expression [Numbers 27:17, Ezekiel 34:5] is not merely a metaphor for an aimless crowd, but refers back to the whole history and destiny of Israel, and brings to mind how God shepherded his people, keeping them together in one flock, and leading them towards the Promised Land.) More pointedly also is the finger indicating the leaders – political and religious – who failed to give the people the guidance they needed. It was due to this neglect and failure to discharge responsibility – especially by the Pharisees and doctors of the Law – that God promised a leader who would be a true shepherd. Jesus knew that he himself was this leader and shepherd: hence he immediately begins to instruct the crowd.

On the other side of the lake

The aim of crossing the lake to Gennesaret seems to have been to reach a part of the area with some hope of peace and quiet. Alas, this did not so turn out – immediately the people recognized him (v. 54), and ran around the whole area, bringing the sick to Jesus to be healed. It was sufficient, we are told, merely to touch the fringe of his garment, to be made well; and this applied not only to this area, but wherever Jesus went (v. 56).

Eighth Sunday after Trinity *(Proper 12)*
25 July (Or see **St James p. 213**) *Principal Service* **Parables of the Kingdom**
Matthew 13:31–33, 44–52

The Kingdom of Heaven

Two short parables – one which appears also in both Mark and Luke, and the second also in Luke.

The point of both these short parables is the same: encouragement and awareness of the Kingdom's hidden beginnings in the ministry and preaching of Jesus. The description of the tree seems to be adapted from Daniel 4:21:

> *'The leaves of the tree were fair and its fruit abundant, and in which was food for all; under which beasts of the field found shelter, and in whose branches the birds of the air dwelt.'*

The idea of growth is put out as important: the mustard tree with its tiny seed – from the smallest seed grows the largest bush, or eventually the tree, which in its wide spread of branches gave shelter to the birds of the air, sufficient for the birds to build their nests, produce their eggs and then feed their chicks, all in real space and safety. The growth of the Kingdom in the world will be parallel to such a growth in the countryside.

Similarly, the story of the yeast mixed into the meal: no less than three measures, a very large quantity, enough to feed a crowd of a hundred or so – the tiny measure of yeast will grow and expand and work its way into and amongst the grain ground to powder, making a useful dough.

Both these examples are to be taken as showing how the Kingdom of God will grow and take over, in a marvellous manner, from the smallest beginnings.

Good and evil

The longer parable, in three parts, is of course also about the Kingdom, seen this time as something unexpected: hidden treasure; the finding of a valuable pearl; and lastly, the separating of the good fish from the bad or useless, when the catch is brought ashore.

Did Matthew precisely mean that these three parables – written, incidentally, in a veiled manner, according to the rules of Jewish teaching, especially about the coming of the Kingdom – were for the disciples only? The emphasis on the finding in each case is not accidental, we may be sure, nor is the joyous determination of him who finds.

The last parable of the three, about the net filled with fish, is based on the separation of the elect from the bad – the evil will be thrown away. Not so much a threat as a promise of good things to the righteous. After all, the fish will follow their nature, we might say, for which they cannot be held responsible! The intention of the evangelist is to make the point that to those well-disposed Jews who have made good use of the old promises, their future will be happy; in contrast, the phrase 'separate the evil' may refer to a cleansing of the Church from false members.

A self-portrait?

The evangelist's concluding remark on the parables (v. 51) makes it clear that a disciple is he who understands, and has seen the full meaning of the parables. Matthew's words about the scribe who has 'become a disciple' (Greek: *matheteutheis*) understanding the coming of the Kingdom, is often taken as a self-portrait of the author of the First Gospel. The order 'what is new and what is old' may be significant in this matter, since Matthew is deeply anxious to relate the 'new' – that is, Jesus as Messiah and his teaching – to the 'old', the promises of the Old Testament.

Eighth Sunday after Trinity *Second Service* The Bread of Life John 6:1–21

'How are we to buy bread, so that these people may eat?' John 6:5

Manna

It appears that no miracle of Our Lord recorded in the Gospels excited and stirred the people like that of the feeding of the five thousand. It seemed to them a repetition of that wonder to which all looked back – the gift of manna to the people in the wilderness – the greatest miracle recorded in the Old Testament. Yet Our Lord never looked on his signs as something contained in themselves; for him, every miracle was to be a parable. Here, then, the Lord discourses on the Bread of Life, later in the chapter after the wondrous miracle of the five loaves and two fishes: 'I am the Bread of Life; he who comes to me shall not hunger, and he who believes in me shall never thirst' (v. 35). But the people wanted to make him a king, so he withdrew into the hills (v. 15).

The disciples
At nightfall the disciples get into the boat to row across the lake to join Jesus on the other side. As so often happens on the Sea of Galilee, surrounded as it is by hills, a storm quickly springs up, and the sea becomes rough. It was Passover time, so there would be a glorious full moon, and the night would be as clear as the day. Jesus, on the hillside, would see clearly the disciples rowing hard amidst the tempestuous waves. They would have been rowing about four or fives miles, and were approaching the shore, when they saw Jesus coming to them, walking upon the water. They were terrified, but Jesus assured them – 'It is I; do not be afraid.' They take Jesus into the boat, and immediately they are at the land, and come ashore.

A miracle
Those who treat this episode as non-miraculous suggest that the phrase 'walking on the sea' can mean 'walking by the seashore'. The disciples cross the sea at the narrowest part, and after three or four miles rowing, would be almost across, in spite of the storm. Then it is that they see Jesus on the shore waiting for them. St John regards the event as miraculous. Jesus greets his disciples with 'It is I.' He claims an authority that is divine.

We think of Jesus on the hillside, watching the disciples as they row across the lake in the thick of the storm. He sees their difficulties and comes to meet them. Jesus watches us – not just as a spectator, but as one who loves and cares. He sees us when we are successful and stand firm for what is right, and we can be sure that he rejoices over us. He sees us when we fail, and he must feel sad when we are untrue to our calling and his will. But always he looks on us with love, a love that will never fail.

Faith in Christ
The crowds search for Jesus, and find him on the other side. Jesus tells them that they have been seeking him because of what they receive: 'Because you ate the bread and your hunger was satisfied. Do not labour for the food which perishes, but for the food which lasts, the food of eternal life.'

God does not turn away from us because we want to use him for something or other. But we have to learn to love him for himself; our committal to Jesus, our faith in him, must be total.

Ninth Sunday after Trinity *(Proper 13)*
1 August   *Principal Service*   **You give them something to eat**   Matthew 14:13–21

'Jesus withdrew from there in a boat to a lonely place apart.' Matthew 14:13

Following Christ
These few words picture for us a considerable movement in Christ's earthly ministry. The crowds followed him. The humble people of Galilee flocked to hear him. They pressed on him from cities, towns, villages and hamlets alike. They went with him into the desert in a spirit of simple trust. Moreover, as St John tells us, the Passover was at hand (John 6:4), and no doubt pilgrims on the way to Jerusalem joined the Galilean crowds, making up the 'multitude' (v. 5) of which St Matthew writes (vv. 14, 21).

Motives
Of course, we know that some of the many followers on this occasion may not have been moved by the highest and most spiritual motives: they hoped to be healed, brought their sick people with them (Matthew 14:14); and there is the question of food. Matthew tells us that Jesus told them, 'You give them something to eat' (v. 16), instead of agreeing to the disciples' 'Send them away to buy food in the villages.' The disciples are baffled – 'We have only five loaves and two fish.' Then follows the miracle of the feeding of the five thousand (vv. 18–21) – that number of

men, 'besides women and children' who might well have doubled the total who were fed!

Not far from the Kingdom?
Some Christians take a rather stern view, and demand sincere and complete belief – 'right faith' – and would want to reject all works done apart from recognition of Christ as Lord and Master. Yet we can be sure that many of those who listened to Christ listened from various motives. It is the same today, and this obvious fact may prompt us to look into the matter. We see that quite a number of honest and unselfish persons seem to have no conscious belief in God, and yet live exemplary lives. They are glad to be of use to their fellow human beings, without being aware of any call to altruistic service.

If we are to accept the Saviour's outlook that 'those who were not against him were for him' then such people may be seen as 'not far from the Kingdom', even if they would not want, or ask, to be considered as serving God or following Christ.

Out motives
We should be ready, indeed compelled, from time to time to examine our own motives for serving God. There are those who think they are serving God, but really may be serving some false God – pride, selfishness, a longing for power. These and others are all too human and all too common.

We should recognize that it is not enough merely to have a wish to serve God; we must be sure that we really *are* serving God, in all our thoughts and deeds.

Ninth Sunday after Trinity   *Second Service*   The Work of God   John 6:24–35

'Do not labour for the food which perishes, but for the food which endures to eternal life, which the Son of man will give to you.' John 6:27

When the people's hunger was satisfied, the sign was not completed. It was continued by the command to gather up the fragments – of the bread, though not the fishes. This task was to be done by the apostles (v. 12), the point being that the bread that has been given will never perish (6:27). The surplus is a sign pointing to something beyond more physical satisfaction. It is a reminder of the excess manna that rotted (Exodus 16:16–21), whereas the food that the Son of Man will give 'endures to eternal life' (John 6:27, 31). The Eucharist itself is a messianic feast, but it is still not completed. It will reach completion in the worship of heaven, when the enjoyment of God can never be lost again.

Jesus Christ, the bread of life

Jesus came to inaugurate the messianic Kingdom. One day he multiplied loaves of bread for the large crowd who came to him, and who had not eaten. This event made such an impression on the first disciples and led to so much reflection among the first Christian communities that the evangelists have given us several different accounts of it. John's version, more than any other, reveals its meaning.

The fact is evident: Jesus satisfied the hunger of the crowd. The Kingdom he proclaimed is not of this world, but it is directly connected with it. It was unthinkable that there should not be an effective response to the fundamental need of humanity: hunger for bread. In speaking of the multiplication of the loaves performed by Jesus, the primary truth must not be forgotten: Jesus gave food, abundant food, to a crowd that was hungry.

Jesus and his Message

The crowds had followed Jesus to hear his message, and this message cannot be reduced to a simple feeding of the body. The essential lies elsewhere; the multiplication of the loaves is only the sign of a Bread of Life, which satisfies human hunger to eternity. In order to comprehend the sign, it was necessary to have a poor heart, or to be poor in spirit, as St Matthew would say.

Jesus came to feed the poor, but the bread which he procured abundantly was the bread of the family of the Father. This bread is the only bread that can fulfil human aspirations. In order to be admitted to the banquet of eternity, we must renounce ourselves – that is, fully accept our condition as creature, and offer ourselves to God. The divine bread which fills us, enables us to love our fellow humans better, here on earth; it creates a human dynamism in us which must lead us to provide bread to those who have none. So we see that the multiplication of the loaves was an integral part of Christ's message, not a mere symbol.

Sharing

The citizen of the heavenly Jerusalem – the child born of the Spirit – cares about the realities of this earth, and the needs of its inhabitants. Thus the sharing of the Bread of Life translates itself into a determination to do all that is possible to ensure justice on earth: bread for the hungry, drink for the thirsty, clothing for the naked (*cp.* Matthew 25). The freedom of the children born of the Spirit becomes the source of our efforts to promote human values, to create a situation in which every child of God will be respected in the fundamental dignity of a person. For Christians today are to translate the Bread received from Christ into a new 'multiplication of the loaves' on a planetary scale, to contribute to the solution of the enormous problem of hunger, in all its dimensions. Then the Church will again be a sign in the world for those who hunger for bread and for faith.

Tenth Sunday after Trinity *(Proper 14)*
8 August   *Principal Service*
Don't be afraid   Matthew 14:22–33

'Peter cried out, "Lord, save me!"' Matthew 14:30

A wild night

It had been a wild, dark night, and the Lake of Galilee had been lashed into fury – 'beaten by the waves' and 'the wind against them'. Jesus was in the seclusion of the hills, in prayer; but in the early morning he came to the weary disciples, on the water. Perhaps it was natural that the astonished disciples took him for a ghost. It was equally natural that he assured them: 'Take heart! It is I; have no fear.' What followed is very true to the character of St Peter: impetuous, enthusiastic for the Lord, and quite unable to measure his own weaknesses. Perhaps there is a touch of humour in this record of what happened; there was no necessity for Peter to walk on the water, even though Christ was doing this very thing. Yet the Lord indulged his whim. In doing so, he used it as a means of showing Peter his recognition of his character – his good aspects and his less good ones. Love is the supreme equipment and qualification for discipleship of any kind.

His work

We may look forward to another brief but important visit by Peter to the Sea of Galilee and his home town. It may have been the last of his life. It was on the lake shore, perhaps close to the place where the Lord called upon Peter to follow him, that Jesus appeared to some of the apostles, and during this last visit commissioned Peter to be a Pastor and Leader of the Christians with the words 'Feed my lambs' – 'Feed my sheep'.

That great task which Peter was to be set by Jesus first brought him back to Jerusalem, where he had received the gift of the Holy Spirit, together with his fellow disciples. Then, after years of work in which he suffered imprisonment and at least one narrow escape from death, he moved on to other places.

The Holy Land

In spite of the differences between the sea-going vessels and the fishing boats on the Sea of Galilee, Peter must have enjoyed seeing once more men handling boats, and fishing.

An important step

Here at Joppa, Peter took one of the most important steps in the history of the Christian Church – he decided to preach the gospel of Jesus to non-Jews, and to admit them to membership of the Church. The decision he took here, under God's guidance, changed the Christian Church from being a Jewish sect to becoming a worldwide religion.

So we see in Peter a man who had deep faith in Jesus, and love for the Lord, who in spite of failures and mistakes, had the courage and resilience to start afresh – a man indeed who served Jesus with all his might.

Tenth Sunday after Trinity   *Second Service*
The Bread of Life   John 6:35, 41–51

'I am the bread of life; he who comes to me shall not hunger, and he who believes in me shall never thirst.' John 6:35

The bread of God

When Jesus used the words 'I am the bread of life . . .' we assume that he is using them in a spiritual sense; he means that as the body has physical hunger, and a loaf of bread will satisfy it, so the soul has its own spiritual hunger, and Jesus is able to satisfy that. It may seem to us that this is a strange way of putting the message, when what Jesus means is that he can satisfy our spiritual needs, and can give eternal life – 'I will raise him up at the last day . . . Every one who has heard and learned from the Father, comes to me' (vv. 44, 45). A strange argument had been forward – 'Is not this Jesus, the son of Joseph, whose father and mother we know?' Scornful remarks are made about Jesus' origin, which is by no means as mysterious as that of the Messiah should be. The Messiah should appear, an unknown, from some secret recess; not like Jesus, whose village background is well known, son of Joseph, 'whose father and mother we know' (v. 42). Jesus corrects this deduction in his solemn phrases which follow.

Eternal life

'Truly, truly, I say to you, he who believes has eternal life' (v. 47), 'I am the bread of life' (v. 48), 'Your fathers ate the manna in the wilderness, and they died' (v. 49), 'This is the bread which comes down from heaven, that a man may eat of it and not die' (v. 50). The incarnation is now explicit – Jesus says, 'I am the living bread which *came* down from heaven; if anyone eats of this bread, he will live for ever.' The allusion to the incarnation implicit in v. 33 is here made explicit; and Jesus goes on to give a pointer to the fact that his self-giving will be complete only in his death, which accordingly – if men are to have life – is necessary (v. 51). 'The bread which I will give is my own flesh; I give it for the life of the world.'

This is the climax of the chapter, 'Eternal life' is attainable here and now, if our relationship with Jesus is right. This is the true goal of our existence, which had been envisaged until then only as a gift which God would give to the righteous after death; but now we learn that after-life language is also a way of talking about a new kind of life, here and now in the present time.

Eleventh Sunday after Trinity *(Proper 15)*
15 August   *Principal Service*   The Children's Bread   Matthew 15:(10–20)21–28

'Jesus answered the Canaanite woman, "O woman, great is your faith! Be it done for you as you desire." And her daughter was healed instantly.' Matthew 15:28

Traditions of the Pharisees

It is very clear from the letters of St Paul that it was in matters regarded as 'clean' or 'unclean' that the tensions between Jews and Christians came most definitely to the front, and we have here the blunt disagreements between the Pharisees and the thinking of Jesus on such matters as what is wrong to eat and whether it is wicked to eat without washing one's hands (vv. 10–20). Jesus points the finger plainly at the ultra-pedantic Pharisees – 'blind guides' (v. 14) who will lead 'blind men', so that both will fall into a ditch. An ultimate foolishness, Jesus declares boldly, as foolish as making a fuss over what kinds of food to eat by supposing that certain foods will have ungodly effects – the old Pharisaic traditions, which confuse the Law with taking 'unclean' food for practical reasons, whereas it is really 'evil thoughts' that defile anyone (v. 19).

However, having made his position and thinking very clear, on the matter of the lack of any reality of these ideas and customs – usually made much of by the Pharisees, who look for what they consider 'traditional' offensive behaviour, in fact, behaving very much as 'blind guides' – Jesus himself is faced by something very similar to the inconsistencies he has just been attacking.

Tired

We know that the Lord must be very tired – note the amount of healing strength that must have gone out of him (14:34) in curing the sick and restoring health; and the amount of often bitter arguments going on between scribes and Pharisees, and the disciples – even Peter is asking for explanations (15:15). How reasonable, therefore, that Jesus should seek out some place to retire to, for at least a short while, and meditate. He withdraws from Gennesaret and its crowds, and the arguments that spring up unwantedly about such petty and stupid things. In Tyre and Sidon, heathen districts, he will have at least a fair chance of some peace and quiet, and be able to recuperate his strength.

Demanding
Alas, he has hardly a moment before some woman – a heathen too – no doubt having heard about this miracle-working preacher, and having picked up the correct way of addressing him – 'Lord, Son of David!' – though doubtless without much know-how concerning the significance of these words, is after his attention and help. Jesus pretends he can't hear her, we may suppose; eyes shut, hand to forehead, no doubt, certainly no reply to her crying. She turns her desperation on to the disciples, and has more effect upon them. They were probably just as tired as their Lord, but less prepared to put up with her fuss and noise.

They come to Jesus and beg him to take some action that will settle the crying woman, now kneeling before him. He answers, in effect, that the gospel, the Messianic salvation, was presented for the regeneration of the Jewish people, 'the lost sheep of the house of Israel', and not of others. But the woman has a strong and humble faith, together with a witty and humorous reply – taking up Jesus' refusal to allow the tossing of the children's bread to the dogs, and yet in contrast, noting that the dogs may get the 'crumbs' (surely 'crusts'?) which fall unnoticed from the rich table! We may imagine the broad smile which spreads over the Lord's face, tired as he is with all the demands upon him, at this combination of faith and wit; and his instant response of healing for the daughter and praise for the mother. We might notice Matthew's pleasure – as a Jewish Christian working in a church which happily accepted gentile Christians – at the faith of Gentiles being glorified.

Eleventh Sunday after Trinity *Second Service* **Mary, mother of Jesus** Acts 1:6–14

'All with one accord devoted themselves to prayer, together with the women and Mary the mother of Jesus, and with his brethren.' Acts 1:14

Mary the mother
From the earliest days, Christians have regarded Mary, the Mother of Jesus, with special affection and love. It was Mary's Yes! to the

message from the angel that made it possible for God's plan for the redemption of the world to go ahead. No doubt in the Divine Providence there would have been some other way of performing this amazing task – the love of God cannot be held back, his will cannot be frustrated – but it was Mary's acceptance of the challenge that gave the will of the Creator success, and that without qualification or query.

She could not have known the anguish, the pain, the sorrows that would come to her as a result of her decision, but in faith and trust she gave her response.

In the Scriptures

After the accounts, in the Gospels of St Matthew and St Luke, of the Annunciation, the Birth, and the other Nativity and childhood stories, Mary becomes something of a 'background' figure, her only 'speaking part' at the wedding in Cana of Galilee. She is mentioned on the occasion when the family, worried by the hostility Jesus was incurring, wanted him to come back to the quiet life of village and home (Mark 3:31 and Matthew 12:46). In St John's Gospel we are told that Mary was there at the foot of the cross when her Son was crucified; and he, with almost his last breath, commended her to the care of his best friend. Mary's last public appearance mentioned is when she joins with the other women and the apostles in prayer after the Ascension (Acts 1:14).

As the Church of England is both Catholic and Reformed, so for us Mary is something of a contradictory figure, strong and courageous, yet devoted and passive. An Anglican theologian has written: 'Mary is wholly one of us and wholly yielded to God. May evangelicals who rejoice in her Son's Gospel take their proper share in calling her "Blessed", she who accepted so fully that grace by which they live.'

Twelfth Sunday after Trinity (Proper 16)
22 August   Principal Service   You are the Christ   Matthew 16:13–20

'Who do men say that the Son of man is?' Matthew 16:13

Jesus and Messiah

We may be sure that when Peter declared that Jesus was 'the Christ', the Anointed One of the Lord, he was speaking for the little band of disciples as well as in his own name. That little band had recognized a very definite correspondence between Jesus and the Messiah of Holy Scripture and the hopes of the Hebrew nation; their minds had been illuminated from above. Even so, there was a point of contradiction in their outlook, and once again Peter voiced it.

Contradiction

Prepared to identify Jesus with the Messiah, they deprecated the sufferings which he foretold. As we look back, we can see the sufferings predicted by the prophets; in fact his death would be the profoundest testimony that could be given to God's righteousness. No proud earthly monarch could occupy the spiritual position of the Christ. So, to the thorough student of prophecy and contemporary life, Messiahship had to include suffering, not as something accidental, but as a necessary qualification. The mistake was in identifying Jesus with Messiah, yet rejecting the way in which his mission was to be achieved. When Peter sought to deflect Christ from the path of suffering, he was doing the devil's work for him. It is clear that Peter did not realize the fullness of the implications which were a definite part of his confession of faith.

Causes

Peter did not, then, realize sufficiently all that had been revealed. He certainly divined the true dignity of his Master, but did not realize all that was involved. We may truly say that a great spiritual truth can be perceived and adopted, long before its relations to practical life are realized. It would be right to say that the disciples needed a deeper spiritual experience, and a clearer understanding of Christ and his mission, before this could take place. Even Peter, at this time, was not capable of that. He was a man of impulse and affection, rather than of calm spiritual intuition, or of deeper, painstaking reflection. His forward and impulsive temperament was such that he was generally confident, spoke for others, and was already seeing the future. Our faith owes much to such bold spirits, but often they have to be kept in check by more sober thinkers, and disciplined by the lessons of Providence.

The Kingdom

Peter had rather worldly ideas of the Kingdom of God to come; he was not upset, for example, by the two sons of Zebedee and their inflated visions of the rulers of the Kingdom (Matthew 20:20), but on the other hand, he certainly carried a sword and was ready to draw it (Matthew 26, 51). Had he cherished purer and more definite spiritual hopes regarding Christ's mission, Peter's impulsive nature could have been tamed, perhaps, though maybe still a source of danger.

But we ought not to be too hard; do we not also rely too much on human wisdom, and our own style of thinking? The motto should be, 'Set our affections on the things above.' If we can get our priorities right, then all will be well for us to engage in the tasks of the Lord.

Twelfth Sunday after Trinity   *Second Service*   Flesh and Blood   John 6:56–69

'He who eats my flesh and drinks my blood abides in me, and I in him.'
John 6:56
'Lord, to whom shall we go? You have the words of eternal life; and we have come to know that you are the Holy One of God.' vv. 68, 69

Bread of life

Christ, the first-born of a new humanity, is the bread of life which alone can satisfy human hunger: and this bread is destined to be eaten by those who do the will of the Father, as we hear today. 'My flesh is food indeed, and my blood is drink indeed. He who eats my flesh and drinks my blood abides in me, and I in him' (John 6:55,56). But it must be supposed, for all that, that the citizens of the heavenly Jerusalem do not care about the realities of this earth, and about the fundamental needs of the people who inhabit it. The sharing of the bread of life translates itself into a determination to do whatever is possible to ensure fair treatment for all, to bring justice over all parts of the earth, to provide bread for the hungry, drink for the thirsty, clothing for the naked (read Matthew 25). The freedom of the children born of the Spirit should become, for the Christian, the source of efforts to promote human values, and to bring about situations in which every person will be respected in human fundamental dignity, in the midst of a community of the human race.

Our relationships
'The words I have spoken to you are spirit and life' (John 6:63). The real meaning of resurrection is that our lives can be so changed, so unified, so integrated, that physical death can no longer really affect us – that is, our real selves, our reality. Resurrection is an event happening now, which we can be part of now, bringing us that immortal life, that immortal freedom, that immortal joy, which is release from all that confines us, cripples us, and holds us back. This is the spirit that gives life.

Do we really wish to be reborn into that new life, are we really ready to be raised with Christ? We must not hold back, like those disciples who drew back and no longer went about with him (v. 66). And if our relationship with God has been renewed, it ought to show in our relationships with others. However joyful and uplifting our celebrations in church, what do we display of our experience of the Risen Lord from day to day?

Living to the will of God
Death and resurrection mean the daily dying to self, so that we may become more alive to the will of God and the needs of others. Just as Jesus reconciled us to God, so we must go out and reconcile others to us and to each other. As we share the sacramental bread, and taste the sacramental wine, so we share the power of the Risen Christ, he who is the true Bread which comes down from heaven, like the gift of manna provided for the nourishing of the faithful in the old Israel. In his power and strength we are sent out, to fulfil the work which he himself came to begin, that nothing should be lost of all that the Father was given him.

Thirteenth Sunday after Trinity *(Proper 17)*
29 August   *Principal Service*
Follow Me!   Matthew 16:21–28

'Jesus turned and said to Peter, "Get behind me, Satan! You are a hindrance to me, for you are not on the side of God, but of men." ' Matthew 16:23

Satan

That is a very strong and abusive name to call anyone, surely, but that is how Jesus described Peter – and directly, to his face, with his friends standing by! Why, we must ask at once – for it was only a short time before that the Lord was, as one might say, 'all over Peter'. Why the sudden change? Why the blunt, even abusive words – quite brutal. The reason is that Peter, no doubt with the best of intentions and indeed with an intense love and caring passion for the Lord, is trying to persuade him *not* to go up to Jerusalem for a final visit – final indeed, because the journey would end in his death, as the Lord himself has been prophesying. Jesus recognizes in Peter the voice of the devil, trying to turn the Lord from his duty, the essence of the Father's plan to redeem the world, through the sacrifice of the Son.

Jesus answers Peter's pitiful argument as if he were really the devil – 'Away with you, Satan! Get behind me! You are a hindrance, a stumbling-block [using a Greek word to give more weight]. You are not on the side of God, but of men!'

For the best . . . ?

How often do we not undergo much the same kind of experience. Well-meaning friends give us advice to tempt us to what they think is the best action in some difficult situation, or maybe to take an unclear decision which we would regret after the event. Do we not sometimes say of some person who has made a mess of his or her life, 'He got into bad company' or 'He couldn't see further than the end of his nose!' What Jesus tells his disciples is, 'If you want to come after me, deny yourself, take up your cross and follow me.' He offers a future not of joy and success, but rather of pain and distress; yet one which will be overturned, altogether changed, when the Son of Man comes in glory, and the lost life will be saved indeed, as is made clear in vv. 27 and 28. All will be made right, everyone will be repaid for what he or she has done. And all this will become reality within the lifetime of some of the present spectators (v. 28).

Thirteenth Sunday after Trinity *Second Service* **Paul the Missionary** Acts 18:1–16

Paul is testifying that the Christ was Jesus. Acts 18:5

Paul had gone to Corinth, after the somewhat disappointing episode at Athens (Acts 17:15–18:1). There he settles in with a Jewish couple, Aquila and his wife Priscilla, tentmakers, and priding himself as being always self-supporting, Paul works with them, being himself in the same trade. Each weekend at the synagogue, he can be found arguing with the local Jews, testifying to the great fact that Jesus is the Christ. However, this does not go down well with his audience, who reply not merely with opposition, but with insults and rejection. Paul therefore turns to the Gentiles, 'shaking out his garments' as a gesture of repudiation and separation, towards the Jews. However, his preaching and teaching is not without results – the ruler of the synagogue, Crispus, together with all his household, comes over, as do many of the Corinthians, converted and baptized by Paul and his preaching.

Trouble

After a year and a half, with the gospel rejected still by the Jews, but making good progress with the Gentiles, Paul is attacked by the Jews, who have enlisted the new Proconsul, Gallio. But their campaign is unsuccessful. The new official points out that Paul has not done anything illegal under Roman law, Paul is accused of no crime, and Gallio's opinion is forcibly expressed, when he has the Jews driven out of the tribunal, making a crushing humiliation of Paul's opponents.

Angry at what has happened, they attack and beat up the ruler of the synagogue, actually in front of the Proconsul – who takes no notice at all! Certainly a triumph, even though over somewhat a small affair, for Paul and his converts and supporters!

Fourteenth Sunday after Trinity *(Proper 18)* 5 September *Principal Service* **Discipline in the Church** Matthew 18:15–20

'Where two or three are gathered in my name, there am I in the midst of them.' Matthew 18:20

Jesus has just said (18:4): 'Whoever humbles himself like this child, he is the greatest in the Kingdom of heaven.' The Lord is holding up the child as the ideal of humility; in the ranks of the Kingdom, here is the symbol of the ordinary, simple, rank-and-file follower of the Lord. All too often such disciples are in some danger from proud and clever people (compare Matthew 25:42–46 and v. 10 of the present chapter). Like the shepherd, who, finding his lost sheep (v. 13), rejoices more than over the rest of the flock who have not strayed.

So it is to be, in the case of a brother Christian who has sinned. He is to listen to the leader – the senior Christian – and accept his correction. If not, he should be brought before one or two others, so that what is said can be confirmed 'by the evidence of two or three witnesses'. If this does not work, then the matter goes before the whole church, and if this last resort is also of no effect, the recalcitrant is to be treated as a 'Gentile and tax collector'. (This last category seems to some of us as being rather pointed, recorded by Matthew, who himself, at least traditionally, is identified with the tax collector – see his Gospel, 9:9).

Jesus here makes it clear that 'binding and loosening' (v. 18) is something of a promise that is of a power which is shared amongst the apostles; and the well-known and well-loved 'Where two or three are gathered together . . .' is a promise from the Lord himself, that Christ is acting with the Church in matters of this sort. What a responsibility we have, and how careful and loving we need to be in dealing with people and problems that come under our jurisdiction, if that is not too strong a word! With all our scientific progress, all our knowledge of this world in which we are set, all our understanding of the life that lives all over our globe in so many differing ways, we are still cherishing illusions in our minds and hopes. We must keep in our minds that we are not here to accomplish merely dreams or illusions as to the future; we have no fixed knowledge of that future, and God does not give us this. Christian witness must primarily be in the life which follows the teaching and example of Jesus. If in some way or other, our lives clearly affirm the goodness of God, by reflecting Jesus, this is witness for him.

Fourteenth Sunday after Trinity   *Second Service*   **Healing**   Mark 7:24–37

'All that he does, he does well; he even makes the deaf hear and the dumb speak.' Mark 7

In pagan territory

Jesus, we are told in our Gospel reading, went into the territory of Tyre and Sidon, went deliberately into a gentile, pagan part of Palestine from Galilee, which was Jewish, to two cosmopolitan seaports. He goes into a house, and stays there, actually accepting hospitality from a gentile family, a thing no observant Jew would do. The point St Mark is making seems very clear – to Jesus, his message, the gospel message, was not exclusive to the Jewish people. This important point must soften what appears to be a sharp response to the gentile mother, who, hearing that a holy man had arrived – 'he could not be hid' – asks the help of Christ for her daughter.

Harsh?

Christ's words seem harsh, and he seems all of a sudden to be obtrusively Jewish. All pagans were typically and contemptuously referred to as 'dogs', while the Jews themselves were, of course, 'children of God'.

But his tone must have been encouraging. Is he not saying, ironically, 'If I really believed all that racial stuff, would I be here?' She answers in the same spirit, that while Christ's mission is first of all to his own people, yet it is not limited to them. Others can pick up the surplus. 'Even the dogs under the table eat the children's scraps!' And the child is healed, and lying quietly at home.

Rome

For St Mark, traditionally believed to have written his Gospel in Rome itself, for the Church there, this incident is highly significant, as is the next, where Christ is again in pagan territory. The 'Ten Towns' or *Decapolis* was a league or alliance of Greek and Roman cities, and the healing of the deaf and dumb man seems most likely to have been the healing of a pagan. Christ not only talked to pagans, he healed them. His message, and his power, were available for all the world.

Illness and disease

These two incidents, and the many others in which Christ showed his healing powers, make it clear that the Lord does not regard illness and diseases as things to be accepted. Too often we still hear people saying, 'It's the will of God.' It is not God's will to have illness and disease any more than it is God's will to have poverty, injustice, racialism, religious bigotry and all the rest. These are all things we Christians ought to be fighting against, never acquiescing in or succumbed to. They are clearly contrary to the rule of God and his Kingdom; contrary to God's will, which is for peace, for justice, for health, for wholeness in every sense. All praise to those who fight these evil things, and may we never be anything but hostile.

Fifteenth Sunday after Trinity *(Proper 19)*
12 September *Principal Service* The King and his servants Matthew 18:21–35

'Peter came up and asked Jesus, "Lord, how often am I to forgive my brother if he goes on wronging me? As many as seven times?" Jesus said to him, "I do not say to you seven times, but seventy times seven." '
Matthew 18:21–22

Forgiveness

Forgiveness, strange as it may seem, is commonsense. There are two reasons for saying so. The happenings of every-day life point to the first reason; Jesus makes the second plain in his parable.

What an amount of harm a lack of forgiveness can make within a family circle. A quarrel blows up over some issue, maybe important, maybe petty. Straight talking can clear the air, sometimes just time passing can work a cure; but if people nurse their grievances there may be unhappiness within the family circle – or within a house – for a long time. Much the same applies to quarrels in sports clubs, in some society, even in a church congregation; while on a large scale there can be internal strife in some of our unions, or even a country may become poisoned by unforgiveness towards some other nation or group.

Forgive to be forgiven

When Peter asks Jesus about forgiveness, and gets the striking answer 'Not seven times but – seventy times seven!', Jesus gives a parable. He tells Peter about a servant who owed his king a sum of money, which in our time would amount to thousands of euros (a 'talent' would be worth something like fifteen years' wages of a labourer). The servant cannot possibly pay, begs for time and patience, and the king very mercifully lets him off. But on the other hand, the debtor is owed a modest sum by one of his fellow servants (a denarius would be about a day's wage for a labourer). Being pressed, the debtor asks for a little time; the other servant refuses, and goes so far as to get the poor devil thrown into jail.

The other servants, disgusted at this savagery, go and tell the king. Not surprisingly, the king changes his mind about letting off the first servant, and has him kept in prison too, until he pays up – which in the state of his finances would probably amount to a life sentence!

We are all in the position of this servant, owing the king thousands of pounds, since our sins of every day since childhood have accumulated, and there is no way in which we can reduce the number of them, because we cannot go back into the past and correct them. Yet, like the king in the parable, God freely lets us off if we are genuinely sorry and repent. He does so because of our Saviour's death on the Cross for us.

We too must forgive

The debtor threw away his chance of receiving mercy, in the second half of the Lord's parable, because he was not prepared to be merciful to another person in his turn. We can only obtain the forgiveness which we each need so much, by ourselves forgiving enemies, people who harm us, and those people whom we dislike without knowing why. There is no use praying, 'Forgive us our trespasses,' unless we can sincerely say the words which follow – 'As we forgive those who trespass against us.'

Fifteenth Sunday after Trinity *Second Service* **Who am I?** Mark 8:27–38

'On the way, Jesus asked his disciples, "Who do men say that I am?"'
Mark 8:27

Peter's confession

Caesarea Philippi was a town rebuilt by Herod Philip, and given his name to distinguish it from Caesarea on the coast, the centre of Roman rule. It would be about a day's walk from Bethsaida, and Jesus occupies the time by questioning his disciples. Did the people have a view about him and his future? They tend to identify him with one of the ancient prophetic figures of the past, perhaps returning to earth and heralding a new age. And his disciples? Peter takes a bold step, 'You are the Christ, the Messiah!' The Lord orders them to keep this quiet, at least for the time being.

He give some deeper teaching: the Son of Man, from Daniel and Enoch, suggests a victorious figure, but only after he had suffered, even been martyred, after rejection by the people. Notice that the title 'Christ' occurs here for the first time in the Gospel; the charge to all the disciples is not to reveal this openly. Mark has Jesus giving a detailed forecast of what is to come – his rejection, his death, and his rising again (v. 31).

Peter is upset and angry; Jesus rebukes him – he does not understand, he is distressing the other disciples (v. 33) – 'Get behind me, Satan!' What God has in the future, is what will be; we cannot make alterations in the divine plan.

Teaching

Jesus calls to him the multitude, the people, with the disciples, and stresses the obligations of being his followers. The reference to cross-bearing need not have alluded originally to the Crucifixion, since it was the normal Roman method of executing those who caused sedition. The final sentence may be read as a subsequent warning that those who might not have the courage to confess their allegiance under persecution, would not be numbered amongst those taking a share of Jesus' vindication at the end of the world.

> *Come, Lord Jesus, do not delay;*
> *give new courage to your people*
> *who trust you in your love.*
> *By your coming, raise us*
> *to the joy of your Kingdom,*
> *Where you live and reign*
> *with the Father and the Spirit,*
> *One God for ever and ever.*

PHG, 349

Sixteenth Sunday after Trinity *(Proper 20)*
19 September *Principal Service* **Work in my vineyard** Matthew 20:1–16

'The kingdom of heaven is like a householder who went out early in the morning to hire labourers for his vineyard ... When evening came, the owner said to his steward, "Call the labourers and pay them their wages, beginning with the last, up to the first." ' Matthew 20:1,8

Matthew puts the moral of the parable, as he understands it, at the beginning: 'The first shall be last, and the last first' (19:30), and at the end: 'So the last will be first, and the first last' (20:16).

To understand ...
The phrase 'the Kingdom of God' or 'the Kingdom of heaven' was often used by Our Lord; but it is very clear from the questions they asked, and what they said from time to time, that the disciples were far from understanding. We should not be critical. We misunderstand Our Lord's words in our own time all too easily. We tend to equate the beautiful pictures of an imaginary heaven which we can read in the pages of the Book of Revelation, with 'the Kingdom of heaven' about which Our Lord spoke in his ministry; and we are misled and even confused.

The true Kingdom?
What did Jesus mean? Not an earthly kingdom, though many, even of his closest followers, thought so for a long time. So it was that the mother of James and John besought Jesus to give her sons places of honour and importance 'in his Kingdom'. She believed that if Jesus said, 'Yes' they would enjoy well-paid and responsible posts in a national government. Jesus contradicted this answer to our question when he said to Pilate, 'My Kingdom does not belong to this world. If it did, my followers would be fighting to save me from arrest. My kingly authority comes from elsewhere indeed.'

Ruler and subjects
Any kingdom must have two parts, firstly its king or ruler, secondly its people, the subjects of the king. Here are the basic elements of an earthly kingdom and of the heavenly Kingdom also.

God is the king in the heavenly Kingdom, but who are the

subjects who make it complete? Surely they are the people who love God, obey him, do his will and order their lives according to that will.

An earthly ruler loses and gains subjects through the passage of time, by death and birth; but in the Kingdom of God this does not apply. Indeed, remember the apostles were members of God's Kingdom on earth, and they continue to so be in the life eternal. Remember also that in God's Kingdom there are no limits of age, of sex, of race or colour, or of worldly position. All are free citizens, all come in as beloved of God; all of them, and us, can serve Jesus Christ, and give him their love, do what he desires; the only thing that can keep souls outside is their sin and hatred, and refusal to accept God's love and care and grace.

Limits
Yet, God's Kingdom has certain limits; but these we can understand in our present life are those set up, not by God, but by us. It is our reluctance to keep God's laws, to serve him, and to give him our love, as well as to share with our neighbours – these are what can keep us out of God's Kingdom. And in that Kingdom there is no question of one soul being in advance, or being placed behind. Whatever the merits or power of whatever works may have been done, God's great and magnificent generosity gives the same reward to the one-hour-worker as to those who have borne the burden of the day; he keeps his promises – 'Friend, I do thee no wrong; is it not lawful for me to do what I will with my own?' We see his justice and his mercy, and even more, his love.

Sixteenth Sunday after Trinity *Second Service* **Difficulties** Mark 9:30–37

'Jesus was teaching his disciples, "The Son of Man will be delivered into the hands of men, and they will kill him; and after three days he will rise." But they did not understand, and were afraid to ask him.' Mark 9:31–32

The Messiah

Yes, they were following a Messiah to Jerusalem, but the deeper messages had not gone home to them, about the true nature of the Messiahship. They believe that they are on the way to the Great City, and once there they will play a major part in the setting of Jesus upon the throne of David. The Romans will be got rid of, and Jesus will reign for ever, together with his friends in positions of power and glory.

Even as he tells them plainly that there is only one way to resurrection – to experience the loss of self in death – the message does not get through. They are too frightened to ask for an explanation (v. 32). It is a hard message in every way for these faltering young men to understand.

It is easier not to worry, but to pass the time by discussing who will have the most important positions in the new government (v. 34).

A lesson

Jesus knows all too well the thoughts going through their minds. He takes a child and points out how they too must be open-minded, without their decisions being taken with prejudices, and desires to be important at any cost. Rather, the sign of his government will be to be servants of all, taking a place behind the people they serve.

It is only by service, by openness, by constant care for the weak and the poor, by using our own strength and power for the benefit of others, that we will ever become disciples, followers of Jesus, to share in the glories of his Kingdom. When we take care of a child, we are taking care of Jesus himself. A little further on (v. 42), Our Lord makes it very clear what kind of fate awaits those who mistreat, seduce, give pain to a child. Would that this message was widely known, accepted, and realistic in our own degenerate times.

Tyrants

Although the story of Herod reminds us of all those like him who were tyrants on a large scale, and lived like dictators in their palaces, heavily guarded against assassination attempts, yet we must realize that there were and are lesser tyrants as well as the great ones, and indeed we can all too easily be tyrants ourselves.

There are tyrants in the home, in places of work, in schools, and in almost every sphere that can be named.

They do not all exercise tyranny by uttering loud threats and a show of force; often subtler methods are employed. The selfish person tyrannizes over those who have to give in to his or her whims; the lazy person can make him- or herself a tyrant over those who have to make up for idleness in the home; the sharp-tongued gossip can be a tyrant in a village or small community; the petty official showing off his authority can be a tyrant in the ground or office over which he or she can lord it.

Then, particularly amongst children, we find all too often the poisonous aspect of perverted sexuality amongst the adults, who have responsibilities over the young, and choose to abuse them. Paedophilia seems to appear in our papers day by day; the problem of how to deal with the corruption of such hideous treatment, the making of indecent films which can be stored in computers, the passing on – probably for money – of pornographic photographs. And in the worst cases, the cruel deaths the innocent children suffer. Protection of children from 'hard-core' pornography should be undertaken by every government.

Seventeenth Sunday after Trinity (*Proper 21*)
26 September *Principal Service* **Asking Questions** Matthew 21:23–32

'Which of these two did the will of his father?' Jesus asks; and, 'What do you think?' 'What will the owner do?' 'Have you never read . . . ?' Matthew 21:28,31

The section begins with a question to Christ, and he turns it against his opponents, 'I also will ask you a question . . .'

More than in previous generations, ours is one which asks questions. Some are trivial, some are impossible to answer, many are important, few relate to life, to death, to the future of the individual, and to the destiny of the world itself.

Answering . . .
That famous open-air debater, Donald Soper, once said, 'The Christian Church is a magnificent institution for answering questions that no one is asking.' Alas, there is much truth in this

remark. Preachers and synods, councils and conferences spend much time, energy and thought in providing answers to what they deem to be significant and important questions of our time – and the great majority of the human race couldn't care less.

The right questions

If Christians are answering questions that nobody is asking, or not giving answers to the real questions, then we ought to be helping people ask the right questions. As an agnostic student remarked in a debate about religion, 'I'm not at all convinced that Christianity has the answers we're looking for – but I do think it has the right questions!'

Certainly the Bible asks the right questions. Many of them are being asked today, if in less elegantly worded language. 'Who am I? Is there a real meaning to life? How can I be just, and right, as well as loving? Who needs religion? Why get involved in the troubles or needs of others? Why be responsible for anyone other than oneself? Why is Jesus Christ necessary to a modern faith? Should we try to scrap the old morality?'

More questions?

On the other hand, here are some more questions which Jesus might ask of us: 'Why have so little faith in God? in your fellow human beings? in yourself? Why don't you do what you know is right – not just religious? Why do you think the Christian base for life and action is nonsense in today's world?'

When opponents or outsiders put their questions – often difficult – to Christians, we ought to be able to come back, as Jesus himself did, and say, 'I will also ask *you* a question.'

Remember

Jesus Christ is himself the answer as well as the basic question. He does more than answer life's dark questions, he gives us the light to see our own true way through life.

Seventeenth Sunday after Trinity   *Second Service*   **In my name**   Mark 9:38–50

'He that is not against us is for us.' Mark 9:40

For or against Jesus

John informs the Lord that a man has been seen who casts out demons in Jesus' own name; but this man is no follower of the Lord – and this upsets the disciples, who try to stop him, somewhat arrogantly! Jesus takes them to task; this man is doing good deeds in the name of Jesus; the Kingdom of God is being spread, and they are wrong to try to stop such actions.

The Kingdom of God is not some kind of political power structure; instead, any and every person who is – intentionally or not – following the example and the teaching and the actions of Jesus, is helping to build up the Kingdom. The Kingdom can be brought into existence by very drastic actions, such as cutting off a hand or a foot, or losing an eye. Can Jesus really mean we should do such things rather than sin, and thus lose the Kingdom altogether?

What Jesus is saying is that the Kingdom is so precious, it would be better to lose something important and even precious, but which we can manage to do without, rather than lose the Kingdom.

Purification

The combination of salt and fire indicates purification; the contribution of a disciple of Christ to the health and goodness of the world depends upon his or her own wholesomeness. (So says a venerable teacher, deep in consideration of the true meaning of passages in the Scriptures which sometimes seem difficult to us.) No sacrifice is too great, if entry to the Kingdom is assured.

Again, each person's call is different and unique; but in a variety of ways, we are called to follow the Lord. Let us consider our life and our way of living. Is there anything that comes between us and our following of Christ? If there is, let us be prepared to put it aside, cast it away; and by so doing we will be at peace with one another (v. 50).

Eighteenth Sunday after Trinity *(Proper 22)*
3 October   *Principal Service*   **Respect for Life**   Matthew 21:33–46

What can be more important, more valuable, than human life? Here is something God created upon this earth, as a supreme example of what life can be – life with all its varieties, from the smallest and tiniest creatures, through the vast developments which have been realized in the self-understanding, the self-growth of the human race. We are able to look back to the mysteries of Creation – the very beginnings, the 'Big Bang' in the universe, the even more mysterious development of life in its many forms, culminating, we would say, in the appearance of human life. Human life into which Jesus himself was born, at the proper time, and the redemption of that human life in the planning of the Creator and the acceptance of his plan by one particular human being, Mary, the mother of Jesus, the Christ. Today's reading of a parable – the gripping story of the man who planted a vineyard and what followed – is indeed an allegory in which almost every detail represents something in God's dealings with his chosen people, Israel. And the life of the Lord Jesus himself, coming to our tiny remote planet, with his message from the Father of love, of hope, and of joyful recognition; but spoilt by greed and sin.

The Song of the Vineyard
The theme of our reading is Disappointment, Betrayal of Trust, and the inevitable results of such betrayal and disappointment.

The prophet Isaiah seems to be writing his poem-parable just about the time when Israel, under King Ahaz, looking for a powerful ally in dangerous times, appealed to the Assyrians. From that time forward, Israel was neither more nor less than a vassal-province of Assyria. Isaiah's message is clear – if Israel does not trust in the Lord and in the Lord alone, then her doom is certain.

The use of the image of a vineyard for God's chosen people is not fully revealed until the end of the song. Then, like Nathan crying 'Thou art the man!', Isaiah drops the mask. God has bestowed upon Israel his grace and loving care, and has rightly expected the fair fruit of justice and righteousness – only to find the foul fruit of injustice and oppression.

It is faithless Israel that is to be given to the thorns and briars; God will remove all defence of her, will care no more for her, will leave her to her fate.

The parable of the vineyard
Jesus, in his parable on the same theme, repeats Israel's details – the careful planning, the hedge, the wine-pit, the tower – but makes the vineyard this time an 'investment' which is let out to

tenants. The details of their wicked and grasping behaviour seem to be deliberate echoes of the history of the prophets, so often rejected by the rulers of Israel; and the final appeal through the beloved son, who is murdered callously, seems a clear reflection of the mission and passion and death of Jesus.

The betrayal of the son, and the greed of the tenants, can have only the one answer – their destruction, and the handing over of the care of the vineyard to others more worthy.

How far this parable is an authentic utterance of Jesus, the scholars wonder; perhaps its present form reflects the troubled conditions of the early Church. It certainly poses a question which Jesus asked of both the Jews and his disciples, during his life on earth – 'What think you of me?'

Questions for us

What do we think of Jesus? How do we receive his claims? Are we among those who reject him?

He is that stone rejected by the builders, but which yet, in the marvellous will and providence of God, became the actual corner-stone of the whole new edifice. The old Hebrew rulers, who heard Isaiah, rejected him and his advice, and as a result the nation became enslaved by its enemies. The rulers of Christ's time rejected him and his claims, and connived at his arrest, trial and death. But, just as the death of the son was by no means the end of the story Jesus told, neither was his own death the end of the story.

And for us, the vital question remains – What do *we* think of Christ?

Eighteenth Sunday after Trinity
Second Service **Like a little child**
Mark 10:2–16

'Whoever does not receive the kingdom of God like a child shall not enter it.' Mark 10:15

Jesus was angry

The only occasion in the New Testament when we are explicitly told that 'Jesus was angry' is when his disciples prevented mothers bringing their small children to him to receive his blessing (Mark

10:13,14 – He was indignant, and said, 'Let the children come to me . . . for to such belongs the Kingdom of God . . .')

We do not easily think of Jesus as angry. Partly because of the words of sentimental hymns, partly by some pictures of Jesus, and partly by misuse of our own imaginations, we all too easily think of him as always very gentle and quiet in word and deed. Certainly he was so, we may be sure, when dealing with the sick, the feeble, the distressed, and with repentant sinners. On the other hand, Jesus could and did show his displeasure in no uncertain terms: if we look at the occasions when he did so, we see that his anger was sometimes calculated, always necessary, and always justifiable. For instance, at the Temple when he drove away the money-changers and the cattle dealers (Mark 11:15 – 17, etc.). He was angry with Herod for his double-dealing (Luke 13:32). He was angry with Peter more than once, and even told him he was like Satan (Matthew 16:23).

Calculated anger
Often – too often! – our fits of anger are sudden impulses, but on occasions Our Lord showed his anger after calculated thought. The abuse of the Temple by the traders, and the failure of the Temple authorities to keep them in check, was surely known to him from boyhood; he must often have thought about it, and prayed about it, and perhaps spoken about it. In the end he decided that only an open and forceful protest would achieve anything. Nor were his condemnations of the scribes and Pharisees, nor his comment about the shifty 'fox' Herod, made on the spur of the moment. His words were severe when he felt that severity was deserved and needed.

Justifiable anger
During his ministry Jesus was training his small band of apostles. It was therefore necessary to show in no uncertain way that he was displeased by their rejection of the children, and no doubt he was angry on other occasions not known to us, but when it was for their good. No parents can bring up their children properly without sometimes showing clearly that they are upset by their wrongdoing, and showing it clearly.

When tackled earlier by some Pharisees (v. 2) who tried to lead him into a no-win situation, on the subject – always tricky – of divorce, Jesus goes back to the original plan of God, as taught by

Moses. But they are able to bring out the concessions made by Moses (Deuteronomy 24:1–4) of divorce (or more correctly, 'dismissal'). Such a practice was, in the eyes of Jesus, wrong and against the will of God (v. 9), who would have equality in sharing life and love between women and men, according to God's original plan.

The children
Children came to Jesus readily, and he took them in his arms and blessed them, laying his hands upon them. They were, and are, specially near and dear to him; with their simple and open approach of reception, so 'child-like' we would say, full of life and love, hope and interest. Alas, all too soon they may become marked by the world, even tainted by evil and self-centred adults who take them on wrong and cruel paths. But to Jesus the children are not to be hindered from coming to him, in joy and love – and we are to remember that unless we can be like the children we will not enter the Kingdom ourselves.

Nineteenth Sunday after Trinity *(Proper 23)*
10 October *Principal Service* **The parable of the wedding banquet** Matthew 22:1–14

'When the king came in to look at the guests, he saw there a man who had no wedding garment; and he said to him, "Friend, how did you get in here without a wedding garment?" And he was speechless.' Matthew 22:11–12

The story about the man without a wedding garment seems to have been attached to the parable of the Great Supper, in order to balance its teaching. The parable of the Supper teaches us that God's love welcomes all, even the most disreputable, unlikely, and unworthy. However, the second part of the story seems to be a warning against presuming upon the all-embracing goodness and love of God.

He didn't bother!

Here we have the sad story of the man who was invited to the great wedding party, but couldn't be bothered to change from his ordinary grubby working clothes into the fresh garments provided.

Do not let us make any mistake – the point is not that he didn't have any fine clothes himself, but that the host, as a matter of course, provided fresh clean clothes for his guests. This man just couldn't be bothered; he just wanted to get at the food and drink.

A very insensitive, greedy and inconsiderate fellow. No wonder he was speechless when the king himself came to him; no wonder he was thrown out, to the darkness of the night – and with his hands tied, which seems a bit rough; but then he has already been grabbing and guzzling at the table, and maybe has had his share!

A warning

We are warned that we cannot take part in the feast of eternal life, and be at home in God's presence, without being changed. Whatever attitudes we may adopt to impress, or baffle, other people, or to conceal our own inadequacies, note that none of these will impress God. The Lord reads the heart, and is not impressed by attempts to 'do better', to 'cover up' mistakes or omissions; he requires inward integrity, and acceptance of reality.

We pray, 'Almighty God, to whom all hearts are open, and from whom no secrets are hidden ... Cleanse our hearts by the inspiration of your Holy Spirit ...'

God will provide

Only God can give us the clothing of salvation to wear. Only God can give us the courage and the determination to become what we are designed and intended to be; then as ourselves, no longer appearing other than we are, we may indeed approach the Table of the God of Truth.

Nineteenth Sunday after Trinity *Second*
Service **Real Treasure** Mark 10:17–31

'How hard it is for those who trust in riches to enter the kingdom of God!' Mark 10:24

The young man who ran up to Jesus and knelt before him was asking the thousand-dollar question: 'What must I do to win eternal life?' Jesus replied by quoting the Commandments; the young man affirmed that he had kept them from his youth. Jesus saw how much good there was in him, and his heart warmed towards the lad. But there was one thing necessary: he must give up his wealth, sell his possessions. Then, and only then, would he be in a position to commit himself. But alas! his wealth came between him and God. He was unwilling to sacrifice his riches – his face fell, and he went away with a heavy heart. We may be sure that Jesus also was disappointed and sorrowful.

Forsaking all

It is not only wealth that Jesus calls upon his disciples to give up. In the case of St Matthew, for instance, it was his work; he left the custom-house and found Jesus. What mattered most was the absolute commitment to Christ. God offers to us through Christ the gift of eternal life. The rich young man was rightly concerned with this – that eternal fellowship with God, begun in this life, and fulfilled in the life to come. Here is the true purpose of our life: it is this which matters supremely, and nothing must be allowed to stand in the way of it. We, each of us, have to examine our lives and see where we stand now.

Questions

The questions we have to ask ourselves about money and how we obtained it are these: Did we get it in a way that harmed or injured anyone? Did we get it in complete honesty, so that we should be unafraid to open every item to the light? Did we give value, by giving honest, hard work for service? Do we regard money as being a friend to be used, used to enrich life for ourselves and for others? The seeking of money and the desire to possess more can mean that we are in danger of having no time for God, and so neglect and forget the One from whom all good gifts come.

Possession of money can make us hard and unfeeling, and divide us from others, and so, less human. Let us examine our lives and see just where we stand in relation to other people, and, above all, to God.

StPeter Pontardawe 6:00r 17/10/9a

Twentieth Sunday after Trinity *(Proper 24)*
17 October   *Principal Service*   **A Question of Authority**   Matthew 22:15–22
'Tell us what you think. Is it lawful to pay taxes to Caesar, or not?'
Matthew 22:17

Questions, questions!
An old trick in arguments and discussions has been to ask questions – questions that may set traps, rather than merely asking for information. Even such a high figure as the President of the United States was put through a gruelling time, as we all know too well through television and newspapers, not long ago. Inquiries of this sort tend to suggest that the person being questioned may be untruthful or naïve. Jesus is not fooled by the approach of the Pharisees. He knows that the obsequious questioner hopes to get him into trouble with the Roman rulers, or at least make him lose popularity with the common people. They hated the invaders, with their ungodly foreign religions, and their regime so often cruel, kept in office by the sheer strength and power of armed force.

Reply
Our Lord's reply to the malicious Pharisee, asking 'advice' as to whether they should pay the taxes imposed by Caesar or rather, Caesar's minions, was simple. If they used Roman coins, the imperial money, and paid the tax with it, they were admitting that they accepted the right of Caesar – the Roman regime – to tax them. Very neatly, Jesus has them 'hoist with their own petard'! They could not grudge the State their taxes and just dues, when the State gives, or at least attempts to give, security from violence and robbery, and looks after such things as good roads, a decent water supply for all, and other public services. The word which

the Authorized Version translated as 'render' means more than 'give' – it has the meaning 'give back', which emphasizes the duality of the running of authority with the support of those who paid their taxes.

The question

All the same, a question still remains: can a Christian accept an earthly authority?

Christ's biting answer can be interpreted as meaning 'Everything belongs to God – and Caesar [the power of human government] has no right to anything.' Some Christians have indeed gone as far as this, refusing to acknowledge the State in any way – and have suffered for it.

Most of us, however, would prefer to take Christ's answer at face value; that is to say, the State has certain rights which should be respected, but God's rights are as important and, indeed, if a conflict arises, then they are over-ruling.

Authority

We should expect, according to St Paul, a tranquil and quiet life with full liberty to observe the precepts of religion and the standards of our morality. Suppose these expectations are not fulfilled?

We should then be in the position of a John the Baptist, who was prepared to stand up and say, 'What you are doing is wrong!', and to suffer for saying so. We see many dissidents in Europe, and indeed in other parts of the world, who have been telling their authorities and suffering still for doing so, sometimes in the most brutal and cruel ways. Indeed death has been, and is, often the penalty; the United Nations has all too often been unable to act, or has taken action which is puny and unsuccessful.

Christians should be prepared to support those who are suffering in whatever ways may be possible, certainly by putting pressure on our own governments. We may not be John the Baptists, but we should be ready to proclaim the truth as we see it, point out injustice, and attack what is wrong, as a part of our Christian vocation.

Twentieth Sunday after Trinity *Second Service* **Hatred – and Love** 1 John 3:16–4:6

'By this we know love, that he laid down his life for us; and we ought to lay down our lives for the brethren.' (3:16) 'Let us not love in word or speech, but in deed and in truth.' (3:18)

Violence

'Nature red in tooth and claw' – this brings up a vivid picture of primeval life, not only in the forests where animals fight and kill, but in our own urban jungles. There in 'civilization' there is plenty of violence, mugging, murder for gain, sexual attacks, brutality because of differing colours of skin and race. And we are aware also of the fierce competitive spirit which often encourages people to 'do each other down'. Just before our first text, St John writes, 'Anyone who hates his brother is a murderer' and warns 'No murderer has eternal life abiding in him.'

The Old Testament taught 'Thou shalt not kill' ... In the New this still holds, but it has added that we must not harbour thoughts of enmity; we must not see our enemy or opponent killed, even mentally, in our thoughts. Nor must we look upon our fellow humans as fools, nor show a contemptuous approach to them. As Our Lord himself said, 'It is out of the heart that come evil thoughts, acts of fornication, of theft, murder, adultery, and ruthless greed' (Matthew 15:19).

If we harbour ill will and bitter thoughts about a person, we will find we are cut off from God; we should not approach the altar of God with our offering, for it will be rejected, like Cain's, until we make peace with our brother.

This world – and that

We are people of two worlds, which are yet closely connected. We live at present in a world of beliefs and unbeliefs, of hopes and fears, of hates and loves, a world where there is lust and cruelty – often most violent and extreme – yet existing side by side with true devotion and deep kindliness.

The world which Christ came to, and in which he gave his life, was no different – the human heart changes but slowly, if at all, down the ages. Christ knew what was in humanity, 'the evil things

... that defile a man' (Matthew 15:18), yet he knew also of the thirst in humanity for a meaning to life.

Christ came to give humanity a way out of darkness, a way to a new world. The life Christ offers is a new life, and he offers it abundantly. 'This is how we know what love is – Christ gave his life for us' (1 John 3:16).

Hatred
Hatred is a contraction of the heart, a poisoning of the human personality. Hatred breeds hatred. 'Whoever hates his brother is a murderer', even if, unlike Cain, we do not proceed to action (Genesis 4:8).

That great leader of the black people, Martin Luther King, showed his nobility of character by never allowing himself to become bitter, despite the hatred and persecution directed against him. He was imprisoned twelve times; his home was bombed twice; and threats of death were constantly hurled against him and his family. He never reacted with hatred to hatred, but sought to transform his own suffering into a creative force. Unlike Cain, Martin Luther King was never 'mastered by the demon'. The source of his power was Christ. 'I have learned,' he said, 'that the Master's burden is light, precisely when we take his yoke upon our shoulders.'

With Christ, there is no hatred, only love.

Twenty-First Sunday after Trinity *(Last after Trinity   Proper 25)*   24 October   *Principal Service*   **The Son of David**   Matthew 22:34–46
' "What do you think of the Christ? Whose son is he?" They said, "The son of David." ' Matthew 22:42

Messiah
We have just heard – that is, if we were amongst the attentive crowd who tended to follow Jesus about, whenever they could, and doubtless impress on their memories the words of the Teacher – the sharp response of Jesus to the query over the tax: 'Render to Caesar the things that are Caesar's; but to God the things that

are God's!' And then there was the seemingly rather comic, almost music-hall to our ears, story about the unfortunate lady who was taken in marriage by 'the seven brothers' one after another, as they died off, and eventually – hardly surprisingly – died herself, poor soul. The Sadducees were taking the opportunity to deny the validity of the Pharisees' comparatively new doctrine of the resurrection of the dead. To prove this doctrine – generally accepted only during the last two centuries – the Pharisees had to resort to pretty subtle interpretation of certain texts in the Old Testament. The risen life, they contested, would be something like ordinary human existence, crudely thought of as desirable for such matters as preserving the family fortunes. The Sadducees ridiculed all this, pointing to the fact that the Old Testament makes no mention of any resurrection.

Jesus then answers the Sadducees' argument by quoting Exodus 3:6, words from the very mouth of God himself. If he is the God of those patriarchs, the words mean more than prosperity and protection by the God of Israel. Words which had been promises made to the living, not to the dead – surely this must imply therefore that the Old Testament did mean there was a resurrection of the dead to a future life, which would fulfil God's promises to the great figures of the past. 'God is not a God of the dead,' a point against the Sadducees who failed to understand the Scriptures!

The Great Commandment of the Law
The Sadducees being silenced, the Pharisees take up the contest. The lawyer may well be truly interested in Jesus' reply to his query, and hoping for a rather technical answer, which might show up Jesus' preference for this scholarly group – the Pharisees – as against the Sadducees. Jesus in fact presents the listeners with a more intellectual summary of Hebrew faith, playing down to a certain degree the ritual and sacrificial worship of the Temple. But then comes for the Pharisees the last of these questions, from Jesus himself. The question that arises from the widely held belief that the Messiah would be a direct descendant of David, is, how could the Messiah, David's 'son', be 'lordly' enough to sit at God's right hand? No answer is given (at this time) by Jesus; but the answer, at least the first Christians believed it was the answer, was shown by the whole life, death and resurrection of Jesus himself.

Twenty-First Sunday after Trinity *Second Service* **Strength and Suffering**

2 Timothy 2:1-7

'Be strong in the grace that is in Christ Jesus.' 2 Timothy 2:1

From one generation to another

St Paul is writing to Timothy at Ephesus; the Apostle is imprisoned in Rome, his mind intent on passing to his successors the duty and the urgency of spreading the good news of the gospel, and the maintenance of the transmission from one generation to another. 'Entrust what you have heard from me, to faithful men, who will themselves – being good teachers – pass it on to others, who will have the ability also to teach clearly and well.' This is clear and positive teaching from the apostle to the young man who has just had the grace of ordination (from Paul himself – see v. 6 of the first chapter – 'The gift of God that is within you through the laying on of my hands'), before many witnesses attending the service.

Even in the early days, there would be considerable numbers of the converted who would attend the regular services, and would doubtless bring friends and companions who would have heard something of the Good News, and Paul encourages Timothy to pass on the gospel – 'following the pattern of the sound words which you have heard from me, in the faith and love which are in Christ Jesus' (v. 13).

Perseverance

Paul follows his admonition to perseverance in Christian leadership, by putting before Timothy the example of the good soldier, who does not get involved in 'civilian pursuits' but firmly carries on, to satisfy the one who enlisted him in the first place. Then, the example of the athlete, who must abide by the rules of the sport or athletics, if he wants to get a crown in the end. Finally, Paul quotes the example of the hard-working farmer, who is the person who rightly receives the 'first share' of the crops he has been tending. All these examples, and all his words of advice, Paul advises Timothy to 'think over' – keep in mind, we might say – for then the Lord will enable the new bishop to have a clear understanding of everything, and be able to make known God's plan for us.

Equality
Timothy, young as he is, is addressed as not merely a friend and partner in missionary activity, but as someone holding long-term responsibility in his church at Ephesus. Paul writes to Timothy as a pastor, established now, and anxious to give fearless testimony to Our Lord.

Do we, in our very different world, all the same follow as far as we can, the directions given by Paul? – to testify fearlessly to Our Lord, to ensure that the work of the Church will continue and expand, however events may go; and that the saving life and death and resurrection of Jesus Christ will be made the centre of fearless testimony and courageous proclamation. Does not all this direction make our own efforts stronger and more powerful?

The Fourth Sunday before Advent
31 October   *Principal Service*   **The Close of the Age**   Matthew 24:1–14

'Tell us, when will this be, and what will be the sign of your coming and of the close of the age?' Matthew 24:3

The Temple
'Anyone who has not seen the Temple of Herod does not know what beauty is!' So Jewish tradition had it; and it was this wonderful building, a great mass of marble, snow-white and beautifully carved, glittering with gold, rising terrace upon terrace, which was reduced to rubble by the invading Roman army. The historian Josephus describes how fire was set to the colonnades, and how a particular soldier took up a burning length of wood, hoisted himself up on the shoulders of his comrades, and thrust the fire through a window of the innermost sanctuary, so that the flames took fierce hold of the most holy place of God. This, then, was what Christ tells his disciples – 'not one stone will be left upon another; all will be thrown down.'

174

The close of the Age

This dreadful end to the wonderful and beautiful Temple is only a part of the general warning – there will be false Messiahs who will attempt to draw away the faithful, and all around there will be rumours and scares, nation against nation, famines, earthquakes – and this is only the start. The war may well be the Jewish War, AD 66–70, which brought extreme despair and initiated the 'Diaspora', that is the dispersal of Jews, to any place where they might be safe, or at least safer, than the cruelty and persecution in the Holy Land.

The 'sufferings' (v. 8) are more correctly translated as 'birth pangs', indicating the New Age, and even the birth of the Messiah, from the pangs of the Old, and the tribulations of the scattering among the nations of God's People, and the hatred between men for Jesus' sake (v. 9). But those who endure to the end will be saved (v. 13) and – most important, above all – the gospel will be preached over the whole world. Indeed, this must be done, and every nation must be reached, before the climax of the post-resurrection situation. And until this is accomplished, false prophets will 'take the stage' and many will be led astray.

St Paul's view

St Paul in his letter to the Thessalonians (1 Thessalonians 2:9–13 is our reading) makes it quite clear that the preachers of the gospel of Christ are in no way money-making sophists; indeed they made themselves self-supporting, working at all hours to avoid having to ask for support from the converts. Paul, we might note, makes it very clear that his practice is to make himself independent by plying his own trade during the mission. By acknowledging Christ as Lord and King, we become citizens of his Kingdom, though we await its full glory in the age to come, providing we 'lead a life worthy of God'.

If the missionaries' message had only been of a man-made philosophy of life, the young Church would not have been able to withstand the opposition as it did.

The new church year

Here are lessons to learn, and instructions to obey, for us who are indeed children of the Light and thus children of God. As for the Temple, our new Temple is not 'made with hands' – as St Paul puts it, 'Do you not know that you are God's temple and that

God's Spirit dwells in you?' He says also, 'God's temple is holy, and that temple you are.' Let us look forward as the new year of the church's calendar begins to unfold, and with prayer and faith begin to aid in the building of the Church of Christ in the year to come.

The Fourth Sunday before Advent
Second Service **A Flame of Love**
1 Thessalonians 2:9–13

'Lead a life worthy of God, who calls you into his own kingdom and glory.' 1 Thessalonians 2:12

Our gospel today reminds us that we are to consider our lives as set between the two comings – the Two Advents – of Our Lord.

Christ came at Christmas; he grew up and shared our human temptations and sorrows in 'this mortal life'. But he is to 'come again', not in lowliness and humility, but 'with power and great glory' (v. 30), and we are to be sure not to be led astray before this, as the Lord himself teaches us in the remarks he gives to the disciples, sitting on the Mount of Olives (v. 3). Many frightening and disturbing forecasts of what will happen are spelt out for us to see and so prepare ourselves (vv. 9–12). However, we may be assured that in the end, if we endure all unhappy persecution, we shall be saved (v. 13), putting our trust in what Our Lord teaches us and prepares us to endure.

Are we prepared?
Will we be ready to meet him? Will we, above all, have learnt the great lessons of Christ's teachings? Do we love one another, as God has taught us (1 Thessalonians 9:10), do we live quietly, mind our own affairs, work with our own hands, as the apostles have taught us? The scholars tell us that the Thessalonians thought that the second coming of Christ was at hand, and so they were tending to neglect their daily duties and tasks. Paul is anxious to correct such mistaken ideas, and for his converts to be seen as regular workers, constant in their attention to their occupations, and therefore to be seen by heathens and others as independent and respectable.

Will Christ come?
At our Eucharists we join in what are called the 'Acclamations'. Immediately after the celebrant has pronounced the words of Christ over the bread and wine, ending 'Do this in remembrance of me', all assert, firmly and aloud, what is called 'The Mystery of Faith':

> 'Christ has died:
> Christ is risen:
> Christ will come again.'

The first two phrases do not cause any difficulty; we recognize the death and the resurrection of Our Lord as central truths of our faith. But do we equally believe and understand the third assertion? Will Christ come again?

Tradition
Let us be quite clear: the third assertion has as much apostolic weight behind it as the others. The same strong, clear voices that assert the Cross and the Empty Tomb also assert the Coming in Glory (Matthew 24:30, for example). The New Testament clearly insists upon what it regards as the final chapter, the glorious climax, of leading a life worthy of God, who calls us then into his own Kingdom and glory (1 Thessalonians 2:12).

Signs of Christ's coming (Matthew 24:1–14)
The beautiful Temple, newly rebuilt by Herod the King, was all white marble and gold leaf; it had cost vast sums of money, taken months of work by skilful builders and carvers, and was the aim of hundreds of pilgrims from all over the known world, Hebrews who could rejoice at the wonderful centre of their faith, at last a masterpiece to dazzle heathen eyes, and perhaps bring them to the True Faith. What a shock for the disciples to hear Christ tell them that all this marvellous building would be destroyed; once again the Temple would be shattered, and the worshippers dispersed to foreign countries. It is a sad and depressing message that the Lord gives to his followers: false 'Christs', wars and rumours of wars, famines and earthquakes. The one hope that is promised is that, in spite of the tribulations, the hatreds, the multiplied wickednesses, he who endures to the end will be saved; and that

end will come when the gospel has been preached through the whole world, as a testimony to all nations.

> O Lord Christ,
> before whose judgement seat we must all appear,
> keep us steadfast and faithful in your service,
> and enable us so to judge ourselves in this life,
> that we may not be condemned on the Day of your appearing;
> for your tender mercies sake.

William Bright (PHG)

Fourth Sunday before Advent *The First Evensong of All Saints* The Communion of Saints Revelation 19:1–10

'I heard what seemed to be the voice of a great multitude, like the sound of many waters, and like the sound of mighty thunder-peals, crying, "Hallelujah! For the Lord our God the Almighty reigns!"' *Revelation 19:6*

Praise
This great act of praise is the act of the redeemed of God, the Church of Our Lord. Here is the worship of the elect of God, who are 'knit together in the one communion and fellowship, in the mystical Body of Christ our Lord.'

What do saints mean to us? Improving stories about good men and women? Ideals that seem almost unattainable? Mysterious figures in colourful robes, fitted into stained glass windows, or elaborate poses carved in wood or stone? The most expressive definition of 'saints' is probably this: 'Saints are sinners who went on trying.' Mostly the saints were ordinary enough people, not many had any special or dramatic gifts – but, they were people who just decided to take God's love for them seriously, and who tried to love him seriously, in return.

The calendar

Throughout the year we commemorate various saintly figures whose names are inscribed in our church calendar. In the old Prayer Book the Calendar came early on, before the actual services; and you would see that many of the names were printed in red – which is why they are often called 'Red Letter Days'. These are the great Bible saints, the Apostles and Evangelists, and others we read about in our New Testaments. Then there are names of saintly men and women, martyrs and confessors – that is, those who displayed their love for Christ openly, sometimes suffering torture and cruel death. Others are confessors, probably teachers, bishops, and so on. Many were included because they were specially loved in some particular area, like Hugh, Bishop of Lincoln, or by their lives showed their devotion to Christ, like St Francis. Contemporary books such as *Exciting Holiness* from Canterbury Press give many more names of modern saints.

Christian history

From these names we gain a sense of Christian history, the work of the Holy Spirit in many places and many times, upon many and varied human beings. What a wealth of Christian talents there are. By no means all are given to bishops or popes or clergy or kings – there are men and women of high and low degree, of great education and of little learning, simple folk and great minds.

And we should remember that for every name recorded in our calendars, there are uncounted others known only to God. Together they make up the 'great multitude that no man can number . . . standing before the Throne.'

Prayer

It is with them, and the holy angels, that we pray 'with all the company of heaven' at every celebration of the holy Eucharist. By their actions on earth they have come to be in the presence of God now. As St Paul puts it, the saints are like a crowd of spectators at a great athletic meeting, cheering on the contestants; they, as they know from experience in their own lives, can share our troubles and acclaim our successes.

As we ask our friends in this earthly life to pray for us, so it seems very reasonable to ask for the prayers of those who are already in the clear presence of God. Here, then, is the true meaning of the expression in our Apostles' Creed, 'the Communion of Saints'.

'O blest communion! Fellowship divine!'

Third Sunday before Advent   7 November
Principal Service   **The Great Day**
1 Thessalonians 4:13–18; Matthew 25:1–13
'Keep awake then, for you never know the day or the hour.' Matthew 25:13

It appears that some members of the Thessalonian church had raised the question as to whether the faithful departed, dying before the Second Coming of the Lord, had lost or forfeited their chance of being received into the heavenly company of the redeemed in the Lord's Triumph. St Paul is very plain: 'You must not be ignorant and you must not grieve, for those who have died; the Lord Jesus will bring with him those who have fallen asleep [v. 14] for we know that the Resurrection of Jesus is the Christian hope of life beyond death.' In the scriptural prophecy which is fulfilled, the human race in principle, in Christ, triumphed over death. For the baptized at their baptism into Christ die, and are raised in him to share in his risen life (4:14). For the baptized death is past, they now live the eternal life.

St Paul is not attempting to give a literal description of the end of the world, but to provide the assurance which the Thessalonians have asked. He teaches that those who remain alive at the coming of the Lord, will not precede those who have died, for those who die 'in Christ' remain 'in Christ' until the final Triumph. So he is able, indeed certain, to say that 'we shall always be with the Lord; so comfort one another' (v. 18).

Keep awake
'When the day comes, the Kingdom of Heaven will be like this' (Matthew 25:1–13). The parable of the foolish and the wise girls is a striking story; we all love a wedding, and rejoice to join in the joy and happiness of the couple, the family and the guests, as

soon as we hear the magic words 'A Wedding!' This is one of a series of stories that Jesus told; all are meant to help us to realize how we should be keeping ourselves ready for the Great Day. They illustrate the suddenness with which the End must be expected, and the error of not taking seriously the teaching 'Keep awake!'

Certainly the early Christians expected the Last Day to arrive before very long, indeed within a lifetime. 'The bridegroom was late in coming' may be directed at all those who relaxed their vigilance, and failed to reckon with the possibility of delay.

The error of the foolish girls was not that they fell asleep, but that they did not allow for the possibility of delay. Perhaps the original point of the parable was to warn Christ's followers that they should be prepared for a longer period of waiting than they thought was probable in the first flush of enthusiasm, and hope.

The lamps

The fault of the foolish girls was not that they had brought too little oil, but that they had forgotten to bring any oil at all. They did not visualize any period of waiting, which would have exhausted what oil they did have in their lamps, so they were caught out by the midnight cry, 'Behold the bridegroom! Come out to meet him!' Alas, while they went off to buy oil, the bridegroom came, the girls who were ready went in, and the door was shut. Too late! was the cry, alas.

New life

This parable falls into place with the story about the man who had no wedding garment at the wedding feast (Matthew 22:11–14). It was not that the man himself was expected to bring a wedding garment, some kind of colourful coat or cloak, but that he did not bother to put on the wedding garments provided by the host. The new life offered so freely to all (often under the image of a feast) is certainly free, but given on condition that the recipients prepare themselves (perhaps with good deeds or repentance). If this condition is ignored, we may well expect to be turned away, or, like the thoughtless girls, locked out. Let not this fate be ours – the answer lies in our own hands: Be ready, be prepared!

Eternal God,
you have warned us,
that your Son the Bridegroom will come at midnight,
at an hour when we are least aware.
Let us ever hear the cry,
'The bridegroom is coming,'
so that we may never be unprepared to meet him,
Our Lord and Saviour Jesus Christ.

Lancelot Andrewes (PHG)

Second Sunday before Advent
14 November   Remembrance Sunday   *Principal Service*   **Encouragement**   1 Thessalonians 5:1–11, Matthew 25:14–30

'God has not destined us for wrath, but to obtain salvation through our Lord Jesus Christ, who died for us so that whether we wake or sleep we might live with him.' 1 Thessalonians 5:9–10

Give each other strength!
As we study the life, the work, and the teaching of St Paul, what strikes us is the practical outlook which he had on life. In spirit, it is true that he could be transported to the seventh heaven, then he came back to his work for our Lord amongst men with renewed inspiration. Here he is giving advice to his people in Thessalonica. He has just been quieting their worries about the End of the World, and in particular why are they worrying about trying to fix actual dates or times. They have been asking for some written advice (v. 1), and Paul is not anxious to give this to them, but devotes the first half of this letter to soothing their worries. He is speaking of things in the future which a Christian should realize are certain, although we cannot tell how or when they will come about. Paul bases this certainty on belief in God, and in trust on him. God has his purpose for humankind, and however much our human ways may hinder and delay him by sinful actions and foolish ideas, God's will is going to be carried through. To us the universe is so vast, time is so endless, that our individual lives seem too tiny and too short to matter. But God wants us to live by his laws, to

give him our love, and to advance his Kingdom, through our love for Jesus Christ, who gave his life for us (v. 9).

Paul has all these matters in mind, we may be sure, when he exhorts his Thessalonian converts to 'encourage one another and build one another up', or as we might put it, 'Go on cheering and strengthening each other' (J. B. Phillips).

I was afraid, and I went and hid your talent

Our gospel reading is about how easy and yet how foolish it is to make mistakes when we are not thinking about how we should advance God's intentions, spread God's love, make the spreading of his Kingdom our aim.

The trouble about the third servant was that he thought small. His mind was conditioned to think always in terms of the minimum. Why? Well, it's safe, isn't it? If you make your aim always the most modest, you can't get into much trouble if you don't achieve it. If you keep your head down and don't ever look up and see what might be, no one will think you could be empire-building, will they? Thinking small has been a curse to too many politicians, investors, traders and business men – and church men and women. Growth has been stunted, opportunities missed, and often the way has been left open for others to benefit, instead of the originators.

Five loaves and two small fishes . . . ?

The disciples took a poor view of the few loaves and small fishes that made up a small boy's picnic lunch. 'What are they among so many?'

Their pessimism was proved triumphantly wrong when the meagre food fed the multitude. Whether the miracle took place in the loaves and fishes, or in the minds of the multitude, it was a magnificent example of 'thinking big' being successful.

And we might remember Jesus' response to the disciples' admiration for the great size and beauty of the Temple:

Jesus left the Temple and was going away, when his disciples came to point out the buildings of the Temple. But he answered them: "You see all these, do you not? Truly I say to you, there will not be left here one stone upon another, that will not be thrown down." ' Matthew 24:1–2

The small ...

We ought, however, in no way to despise the world of small opportunities – the 'little man' and the 'little person', the ordinary human being living an ordinary, small human life.

Equally we must not despise the small, local congregation of the Great Church of Christ Universal. And remember how in Advent and at Christmas we adore 'God in-human-life' who came as a 'tiny baby thing' in a small town in an obscure province of the mighty Roman Empire. Christ's human parents were from the 'little people' – but the Child grew to manhood and became the world's most powerful 'factor' in the transformation of both individuals and nations.

The world

In our time we can be sure that God is telling us to 'think big'; for the whole world is so closely linked nowadays that an event in one tiny corner can have repercussions immediately all over the globe. As Christians in a world that has become a village through technological progress, we must think of the whole world and not just our own small region.

'God so loved the world, that he gave ...' says St John (3:16), and the Lord Christ himself said ... 'the field is the world' (Matthew 13:18).

As Christian men and women we have given our allegiance to the cause of Christ in one world under God, a world indivisible, a world to be transformed.

Second Sunday before Advent   *Second Service*   **Sacrifices**   Romans 8:28–38

'If God is on our side, who is against us? He did not spare his own Son, but gave him up for us all.' Romans 8:31,32

Remembrance Sunday comes round again, with its recollections, its parades, its reminders, and its inspirations. We wear our poppies, plant our crosses, and make our resolves. For some, the memories will be such that they find sadness mingled with gladness as they recall their dear ones. An era ended on that fatal 4 August of 1914; few realized how far-reaching would be its effects.

Another tragic day was 3 September 1939; and the effects of that day are not fully experienced even now. And we remember also the Falklands campaign, still recent, and how that affected the national life; and the Gulf War, even nearer to us.

Those who served in the wars, those who lost relatives, those who experienced wounds and disease, or the terrors and despair of bombings, deaths, refugees, those whose whole families disappeared in hideous prison camps, still hold to moving ceremonies – the Cenotaph, the shower of crimson poppies that falls in the Albert Hall, each petal a life destroyed; the reciting of those heart-rending verses by Laurence Binyon 'At the going down of the sun, we will remember them.'

Remember

Here in our Eucharist today we have a remembrance service – 'Do this, in remembrance' of Jesus, Our Lord, who gave his life for us. A remembrance service, indeed, which ought to be truly alive for us.

The Eucharist is not just a piece of folk-lore, for our service is not just a memorial service. In the expressive words of the hymn,

> *'And having with us him that pleads above,*
> *We here present, we here spread forth to thee,*
> *That only offering perfect in thine eyes,*
> *The only one true pure immortal sacrifice.'*

By making effective now something that happened days, months, years ago – in the case of the Eucharist, two thousand years ago – we are taking part in an act both of Remembrance and of Healing. The healing comes in the repeating of the action, the making of the Saviour's life effective in our lives; a process of remembrance and memorial which is also a resurrection, a new life.

Tribute

A great many men and women gave up home life and comfort, sometimes their prosperity and hopes as well, in order to serve their country and preserve world freedom. Many lost their lives in doing so. Many of these were not Christians, many who were did not act with any Christian motive in mind. Yet we remember them and pay our tribute to them in our church services on Remembrance Sunday. Truly, the sacrifices they made were in principle – or even unacknowledged – examples of the Christian ideal of sacrifice.

Variety of sacrifice

We should remember that the variety of sacrifices made, or which can be made, are of many kinds, great or small, magnificent or homely. Remember also that even if conscious or not, these are sacrifices to some extent copying our Saviour. This may be very obvious, when in an act of great heroism one man lays down his life for another, or scarcely noticed when we do something small but generous and unselfish; but each is following none the less in the Master's footsteps, the Master who set us the supreme example of sacrifice, when he died for us in agony upon the Cross.

Peace

And we believe we keep Remembrance Sunday for peace. In praying for peace, as we all do, we should remember that not all 'peace' is good peace. 'You make a desert, and call it peace' was the bitter comment on the brutality that formed the Roman Empire; too many opponents of other peoples, other religions, other convictions, try to make 'peace' by brutality, by slaughter, by oppression, by fear.

We should always pray for peace – yes, indeed! – but for a just peace, a fair peace, a right peace, and the bringing of freedom. How wonderful has been the 'Good Friday' settlement in Ireland, and what an example to other nations and places. A peace based on surrender to evil, by contrast, is hateful to God and humanity alike, and will never bring a lasting result.

Inward peace

Jesus Christ spoke of 'peace' to his followers, meaning inward peace, the peace that is not disturbed by outward events, that can carry the holder through fire and torture, evil happenings, through sorrow and distress.

That inward peace comes from centring our thoughts and lives on Jesus, and from really trying to follow his teaching and example day by day. If we can only place our final trust and confidence in God, we will gain that inward peace. If all people, if all nations, could do the same, there would indeed be no problem left about possessing outward peace also.

Grant us grace, Lord, to take to our hearts your judgements which overtake us when we set brother against brother and nation against nation. Give us wisdom and strength to fashion better instruments for our common life, so that we may dwell in concord under your providence; and may your Kingdom come among us, through Jesus Christ Our Lord.

Reinhold Niebuhr

Sunday next before Advent
21 November   *Principal Service*   **Christ the King**   Matthew 25:31–46

'When the Son of Man comes in his glory, and all the angels with him, then will he sit on his glorious throne.' Matthew 25:31
'The kingdom of the world is to become the Kingdom of our Lord and of his Christ, and he shall reign for ever.' Revelation 11:15

The Kingdom
In today's collect and readings we remind ourselves that Christ is our King; and because of that claim, we assert that the world is his Kingdom. Jesus often spoke about 'the Kingdom of God' – what does this title mean?

The Kingdom of God is both a personal and a social realm. It is set up in us when our hearts are fired by the love of God; when our wills are loyal to his will, and our desire is to serve him. This is the Kingdom of Heaven which in the words of Jesus is within us – the reign of the Lord in each of us.

Similarly, the Kingdom is set up in our social life when, acting together, we seek to express the purposes of God in all the affairs and conditions that surround us, so that all our corporate, political and economic habits accord with the will of God, and forward his aims. This is the Kingdom of God which Jesus tells us is 'at hand', and is the work of Christians to put in hand.

Adventure

The Kingdom of Heaven, in becoming a reality and a realm, is an adventure in which we follow the gleam of the Divine Love which will lead us all to higher and yet higher ranges of our personality and spiritual life. As we journey on, so will our fellowship be the more complete, and the family of God reunited. Yes, this Kingdom begins on earth, but it continues after we have moved out of this material place of ours, into other environments.

This world is a fit place in which God's family can make, or begin to make, their home. Here is the promise and the challenge of the Kingdom of God.

The power of love

If only we can make up our minds to believe in the power of God to give us his Kingdom on earth, if only we can assert that faith which Jesus said can move mountains, then we shall be ready to do his will, if we surrender ourselves to God, allowing nothing to stand between us and him and the extension of his rule. The road to the Kingdom of Peace and Love is the same as ever; the new tyrannies of nationalism and of racism have not changed its course, violence has not destroyed it. It is still the way which the Master took, the way of love, and a new age of peace and joy, when the whole created order will come to worship at his feet.

Sunday next before Advent   *Second Service*   The Great Commission
Matthew 28:16–20

'Now the eleven disciples went to Galilee, to the mountain to which Jesus had directed them.' Matthew 28:16

Always with us

Today we celebrate the bold proclamation that Jesus is always with us (v. 20). He chose to meet the disciples at the top of a mountain (v. 16) in his risen human body. Only the women have seen him, and to them he gives his instructions to be passed on to the disciples ('Go quickly!' v. 7). Jesus meets this group, who fall at his feet in worship; then Jesus gives the further instruction, to go to Galilee, and presumably he mentions the mountain there, which they will already know.

At the mountain, the disciples worship Jesus again, though some still refrain (v. 17). How typical of disciples of all times – for to believe is one step, but to live by the commands and demands of the Lord is another. Do we in truth so take the words and example of Jesus to our hearts and minds, that we follow his words and example? Do we really live holding the belief in Jesus as Lord and King?

All authority
We are to take seriously the Risen Lord explaining how he will be always present, always with us, we who are the new People of God, who firmly believe in Jesus and try to live obeying his rules. Above all, we are to make disciples for Jesus, from all nations, with the solemn sacrament of Holy Baptism, the new initiation rite. Once upon a time only males could be made members of the People of God; now the universal entrance is offered to all human beings, women and men. The new rite is – let us notice – a baptism in the threefold Name of God: Father, Son and Holy Spirit. Not merely in the name of Jesus the Saviour, but also in the name of the Creator God, and the Sanctifying Spirit.

The Kingdom
'Jesus, remember me when you come into your Kingdom!' So spoke the good thief on his cross, suffering the same fate or punishment as the Lord; no doubt duly caught out in some criminal attempt – theft, murder, blackmail or whatever. Yet in his pain, distress and agony, he somehow took from Jesus, in some glimpse through darkening eyes, a belief in a power to help. 'Remember me, when you come into your Kingdom,' he manages to articulate through cracked, dry lips.

The kingship of Jesus, living and in our hearts and souls, is shown throughout his life and his death as a man caring for others in pain, in torture, in despair. His life upon earth was spent in seeking and saving the lost, the unfortunate, the despairing. 'Come to me, all who labour and are heavy laden, and I will give you rest. Take my yoke upon you, and learn from me; for I am gentle and lowly in heart, and you will find rest for your souls' (Matthew 11:28).

*We adore you, O Christ, and we bless you,
because by your holy Cross you have
redeemed the world.*

Sermons for Saints' Days and Special Occasions

30 November   *St Andrew the Apostle*   Sharing the News

Isaiah 52:7–10, Psalm 19:1–6, Romans 10:12–18, Matthew 4:18–22

The call

The calling of his closest disciples by Jesus is recorded in all four Gospels; but St John tells us that Andrew heard the Baptist preaching and saw him baptizing Jesus. Andrew and another disciple then followed the Lord. What he told them had such a profound effect on Andrew that he sought out his brother Peter, with the news that Jesus was the Messiah. May we, too, show such alacrity in sharing our knowledge of Jesus – not only with strangers half a world away, but also with those of our closest family who may yet be in ignorance of him. Andrew was not only the first disciple to be called: he was the first Christian missionary to bring someone else to Christ.

Increase of faith

When the crowd of five thousand milled around Jesus, hungry and eager, it was Andrew who had faith enough to seek out a boy with at least some scraps of food: 'But what are they among so many people?' (John 6:9). He was quickly to be shown how a little faith could produce a mighty increase.

Jew though he was, Andrew did not hesitate when Philip told him that some Greeks were seeking a word with Jesus (John 12:22). He was open to the gospel being shared with Gentiles.

Sharing in prayer

There was Andrew again, with the ten apostles in the upper room where they met for prayer after the ascension of Jesus (Acts 1:13). He would never have the high profile ministry of his brother; but his was an outgoing ministry none the less: whenever we meet Andrew, he is sharing his faith with others – personally, intimately, one-to-one.

It can be uplifting to speak to vast crowds and great congregations; but there are countless Andrews in the world today who continue quietly, unobtrusively, but with dedication and loyalty, to share their faith wherever 'two or three are gathered together' – when the third member may be Christ himself.

26 December *St Stephen, the First Martyr*
A Glimpse of Heaven

1 Chronicles 24:20–22, Psalm 119:161–168, Acts 7:51–60, Matthew 10:17–22 or Acts 7:51–60, Psalm 119: 161–168, Galatians 2:16b–20, Matthew 10:17–22

Server of tables

Stephen's example shows us that the nature of our work need be no inhibitor to sharing the gospel message. Table-waiter though he was (Acts 6:2f.), he exuded 'grace and power' and 'did great wonders and signs among the people' (Acts 6:8). He countered the arguments of many foreigners (v. 9), and – predictably – attracted unwelcome attention. Hauled before the high priest, he gave a spirited defence of his faith, tracing the purposes of God through giants of the Old Testament – Abraham, Jacob, Moses – or Christ himself.

Persecuted in the name of God

Jesus had said: 'The hour is coming when those who kill you will think that by doing so they are offering worship to God' (John 16:2). For Stephen, the hour had come. While a man called Saul looked on, the first Christian martyr prayed: 'Lord Jesus, receive my spirit' (Acts 7:59). Saul was soon to meet Jesus himself – and not on his own terms.

Jesus is as close to each of us as a single breath. We may be prepared to meet him, as was Stephen; or we may be as unprepared as was Saul on the Damascus Road. Whichever is the case, Jesus does not arrange the interview ahead of time.

Seed for the Church

Semen est sanguis christianorum ('The blood of the martyrs is the seed of the Church'), said Tertullian, a Christian preacher of the late second and early third centuries (*Apologia* 50.14). As the seed has been sown across the world over the past two thousand years, it has given rise to new growth, new fervour, new life, where before there was stagnation, apathy and spiritual death.

Stephen 'saw the glory of God and Jesus standing at the right hand of God' (Acts 7:56). Can we hold this version in our hearts today, of the Saviour of the world *standing* to receive the table-waiter who had been faithful unto death?

And with his last breath, Stephen asked that forgiveness be shown to his murderers.

27 December   *St John the Evangelist*   Beloved Disciple

Exodus 33:7–11a, Psalm 117, 1 John 1, John 21:20–25

Who was John?

The author of the fourth Gospel, the three Johannine Letters, and the Book of Revelation may indeed be one and the same, and many Christians observe today as the Feast of St John the Divine – writer of Revelation's visions, exiled to Patmos for his zeal in preaching. Many more believe that John the fisherman-brother of James, and especially beloved disciple, was not the visionary, and focus on the Gospel and letters as the sum of his canonical writings.

Certainly John the evangelist had a special place in Jesus' heart, if – as is generally thought – it was he who sat next to the Lord at the Last Supper (John 13:23). At Calvary, there is even less room for doubt: John it was whom Jesus placed in charge of his mother (John 19:27). Then, on the Galilean shore after his resurrection and the re-commissioning of Peter, John is also there with

Jesus, and there is a hint that his ministry will somehow last until the Second Coming of Jesus (John 21:23). If this John is also the author of Revelation, then indeed his work extends in a very special way to the End-Time.

From the beginning
In his gospel (John 1:1), and this first letter, John is at pains to 'earth' his narrative (1 John 1:1) 'from the beginning'. There has never been a time when God was not, and there will never be a time when he will not be. John's is not a world of chance, where good and bad intermingle at random. For him, God is forever in charge, and working out his almighty purposes.

Of the four Gospels, John's is the most theological by far, as he sets out the life of Jesus against the background of history and prophecy. John quotes the Old Testament more than the other three writers; and he is not concerned with the nativity stories, but with the pre-existence of God's *Word*, its earthly manifestation in Jesus, and its message and meaning for the Church.

God is light
'God is light' (1 John 1:5). In Jesus 'was life, and the life was the light of all people' (John 1:4). John's is a wide, cosmic view. Perhaps, indeed, it was the same 'John' who wrote, of the heavenly Jerusalem: 'The glory of God is its light, and its lamp is the Lamb!' (Revelation 21:23).

Can we pray for some of this Light to brighten our lives, and the lives of those whom we meet today?

28 December   *The Holy Innocents*   Suffering Children
Jeremiah 31:15–17, Psalm 124, 1 Corinthians 126–29, Matthew 2:13–18

Cruel slaughter
It comes as a shock, in the midst of Christmas celebrations, to focus on the cruelty and pathos of this episode. Why did God permit such carnage, even though it had been foretold (Jeremiah

31:15)? It is disturbing that the birth of the world's Saviour should – albeit indirectly – include such a tragedy.

Yet, if we reflect how Satan must have felt when Jesus came to earth to save those whom Satan considered his own, it is understandable that attempts should be made to halt the process of redemption. The same applies today. Whenever light and goodness come on the scene – a new church dedicated, a cure for some disease or other, a new advance in science, an increase in Christian zeal ... Satan motivates someone to move against the work.

The Devil's limits

St John tells us: 'The devil has come down to you with great wrath, because he knows that his time is short!' (Revelation 12:12). He has recognized his limits ever since his plans to kill the infant Jesus were confounded. So we have hope. St Peter spells it out: 'Like a roaring lion, your adversary the devil prowls around, looking for someone to devour' (1 Peter 5:8). He prowls, but he can be heard before he pounces. With the indwelling Holy Spirit, bequeathed to us by Jesus as our Comforter, Guide and Sustainer, we have – if we train our spiritual ear to hear – a twenty-four hour, round-the-clock early warning system, which the distraught Bethlehem mothers did not have. The Spirit had not then been given.

If not murder, then doubt

But Satan, forever on the prowl, is never short of listening ears tuned to his wavelength rather than that of the Holy Spirit. He will tell a young person hooked on narcotics that there is no way back to normality. He will tell the poor that there is no way out of the trap. He will tell the terrorists that their only way to freedom is through more violence. Today innocents are still being killed. Can we do nothing to stop the massacre?

1 January 1999   *The Circumcision of Christ*
The Saviour named
Numbers 6:22–27, Psalm 8, Galatians 4:4–7, Luke 2:15–21

Who are You, Jesus?

Since the sixth century, this day has been observed as the Circumcision and formal Naming of Jesus. 'Jesus' (Joshua) was not an uncommon name: yet there is no room for doubt as to Christ's identity when, for example, Saul meets Jesus on the Damascus Road. 'Who are you, Lord?' 'I am Jesus, whom you are persecuting' (Acts 9:5). Angels had announced his birth; magi were to come from far away to worship him; Herod was to shed the blood of innocent children the length and breadth of Bethlehem, in an attempt to kill him; he and his parents were to seek refuge in Egypt . . . This was no ordinary child: he could bear the name of Jesus with unique authority and distinctiveness.

The shepherds' ministry

They came, these men of the fields, to look in awe and reverence at a little child. And, having seen this wonder, they spread the news (Luke 2:17,18). Often we overlook their ministry. Whom did they tell? How many believed them? How many, in turn, sought out the Holy Family? Luke tells us that the people were 'amazed': who, indeed, would not be amazed? Yet what did they *do*?

The challenge of Christ

When Jesus meets us today, we rarely have a warning in advance. Many times his coming amazes us. Sometimes we do not notice him. Yet he still comes with the same purpose as when he was born in Bethlehem, hung on the cross, or appeared to Saul. He challenges us, first, to recognize him – and then to turn that recognition into faith and service. He does not take away our freedom of choice: we can recognize him – or not. We can build on the recognition – or not. Many of those whom the shepherds told, would not take the trouble to visit the child. Many today, when Jesus crosses their path, either do not see him, or do not take the trouble to hear and act on the message he brings.

The blood shed at the circumcision was a sign of more to come: innocent red life-blood being spilled because God had given his most precious possession for a world which was – for the most part – looking elsewhere.

Yet the challenge remains. We still have time to accept it.

Sunday 17 January   *St Antony, Abbot*   Go and sell all

'Jesus said: "If you wish to be perfect, go, sell your possessions, and give the money to the poor, and you will have treasure in heaven; then come, follow me."' Matthew 19:21

A call from God

Antony was born the son of a prosperous farmer in a village some miles south of Memphis, Egypt. His parents died when he was nineteen. One day, while the gospel was being read in his village church, these words of Jesus in Matthew 19:21 burned into his heart. Selling the farm, he gave the proceeds to the poor, and went to live with a hermit on the outskirts of the village. Memories of wealth and luxury followed him, and he retreated further into desert isolation.

Seeking solitude

Many like-minded men followed him, and it seemed the further they went from civilization, the worse their temptations became. But the community of monks persevered, and Antony formed a special friendship with the saintly Athanasius, Bishop of Alexandria – a friendship which continued until Antony's death, at the great age of 105.

Inheriting the monk's most cherished possessions – an old sheepskin tunic and the mantle he had used as a mattress – Athanasius wrote a *Life of Antony*, which has helped many Christians struggling to escape the snares of wealth.

Simplicity

Antony's *vade mecum* was the Bible. He told his monks: 'The Scriptures are sufficient for instruction and encourage purity of heart.' (In Coptic, the word for 'heart' and 'mind' is the same.)

Anyone whose life has counted for Christ has been in danger of being misunderstood, not only by the world at large, but also by those nearest to them. Antony was no exception. 'The monk is pursuing only his own salvation, while the Church believes she is also serving the souls of others,' was a charge he fought against all his life. It is significant that Eusebius, Bishop of Caesarea, who gave us the tome of *Church History*, chose to omit an account of Antony. In theological outlook, the two were poles apart: Eusebius advocated full participation of Christians in the life of the Empire, and considered that Antony had withdrawn from that life. But, as has been seen with popes, princesses, nuns and noblemen, the world will criticize, wherever someone is bold enough to do, say, write or preach in the name of Christ.

What of today?
We have a far longer and richer monastic history to weigh in our deliberations, than had the fourth-century Egyptian Church. How much is the solitary or secluded life a valid part of today's Church? Modern Christians in Egypt are a persecuted minority; but George Herbert looked back to the days of Antony, and the devotion of Egypt's many hermit-monks:

> *'The Ten Commandments there did flourish,*
> *more than the ten bitter plagues had done before.'*

> *Church Militant*

25 January *Conversion of St Paul* **Early Recognition**
Jeremiah 1:4–10, Psalm 67, Acts, 9:1–22, Matthew 19:27–30, or Acts 9:1–22, Psalm 67, Galatians 1:11–16a, Matthew 19:27–30

Before the day of birth
Known and consecrated for the Lord's service even before he was born, Jeremiah was destined for great things. Did he have a choice, or was this pre-destination carried to the limit? Taken at face value, it would appear that God gave his prophet no let-out clause in his contract of ministry employment. And Jeremiah responded positively – unlike Paul, who, as Saul, had for some time persecuted the earliest followers of Jesus (1 Corinthians 15:9).

Personal encounter
Jesus had taken Saul's venom personally: 'I am Jesus, whom you are persecuting' (Acts 9:5). To attack the Church (and anyone in it) is to attack the Lord himself. Jesus, in this encounter, intends

Paul to be under no illusions as to the victim of his animosity – or to the engineer of his conversion. Paul must have wished the 'letters to the synagogues' (Acts 9:2) anywhere but on his person, as the light of Jesus floored him and blinded his vision. Whether in an innermost pocket, or even in his saddlebags, he would know in an instant that Jesus could see every incriminating word.

What is there to say, in such a personal encounter with God? Well, as Christians we have such encounters every day, the instant we lift our hearts in prayer, the second that God steps in, be it an emergency, or the gentlest of whispers. He stimulates us to a recognition of his presence in a million different ways – and we are there, as Paul, on the Damascas Road: 'Who are you, Lord?' 'I am Jesus.'

Living in confidence

If we are keeping our prayer, worship and heart-lines of communication open to God, we shall not suffer the trauma that Paul went through. Our encounter with God will be a positive step along our spiritual journey, rather than a cataclysmic hiatus. It may also be, that – like Ananias – God will call us to minister to someone with whom we would not normally seek contact. Let us be open to the Lord's guiding, as today we are given another chance to consider the great outcome of Paul's Damascus Road encounter.

19 March *St Joseph of Nazareth*
A Life Unobserved

2 Samuel 7:4–16, Psalm 89:27,28,34–37, Romans 4:13–18, Matthew 1:18–25

Requiescat in pace?

So often, even in these times of what we like to call 'advanced communication', men and women die before their real worth is recognized. As their bodies 'rest in peace', slowly the world wakes up to the great deeds they have been doing so quietly over the years. So it is with Joseph: the gospel references to him are brief in the extreme; in fact, we never hear of him speaking a word. Yet he was the earthly father of the world's Saviour!

We know, at least, that Joseph was still alive when Jesus, at twelve years of age, lingered to converse with the doctors in the temple (Luke 2:41ff.). How long he lived after that, we can only guess.

The model of parenthood

Joseph was 'righteous' (Matthew 1:19). God would surely not have chosen a less upright man as the custodian of his child. He was open to God's directions, accepting the strangeness of Mary's conception, without panic or confusion. He tried valiantly to find suitable accommodation for his pregnant wife in crowded Bethlehem, and was successful in that Mary did not have to give birth in the open fields.

Apparently Joseph coped well with the unexpected visit of the Magi, and was able to prepare his family for the long journey into Egypt. Did he have time to pack his carpenter's tools? Was there work for him to do in Egypt? It was a big step into the unknown – but Joseph made it.

A stable home

Joseph was the husband God has chosen for Mary, the father he had selected for Jesus. Physically, Joseph was unnecessary for the birth of Jesus: yet as the titular head of the little household, he was very significantly a part of the divine plan for Jesus to grow up in a loving, complete, stable home environment.

Today, Joseph's example stands as a model for all fathers. God could so easily have effected the coming of the world's Saviour without recourse to Joseph: that the Almighty chose otherwise is an encouragement for every family to build a similar domestic stability.

Let us today hold the families we know – and are – in the love of God.

23 April *St George, Patron Saint of England*
A holy bargain

1 Maccabees 2:59–64, or Revelation 12:7–12, 2 Timothy 2:3–13, John 15:18–21

The Great Dragon

According to legend St George visited a city in Libya where the population had long been terrorized by a ferocious beast. When the supply of domestic animals had been exhausted, the citizens in desperation resorted to satisfying the beast's hunger with humans. St George struck a holy bargain: if he killed the dragon for them, the citizens must accept Christianity. Both sides honoured their part of the deal.

St John, in his Revelation, sees Satan as 'the great dragon' (Revelation 12:9), defeated by Michael Archangel and his forces in heaven, and exiled to earth, where he is a dangerous enemy, knowing that his time is short, but causing as much trouble as he can while he has the chance.

Two-pronged attack

Whether or not the legend of St George is true (and it is one of many), its message surely has relevance today: while we are fighting evil, can we endeavour at the same time to bring the gospel to non-believers? Can we be seen to be fighting Satan *to make God known*, rather than merely as an altruistic exercise in oiling the wheels of daily living?

St Paul puts it this way: 'The love of Christ urges us on' (2 Corinthians 5:14). The apostle's past was sufficient to give rise to innumerable accusations of improper motives, self-seeking or evil conspiracy. He could rise above these, because of Jesus' love impelling him on, 'forgetting what lies behind and straining forward to what lies ahead' (Philippians 3:13).

God's unchained Word

Paul expands this teaching, in his second letter to Timothy. As the gospel is not restricted, so we should wear our Christian colours openly and proudly. 'If we deny him, he will deny us' (2 Timothy 2:12). It is always sad when the obituary notice of a person is the first indication of a Christian life. If this touches our hearts, let us take immediate steps to ensure that God is not only moving in us now, but *can be seen* to be moving in us, while we have the chance to make him known.

No compromise

Among the other legends of St George, is one reminiscent of Old Testament times: as Daniel disobeyed a king's edict against praying (Daniel 6:6ff), so George is said to have torn down the emperor's edict ordering Christian clergy to sacrifice to pagan gods. George paid the price for this bravery by martyrdom (*c.* AD 303).

When we are brought to a time of decision for God – and it is likely to be on a less dangerous issue than that faced by Daniel or George – let us pray for courage to show our Christian colours boldly and unequivocally.

Sunday 25 April *St Mark the Evangelist* Accurate aim

Proverbs 15:28–33, Acts 15:35–41, Mark 13:5–13

Committing the gospel to writing

Almost certainly, Mark's was the first of our four canonical gospels to be written. Eusebius of Caesarea, the church historian, tells us: 'This also the elder used to say, Mark, having been the interpreter of Peter, wrote accurately, though not in order, all that he recalled of what was said and done by the Lord. For he neither heard the Lord, nor was he a follower of his, but at a later date of Peter – who used to adapt his instructions to the present needs, but not with a view to putting together the Dominical oracles in orderly fashion; so that Mark did no wrong in thus writing some things as he recalled them. For he kept a single aim in view: not to omit anything of what he heard, nor to state anything therein falsely.' (*H.E.* III.39).

'Telling it as it is' is not always the modern way. It is easy – particularly with the English language – to imply several meanings other than the one intended. Translators are constantly battling against unreproducible phrases and expressions. The maxim *Tra-*

duttori traditori ('translators are traitors') grew out of this very problem. We must be grateful today to the scholars whose mission it is to examine and compare the ever-growing number of ancient texts, in order to assess primacy and accuracy.

The end will not be yet
To those who asked when the End would come, Jesus replied: 'The good news must first be proclaimed to all nations' (Mark 13:10). It is significant that these words are found in our earliest canonical Gospel. Yet the Church has taken two millennia to translate the Scriptures into a mere third of our six-thousand-plus languages of the world. True, the two thousand one hundred or so that presently have Bibles, are the most widely-spoken languages; but we still have a long way to go.

Honest to God
Mark's efforts, which were to inspire more readers than he could ever have envisaged, are noted for their simplicity of language, and for their honesty. If Peter indeed was dictating the material, it is a measure of his integrity that his faults and failings are recorded no less than his loyalty and courage.

May we show the same measure of honesty in confession, as Peter; and accuracy in adhering to the gospel, as Mark.

1 May *SS Philip and James, the Apostles*
High calling
Isaiah 30:15–21, Ephesians 3:1–10, John 14:1–14

Close to the Lord
On 1 May 560, the church in Rome where, it is said, lie the remains of SS Philip and James, was dedicated, since when this day has been kept as their dual festival.

We first meet Philip of Bethsaida when, having been called by Jesus, he immediately seeks out his friend Nathanael and brings him to Jesus (John 1:43ff.). Later, Philip is the disciple whom Jesus questions as he prepares to feed the five thousand (John 6:5ff); and, in the Last Discourses, it is Philip whose question draws forth

Jesus' teaching on the unity of Father and Son (John 14:8).

St James ('the Less', to distinguish him from James, the son of Zebedee) was the son of Alphaeus. According to Mark, his mother Mary was one of the women brave enough to stay by the cross (Mark 15:40).

What a privilege to be able to question, and be questioned by, Christ! What an honour to have a mother brave and loyal enough to follow Jesus to the cross!

All we, like saints ...
In the ever-increasing pace of modern living, how often do we take time to assess the privileges and honours God has given us? Our access to the open Bible; freedom of worship; wonderful electronic aids for sharing the gospel more widely than ever before ... The list is inexhaustible. We can, like Philip, bring others to Jesus: we can tell them of the Christ who lives in us. And, like James, many of us can surely give thanks for the example of parents and loved ones whose example has led us to Jesus and has kept us in his love.

The blood of the martyrs is seed
Throughout the Christian centuries, blood has flowed wherever the gospel has been preached. Persecution has produced its martyrs, and their examples have produced resurgence, reform, revival and renewal. It has often been said that the Church *needs* persecution. Certainly many of those whose lives have impacted on Christian history have had to go through the pain barrier to fulfil their mission.

Called to be saints
We are all called to be saints: perhaps even to be persecuted, indeed to give our lives – spiritually, if not physically. In the world, we are nevertheless to set our sights beyond the world. This is one of the hallmarks of a saint: even in the worst chaos, he has an inner peace; in the midst of fear, he has a joy not even death can take away.

14 May   *St Matthias the Apostle*   **Chosen by Lot**

Isaiah 22:15–25, Psalm 15, Acts 1:15–26, John 15:9–17 or Acts 1:15–26, Psalm 15, 1 Corinthians 4:1–7, John 15:9–17

Moment of truth
When grey smoke rises from a certain place in the Vatican, those watching know that the moment of truth has not yet come; but as soon as white smoke is seen, there is a relieved response: *'Habemus papam!'* We have a pope! There must have been a similar relief when the lot fell on Matthias (Acts 1:26), and once again the senior apostles were 'The Twelve'.

We know very little about Matthias as a man, but Peter here tells us that Matthias had been one of Jesus' disciples ever since 'the baptism of John'. We can only guess at the quiet loyalty and dedication of a man who could follow Jesus for so long – even witness his resurrection – yet remain unchronicled until the defection of Judas had left vacant an apostolic place. Justus, also, seems to have had a similar tenure of service; but his was the fate to lose the election.

The ministry team
According to Acts, there were more disciples in Jesus' ministry team of whom we know nothing (Acts 1:21). Who can tell how many, in turn, they ministered to? Each one known to God, yet unknown to men. Each one playing his part as a member of Christ's mission, quietly, without fanfare, without any recognition save that he (or even she) was fulfilling a duty as servant of the Most High.

God's over-riding plans
The election of Matthias to the apostolate gives us encouragement to acknowledge the involvement of God in all our endeavours. The means we use may seem crude; but if we employ these means prayerfully, truly believing that what we are attempting is in line with the high principles of God, we may expect his blessing on the work.

We often hear that 'small is beautiful', and so it can be; but not when reduction should really be enlargement. The apostolate could have remained at eleven men; that it very quickly needed to be returned to twelve was surely not only because twelve had an important significance for Jacob's descendants – but also because the emerging Church must not be seen to be reducing, but increasing.

Can we examine our local church and community today, and apply these principles where necessary?

3 June Thursday following Trinity Sunday (Also called, Thanksgiving for the Holy Communion) *Corpus Christi* Living Bread

Genesis 14:18–20, Psalm 116:12–19, 1 Corinthians 11:23–26, John 6:51–58

Food from heaven

God-given food was not a novel concept for the Jews. Melchizedek had provided bread and wine (Genesis 14:18). The Israelites had been given bread in the wilderness (Exodus 16:15). God had fed Elijah in the desert (1 Kings 19:6). But this was different: Jesus was saying: 'I am the living bread that came down from heaven' (John 6:51). Whatever else they were, the Jews did not class themselves as anthropomorphic. Jesus was preaching a theology beyond their comprehension.

Coping with the unexpected

They had been looking for a warrior, a kingly Messiah who would repel the occupying Roman power, and restore the Jerusalem monarchy. They got a Servant-Messiah, who preached peace of a kind they did not understand. They had been looking for a high priest of the ilk of Melchizedek, who would take over the Temple and its worship. They got a carpenter's son who did not fit the mould. They were looking for a god to fill their egos, and they got a Lamb who offered them his Body and Blood.

If we allow it, the unexpected can catch us ever as unawares as did Jesus the first-century Jews. Yet God has always worked in unexpected ways. Familiarity with the Scriptures may have dulled our appreciation of this; but the Almighty through the centuries has shown no sign of changing his *modus operandi*.

'Between two Masses'

The aristocratic Russian catholic, mystic, nurse and down-to-earth animation of love, Catherine de Hueck Doherty, used to say: 'Anything can be endured between two Masses'. We give thanks today for the Body of Christ which he offers us in the Eucharist: for the strength he gives, the love he shares, the sacrifice he made. Because the price of our ransom was so high, God keeps faith with us. Imperfect members of his Body though we are, he holds us by the strength of the love which shed blood for our sakes.

With such love and strength in us, can we not, with Catherine, believe that anything can be endured until we next come to share his Body, his Blood?

11 June   *St Barnabas the Apostle*
Man of Strength

Job 29:11–16, Psalm 112, Acts 11:19-30, John 15:12–17 or Acts 11:19–30, Psalm 112, Galatians 2:1–10, John 15:12–17

Disposing of land

Barnabas is introduced as 'Joseph', a Cypriot under conviction to dispossess himself and use the proceeds to benefit others (Acts 4:36). This 'son of encouragement' was to be one of the first to realize the genuineness of Paul's conversion. He went to Tarsus, found and allied himself to Paul, and broke the ice for him when the apostles (understandably) were wary of the one-time persecutor's change of heart.

A strong character

Paul was a dominant man, yet he had a worthy ally in Barnabas, when the apostles were challenged by a pro-circumcision faction in Antioch (Acts 15:1f.). But when Mark, having deserted them in Pamphylia, wanted to re-join the team, Paul and Barnabas had a major clash of wills. Eventually, the mission team split into two, Paul taking Silas through Syria and Cicilia, while Barnabas and Mark went to Cyprus (Acts 15:36–41). Thus God used the integrity of two strong men to increase the mission outreach, and expand its preaching and teaching capacity.

Strength for service

Remember how lukewarmness in service in the church at Laodicea is castigated in the Book of Revelation (3:16). God did not water down the fire and brimstone of either Paul or Barnabas, but channelled their power into service for the gospel. Before we smother similar characteristics – in ourselves or others – let us pray that God may give guidance into the positive employment of such strength.

Jesus, on occasion, could display righteous indignation, as in the eviction of the entrepreneurs from the temple courts (Mark 11:15f.); even anger, at the unsympathetic attitude of people towards the man with the withered hand (Mark 3:5); and could turn sharply on his closest disciple: 'Get behind me, Satan!' (Matthew 16:23), when Peter tried to limit God's purposes.

Can we, from this, believe that God wants *real* people, not bread-and-butter saints, in his Church?

24 June *Birth of St John the Baptist*
Genuine Simplicity
Isaiah 40:1–11, Acts 13:14b–26, Galatians 3:23–29, Luke 1:57–66, 80

A Birth to remember

Speech restored, and a song that was to last for thousands of years. Who could forget the strange happenings that marked the birth of this child? Small wonder that even before Jesus began preaching, John's congregations were well established, and he already had a team of disciples to whom he had taught the rudiments of prayer (Luke 11:1).

Preaching with power

John's preaching was powerful, and he was utterly fearless in his denunciation of the religious and secular officials of the day. The miracle is, not that in the end it was his criticism of Herodias and the Herodian morals in general that brought about his imprisonment and execution – but the fact that he had been free to preach for so long, before being apprehended.

Jesus was to continue the fight against immorality and misplaced devotion in high places; and this sustained attack was to produce such confusion in Herod's mind, that when news of the miracles of Jesus were brought to him, he declared: 'This is John the Baptist . . . raised from the dead' (Matthew 14:2).

Poor living, high thinking
John's lifestyle was severely simple: his message so advanced that it set the best theological brains of the day questioning and researching: but they could not fault John's theology, and stood convicted by their own deviations from the Law. Successive generations of Rabbis had compiled interpretations and additions to the original *torah*, until the commentaries outweighed the ancient laws. John cut through this plethora of oral, man-made traditions, and focused his message simply on the One to whom the old Scriptures had pointed.

Dangerous obfuscation
John the Baptist challenges us to re-examine our faith. Is it simply genuine? Or have we, like the Pharisees of old, added portions along the way – and, if so, are these obfuscating the original gospel? For the simple teaching of Jesus speaks to us in *every* situation into which God may bring us: there may be modern trappings, but at the heart of every problem there is a biblical precedent, and guidance there for resolving it. God does not change; his created beings do not change. St Paul's teaching is ever as relevant in 1999, as it was nearly two millennia ago: 'No testing has overtaken you that is not common to everyone . . .' (1 Corinthians 10:13f.).

We need to see that, like John, we meet the common test with uncommon zeal.

29 June   *St Peter*   God's faith in us
'Jesus said: "Blessed are you, Simon son of Jonah! . . . And I tell you, you are Peter, and on this rock I will build my church." Matthew 16:17,18

Many gifts
Under his rough fisherman's skin Peter combined many gifts, many characteristics of the Spirit: a complexity which has affinities with the trio who once argued whose profession or calling had

the primacy: the doctor said: 'Medicine, definitely, for God created woman out of Adam's rib: spare-part surgery, at the world's beginning.' 'Not so,' said the architect, 'God designed the world: architecture was right up front. God (according to Genesis) made everything out of chaos.' 'And who do you think made the chaos?' asked the politician.

Who would have imagined a fisherman could become a politician, able to meet with statesmen and high-ranking officials, in different countries – an architect, building the Church on preaching and teaching – and a doctor, healing the sick in the power and name of Jesus?

Realizing potential
God 'calls into existence the things that do not exist' (Romans 4:17). When Jesus told Peter: 'On this rock I will build my Church' (Matthew 16:18), he was showing faith in Peter's potential, and giving the rugged fisherman confidence of realizing. Not long after this, the disciples were unable to cure a case of epilepsy, and Jesus was seemingly caustic in his response. It was because of their 'little faith. For truly I tell you, if you have faith the size of a mustard seed, you will say to this mountain, "Move from here to there", and it will move, and nothing will be impossible for you' (Matthew 17:20).

What faith God has in us! This was a challenge. God has contracted to do the impossible; we only have to move mountains.

Mind-stretching
Time and again in his teaching, Jesus encourages us to stretch our minds and hearts, to keep up with him. And rightly so: God has given us minds capable of being stretched. He is their creator, and we are capable of standing any strain he puts on us.

Falling – and rising
Peter fell as low as a man can fall, on the night of Jesus' arrest. Reinstated to apostolic mission by the thrice-repeated question: 'Do you love me . . . ?' (John 21:15ff.), he gives hope to everyone else who has fallen. In the first letter that carries his name, there is a prayer which we can personalize for use in our daily walk with God:

> 'Though I have not seen him,
> I love him;
> and even though I do not see him now,
> I believe in him
> and rejoice with an indescribable and glorious joy,
> for I am receiving the outcome of my faith,
> the salvation of my soul.'

1 Peter, 1:8,9 paraphrased

29 June   *St Paul [combined with St Peter, q.v.]*
Whiter than snow

Acts 9:1–19 [not RCL], 2 Timothy 4:6–8, 17–18, Matthew 16:13–19

The good fight

Paul had a bad past: blasphemer, persecutor and man of violence
(1 Timothy 1:13); but now near the end of his life he can stand
before God, totally uncondemned (Romans 8:1). God has blotted
out every sin that Paul has confessed, dropped them into the deep
sea of his magnificently-unfair forgetfulness; and Paul's slate is
wiped clean.

It can be easy to sin, and often relatively easy to confess; but to
allow God to take the sin is hard. We cannot 'un-sin the sin' – but
we can and must let it go, once we have confessed and repented.
If Paul had continued to bear the weight of his past sins, he would
not have had the strength to take the gospel to others. We cannot
fight the good fight encumbered with excess baggage.

In God's strength

How had God strengthened Paul? (2 Timothy 4:17). By removing
the weight of accumulated sin. Paul is not talking here of physical
frailty, but of the anguish when one after another of his companions had deserted him. At such times, our sins are often the
first hazards that come back to weigh us down. In Paul's case, he
had a much more wicked past to recall, than most of us have.

While John reminds us that Jesus' blood is sufficient to cleanse
us from *'all'* sin' (1 John 1:17), this is not a divine *carte blanche* to

sin with impunity; but it is a 'way out', such as comes in every trial (1 Corinthians 10:13), for us to seek God's forgiveness *and forgetfulness*. God hates the sin, but loves the sinner, and has promised to remember confessed sin no more.

Cleansing power
And with the cleansing of our sins in the blood of Christ, comes power to strengthen us for fruitful service. When we commit sin, we weaken our spiritual system; and there is only Jesus who can restore the strength we have lost. Paul's confession and contrition was so deep, he was able to let his sinful past go, until he exceeded the other apostles in evangelistic vigour: 'By the grace of God I am what I am, and his grace towards me has not been in vain. On the contrary, I worked harder than any of them – though it was not I, but the grace of God that is with me' (1 Corinthians 15:10).

And this same grace is still available to all who seek it.

3 July   *St Thomas the Apostle*   Seeking faith
Habakkuk 2:1–4, Ephesians 2:19–22, John 20:24–29

Is doubting dangerous?
The short answer is: Yes, it can be dangerous. Thomas' doubting takes up a sufficiently large part of John chapter 20 to emphasize this; and yet Jesus in his mercy kept the apostle waiting only one week before comprehensibly demolishing his doubts.

One of our leading preachers of a century ago commented: 'Doubting, like toothache, is more distracting than dangerous. I never heard of its proving fatal to anybody yet' (C. H. Spurgeon). Perhaps we judge Thomas too harshly. His courage, after all, was of the first degree (John 11:16). Was God bringing this post-resurrection doubt into the open, in order to give us all the precious revelation of John 20:26–29? Who, after all, can fail to be stirred by the simple, stark invitation: 'Put your finger here and see my hands. Reach out your hand and put it into my side'?

Lack of faith

It is natural to doubt. Each of us does it, time and again. Usually, we do not doubt so much our own capabilities, as God's. We believe we can fulfil our part of any bargain (or we don't enter into the bargain); but often the worry is: will God, for his part, come through in time? If we had as much faith in God as we have in ourselves, we should have far fewer doubts. But Thomas' doubts have many reflections in the modern age. While we aspire with Paul to 'walk by faith, not by sight' (2 Corinthians 5:7), and to avow that 'faith is the assurance of things hoped for, the conviction of things not seen' (Hebrews 11:1), it is tempting to latch on to the latest archeological discovery that 'supports' the biblical narrative – or on to the latest scientific theory which leaves open the date of the Turin Shroud.

'Do not doubt'

'Do not doubt but believe' (John 20:27). It's not a suggestion, but a command. If our doubts lead to belief, we are making for the right track. If our belief is strong enough to keep doubts at bay, we are already on track. Thomas was allowed a week in which to find belief. In the end, it was presented to him. Jesus, in his mercy, deals with us as we are able to bear. Perhaps our generation has *needed* the plethora of recent discoveries, visions and revelations.

Perhaps a subsequent generation will need *more* proof. We do not know how far God will go, to see that his wedding hall is 'filled with guests' (Matthew 22:10).

22 July   *St Mary Magdalene*

Song of Songs 3:1–4, Psalm 42:1–5, 2 Corinthians 5:14–17, John 20:1–2, 11–18

Devotion and loyalty

When the body of Jesus was interred in Joseph's tomb, Mary was there (Matthew 27:61). She was back outside the tomb at dawn two mornings later (Matthew 28:1). Startled at the yawning gap where the sealed stone should have been, she ran to fetch Peter (John 20:2). Her devotion and loyalty were rewarded: Jesus allowed her to be the first to greet him, that first Easter morning

(John 20:16f.). Mark's 'longer ending' (16:9ff.) tells us that Jesus had 'cast out seven demons' from Mary. This could mean she had been a harlot; but it could also be that she had been cured from a form of mental illness. Certainly she had reason to be grateful, and her gratitude was shown in her loving devotion to Jesus.

When convention gives way
Mary does not appear to have been a slave to convention. She was at the tomb for Christ's interment, albeit with other women; but on the resurrection morning she came alone – and the privilege of being the first to see her risen Lord was her own.

Sometime God calls us to service in the company of others, but there are times when we need to go forward on our own, trusting him for everything – and this is often very hard to do.

> *Trust him when your wants are many;*
> *Trust him when your wants are few;*
> *Trust him, when to trust him only*
> *Seems the hardest thing to do.*

Perhaps it is not so much distrust in God, as reliance on convention that places an obstacle in our way. We should remember Mary, and how her love overcame convention and protocol.

Love beyond explaining
How often do we act in love, simply, and without complications or ulterior motives? Has God such a hold on our devotion and loyalty that we, like Mary, will go to great lengths to show him our love? There was once another Mary, who – as a meal was being served – managed to gain everyone's attention by anointing her beloved Jesus and filling the room with perfume. Judas Iscariot sneered, but Jesus' response was full of love: 'She has done what she could' (Mark 14:8).

That is what Mary Magdalene did.

May we be given the grace to do likewise.

Sunday 25 July   *St James the Apostle*   Soldiers for Christ

Jeremiah 45:1–5, Acts 11:27–12:2, Matthew 20:20–28 or Acts 11:27–12:2, 2 Corinthians 4:7–15, Matthew 20:20–28

Disciples, apostle, martyr

Often called 'the Great', to distinguish him from another James, son of Alphaeus, James the apostle was one of the quartet of fishermen called from mending their nets, when Jesus was recruiting his first disciples on the Galilean shore. He remained in the innermost circle of disciples, being permitted to see the Transfiguration, and also to watch – and sleep – on the night of Jesus' arrest in Gethsemane.

Tradition has it that James left Judaea soon after the death of Stephen, returning some ten years later to suffer martyrdom on the orders of Herod Agrippa, in or around the year 44 (Acts 12:2).

Son of Thunder

James and his brother John were given the nickname 'Boanerges – Sons of Thunder', by Jesus. On one occasion, they asked if they could call fire down from heaven, on a group of inhospitable Samaritans (Luke 9:54); and perhaps this was not the only instance of misplaced zeal: we have Matthew telling us of their mother pleading for high positions in glory for her sons (Matthew 20:21), while Mark places the blame for this in the disciples' court (Mark 10:35f.). Yet we can recall that Moses, in his early days, was strong-willed and impetuous: it took a forty-year wilderness period for God to mould him into the wise leader necessary for the Israelites' transition from slaves to potential landowners.

Fervour and loyalty

Similarly, James was gradually guided by Jesus, from being a humble Galilean fisherman, to an apostle of the Church, a man of the gospel, a preacher and teacher for God. Fervour was needed, as it is today; for after two thousand years the world and its forces – whether openly antagonistic to the gospel, or merely apathetic – call for a vibrant courage on the part of Christian witnesses – and loyalty, without which the body of Christ is presented as a house divided against itself.

A poised sword

Knowing of Stephen's martyrdom, James would always be conscious that a similar fate could be his at any time – whether or not he was in Jerusalem. So we today – though perhaps not actually threatened by cold steel – know that Christians by virtue of their calling are vulnerable, even as Jesus was vulnerable in Gethsemane, and on Calvary.

Yet, though we have no physical defence, ours is a spiritual force that makes the devil himself tremble. As John reminds us: 'The one who is in you is greater than the one who is in the world' (1 John 4:4).

6 August *Transfiguration of Our Lord* Vision of glory

Daniel 7:9–10, 13–14, 2 Peter 1:16–19, Luke 9:28b–36

Exaltation

'The daily round, the common task' is an essential part of life; but no less essential is an acceptance of the breaking-in of God's glory. This is not ours to command: God gives it to us as and when he pleases; but we can allow ourselves to be so preoccupied with the mundane, that we fail to see the glory when it comes: a rainbow, the laughter of a child; light in the eyes of a friend; a precious flower blooming by the wayside. God is a master of the ingenious, and he rarely gives advance warning of his actions.

The art of wonderment

Our lives have been impoverished, if we have lost the art of wonderment: if we have become so conditioned to novelty, so stoical, so accustomed to normality, that we have forgotten, or are unwilling to accept, that there are many things for which we have no rational explanation: wonders that defy understanding, but nevertheless invigorate the spirits.

We are not alone. The disciples on the Mount of Transfiguration were caught off spiritual balance, totally unprepared for the wonderful breaking-in of God's glory. Was it a dream? an omen? a warning? an encouragement? We can only wonder at their discussions and reasonings, which would continue long after the event.

Letting God have his way

If we can be bold enough to pray God to move mightily in our lives, we need to be prepared for him to take us at our word. Whatever *we* do, we shall not leave God tagging along behind. But are we prepared to keep up with him? St Paul believed that he and his friends (and, by extension, we ourselves) shared 'the mind of Christ', yet acknowledged that even such participation in Jesus did not qualify us to 'instruct the Lord' (1 Corinthians 2:16). God's ways are not ours, neither are our thoughts on a par with his (Isaiah 55:8). So we can be sure that God will do the unexpected in our case, as happened to the disciples on the mount.

Back from the glory

And after the breaking-in? Do we return to normality unchanged? Surely not: light has been shone into corners of our lives where ordinary daylight cannot reach. Whether we admit it or not, we have been changed by the experience. God is not a waster of time, and he does nothing without a purpose. Can we accept this? Can we admit, once in a while, that something for which we have no explanation has broken-in and changed our lives?

It may be a small change – or a matter, literally, of life and death.

Sunday 15 August   *Blessed Virgin Mary*
Full of grace

Isaiah 61:10–11 or Revelation 11:19–12:6,10, Galatians 4:4–7, Luke 1:46–55

God has done great things

Since nothing is impossible with God (Luke 1:37, 18:27), the work of salvation could have been ushered in without recourse to Mary. That God chose to involve her – and to such a degree – is a mystery, and a cause for awe. How was she special? She 'had found favour with God' (Luke 1:30). But in what way? We do not know – and perhaps it would not help us if we did know. But

216

Mary was unique – as we are unique. And God chose to use her individuality in his greatest plan for the world.

> *'I'll sing a hymn to Mary,*
> *The mother of my God . . .*
> *To live and not to love thee*
> *Would fill my soul with shame.'*

> John Wyse (1825 – 1898)

Mother-love

In the great Father-love of God for his children, we may see qualities which, on a simpler scale, would lie at the heart of Mary's mother-love for Jesus: tenderness, patience, constancy, guidance, and the like. While Joseph steps into the background, after the family's visit to Jerusalem when Jesus was twelve years old, Mary is seen as being with her son through his formative years and into his ministry. At Calvary, she is still with him; and in his dreadful agony he fulfils his last filial duty, and gives her into the care of the disciple whom he loved (John 19:25 – 27).

Many believe that because Mary was specially favoured by God, most poignantly loved by Jesus, her body at death was not allowed to see corruption, being assumed into heaven. It is understandable that Jesus would not permit the decomposition of the body of his beloved mother. Yet this should in no way affect our regard for Mary: God had done great things for her when Jesus was yet unborn (Luke 1:49). Would he abandon that precious womb at death?

Fiat – so be it

'Let it be, Lord, let it be' (Luke 1:38). By her *fiat*, Mary opened the door wide for God to enter her life as fully as he desired. In the natural, there was no sense in her words: a young virgin, accepting life into a closed womb! *Impossible!* Mary knew she could not accomplish the work: it was God's responsibility to do the impossible – she only had to move the mountains of anxiety and unbelief. Only one word was required – and she gave it trustingly, lovingly: *Fiat*, let it be.

Can we today, faced with impossibly difficult tasks, circumstances, challenges, rise to the occasion as Mary rose? Can we have the faith and courage to give God our *Fiat*? God always offers grace sufficient for every challenge: the choice of taking up the offer is left to us.

ſ Coulus 24/8/07

24 August   *St Bartholomew the Apostle*
All sorts and conditions
6?~

Isaiah 43:8–13, Acts 5:12–16, Luke 22:24–30 or Acts 5:12–16, 1 Corinthians 4:9–15, Luke 22:24–30

Son of Talmai
While the often-suggested identification of Bartholomew ('Son of Talmai') with the 'Nathanael' of John's Gospel (1:43ff.) may be valid, at least there is no doubt that Bartholomew was one of the Twelve apostles, being named in all four lists (Matthew 10:3; Mark 3:18; Luke 6:14; Acts 1:13): one of the Eleven who remained loyal to Jesus, and survived the trauma of the Passion weekend, to see the Church (*ecclesia*) begin, and the gospel to spread out from Jerusalem.

Legend has it that Bartholomew travelled to Egypt, and then to Persia, India, and Armenia, where he was beaten to death.

Gospel of Bartholomew
In his commentary on Matthew, Jerome mentions a 'Gospel of Bartholomew', which is also cited by other historians, including the Venerable Bede. It is a fairly short work, but includes a question to Jesus. Bartholomew asks: 'Tell us, Lord, which sin is more grievous than all other sins?' And Jesus replies: 'Indeed and in truth I tell you, hypocrisy and slander are more grievous than all other sins.' One is invariably reminded of Jesus' words in Mark's Gospel: 'Whoever blasphemes against the Holy Spirit can never have forgiveness, but is guilty of an eternal sin' (Mark 3:29).

Uncharted territory
The relatively unknown missionary years of Bartholomew remind us that God uses all sorts and conditions – of manpower and means – in his service, whether famous in the eyes of many, and the stuff of which history is made – or small and unnoticed save by a few. Of the Twelve, some like Peter and John had high-profile

ministries; but who is to say that the ministries of such as Bartholomew or Thaddaeus were any less important?

To see ourselves . . .
In 1 Corinthians 4:9–15, Paul is taking a long, hard look at himself and his ministry, as he imagines outsiders viewing it. He, and others like him, are 'fools', 'weak', 'in disrepute', 'hungry and thirsty', 'poorly clothed, beaten and homeless', and 'weary'. It's not the type of job description likely to encourage queues of prospective applicants.

After his conversion, Paul had had long discussions with Peter and the other apostles. He had probably met Bartholomew. Perhaps, if he had learned of Bartholomew's mission, that apostle was in his mind when he wrote this letter to the Corinthians.

Prayer – as has recently been remarked by a Chinese Christian – is 'God's bungee cord', so Bartholomew, and those whose mission takes them to faraway places, would always be conscious that others' prayers were constantly linking them to God, no matter where they ministered.

May we, too, hold others – far and near – in our prayers, and so keep the prayer cord between ourselves, those for whom we pray, and God, in perfect working order.

21 September   *St Matthew the Evangelist*
Called from the custom house
Proverbs 3:13–18, 2 Corinthians 4:1–6, Matthew 9:9–13

A gospel for the Jews
Matthew was a Jew, writing for Jews. He portrays Jesus as the One to whom prophets of old had looked forward: the fulfiller of the Law, the Messiah to save his people. But Matthew's Gospel is wide-ranging in its provenance; Eusebius of Caesare wrote: 'So, therefore, Matthew compiled the oracles in the Hebrew language; but everyone interpreted them as he was able' (*H.E.* III.39).

This is the major difference between Holy Writ and all other books. God is understood as having inspired the various Bible writers, and thus speaks himself through the text of Scripture –

which means that even if a certain passage is read day after day, God may give a unique meaning from it each time. Call it revelation, insight, or truth: it's the extra dimension that makes the Bible unequalled among books.

Breadth of vision

Though primarily for his fellow Jews, Matthew's Gospel alone tells of the visit of the non-Jewish Magi to the young Christ child. From Matthew, too, we get the well-structured Sermon on the Mount (chapters 5–7), the only mention in the Gospels of the *Church* (16:18), and the parable of the sheep and the goats (25:31ff.), when 'all the nations' will be gathered before Jesus in his glory.

Matthew thus challenges us not to set our religious parameters too closely together. Can we explain our faith to anyone, of any persuasion? Can we simplify it, in order to be understood by anyone who is looking to us to lead him to Christ?

The best persuasion of all

There are religious barriers and divisions today, of which St Matthew knew nothing. We need to guard against them inhibiting our proclaiming of the gospel.

The American evangelist of a century ago, Dwight L. Moody, was once asked: 'What is your persuasion?' He replied, quickly: 'The best persuasion of all – for, like St Paul, "I am persuaded, that neither death, nor life, nor angels, nor principalities, nor powers, nor things present, nor things to come, nor height, nor depth, nor any other creature, shall be able to separate us from the love of God, which is in Christ Jesus our Lord', (Romans 8:38,39).

From duty called

Matthew's secular work was important, but he was called to higher duty. The place of our calling, likewise, is less important than the work to which God calls. When once we are complacent with our mission, it is time to watch. We are not called to be satisfied until, mission accomplished, we see God face to face.

29 September *St Michael and All Angels*
Angelic guiding

'And war broke out in heaven; Michael and his angels fought against the dragon. The dragon and his angels fought back, but they were defeated.'
Revelation 12:7,8

Legions of angels

The Bible records, in around three hundred places, that there are many angels in God's Kingdom. They were made by God, so even angels, like us, depend for existence on God's power. They differ from us, in that they can change their appearance and move great distances at a speed we cannot fathom. They neither marry nor reproduce, but their knowledge is greater than ours. Their prime function is to work on our behalf, motivated by love and loyalty and a desire to see God's will at work in our lives. Day and night, they are available to guide and direct and protect us.

The words of a children's hymn underline perhaps the most important difference between us and angels: while we have a Saviour who died to redeem us, they know and regard Jesus, but they do not experience his saving grace:

> *'There's a ... song which even angels*
> *Can never, never sing;*
> *They know not Christ as Saviour,*
> *But worship him as King.'*

> *Albert Midlane, 1825–1909*

Archangels

In 1 Enoch are the names and functions of seven archangels:
Uriel, who is over the world and over Tartarus
Raphael, who is over the spirits of men
Raguel, who fights in the world of the lights
Michael, who oversees much of mankind and chaos
Saraqael, who oversees sinful spirits
Gabriel, who is over Paradise, serpents and Cherubim
Remiel, who is over the resurrection
Michael Archangel is described in the Book of Daniel, as guarding the Israelites against Persian and Greek infiltration. In Jude, we

221

find him contending with the devil for the body of Moses (v. 9). Jude commends the approach of Michael, who pays Satan the respect due to a fellow barrister. While there are sinful humans to accuse, Satan's presence must be accepted, since even God sees the justice of the indictment.

War in heaven
Daniel has seen Michael as Israel's protector. John portrays him as fighting in heaven for victory – and winning, in the final analysis. But we, this side of the final day, need to accept that God has not yet taken Satan out of our lives. We still need all the help and protection that the angels can give. Each night, the Office of Compline opens with a Petrine warning: 'Keep alert. Like a roaring lion your adversary the devil prowls around, looking for someone to devour' (1 Peter 5:8).

Angels are part of history, but also of history-in-the-making. As St Paul says: 'For the Lord himself, with a cry of command, **with the archangel's call** ... will descend from heaven...' (1 Thessalonians 4:16).

May we be there, to hear that call.

4 October   *St Francis of Assisi*   **Poor for Christ**
'Jesus said: "Blessed are you who are poor, for yours is the kingdom of God."' Luke 6:20

Lady poverty
Today is the festival of *Il poverello*, the 'little poor man' of Assisi, who gave up wealth and position for a love he called 'Lady Poverty'. He would say he gained far more than he lost. We, with seven centuries and more of his example and writings, can say much of the world has gained also. Many who marvel at his courage, and who would never attempt to follow his example, nevertheless have found a spark of life in his poverty and simplicity, which has revitalized their own Christian life.

Abandoned to Christ

Whether one imagines a brown-robed, gentle man with animals clustered round him, or delves deep into the precious writings of Francis or his fellows, the example is one of simple abandonment to Christ: a turning away from what the world and society have to offer, to humility and a complete disregard for convention and status.

For love – not of the man, but for what God was doing in and through the man – the wealthy Clare followed Francis into a life dedicated to poverty and simplicity, and the service of others; thus the Order of the Poor Clares took shape.

The attraction of possessions

Francis, in his determination to be as poor and uncomplicated as possible, would permit nothing to be owned by his brothers – not even books, for books need shelves and shelves need a house to hold them. It was not poverty, he reasoned, to be without possessions; only to want what one did not have. Later, however, as the brotherhood grew, so did a relaxation of the initial vision, and eventually Francis stepped aside from leading the Order. It was not a sea-change: the Order continued to grow; but the *Poverello* knew that time and numbers had subtly altered the 'first white days' of his experience.

History's wheel

It has always been so. Throughout the Old Testament centuries, laws were received – from God, or through the prophets; time brought a relaxation of standards, until a reform was initiated to redress the balance ... only for time once again to lower standards ...

Where are we now, in this wheel of history? Near the zenith, or wallowing in the apogee? Do we, like Francis, see life in its plain simplicity, stripped of the glitz and glamour the world tries to overlay? Do we take the opportunities that the stripping of the overlay uncovers? Or, is it simply easier to look back to a better time, and wish we could do something to improve the present age?

Perhaps, like Francis, we may be even now in the process of being called to do something that God alone can understand.

15 October *St Teresa of Avila* **Practical Christianity**

'I regard everything as loss because of the surpassing value of knowing Christ Jesus my Lord. For his sake I have suffered the loss of all things.'
Philippians 3:8

The way to God
Though she lived and died a Spanish Catholic, the 'way to God' of Teresa d'Avila was so different from that advocated by Catholics in Rome, that the Lutheran Church was later to build on her example, and so bring about the spread of Protestantism across Western Europe.

Teresa lived for 67 years, most of which were spent in weakness and pain. Her mother died when she was twelve, and her father twelve years later. She was almost continually fighting against slander and vindictiveness – from the clergy, from local officials, and even from her own family.

On entering her local Carmelite convent, she took vows of poverty, chastity and obedience – but not silence. She was always to speak her mind; and while in the short term it was often not the best way of making friends, her life and example left a legacy which has been the means of influencing very many people.

Ecumenism
She constantly tried to heal the ever-growing divisions in six-teenth-century Europe between the long-established Catholic Church, and the emerging Protestant Church. As she founded convent after convent, she was able to draw up her own rules, which divided the nuns' time more evenly between prayer and work. Teresa saw to it that each nun developed severely practical skills, in the kitchen and garden, as well as the rules for prayer and devotion. 'Let everyone understand that *real* love of God does not exist in tear-shedding, nor in that serenity and tenderness for which we usually long, just because they console us; but in serving God in justice, fortitude of soul, and humility.'

This was a 'catholicism' which found little favour at Rome, and Teresa was opposed by a number of Italian bishops as she sought to found yet more convents. But she held to her course, in seeing and teaching the 'way of God' in personal terms – a direct relationship with God, which was to be expanded some 200 years later by a young Anglican preacher called John Wesley. There is a touch of irony, in that it was this difference between the Roman, and Teresa's Spanish, catholicism, which led to the rise of European Protestantism, emphasizing a personal, biblical faith:

> 'Taught by the Bible,
> led by the Spirit.'

> Palmer Hartsough, 1844–1932

Vision of the spear

Teresa had a vision in which an angel appeared to her, carrying a fire-tipped spear. He plunged the spear deep into her heart, leaving her on fire with a burning love for God. She saw the painful but beautiful experience as symbolizing the spiritual union of a believer with God. By contrast, the accepted Catholic view of the time was 'the right use of reason'.

Perhaps, in the world of 1999, we need a fresh surge of Teresa's practical and personal Christianity, before we become sophisticated beyond the point of no return.

18 October   *St Luke the Evangelist*   Beloved physician

St contes Healing 15/9/99 7.00am

Isaiah 35:3–6 or Acts 16:6–12a, 2 Timothy 4:5–17, Luke 10:1–9

'Only Luke is with me'

We know the feeling, do we not? Circumstances and people seem set against us: yet one friend stays alongside, and saves us from black despair: one trusted companion, for whom we thank God.

The worst calamity, the problem to end all problems, the severest devastation – all are bearable, if that one precious friend sticks with us.

Luke, the 'beloved physician' (Colossians 4:14) has probably had more involvement with the writings we know as the New Testament, than any other non-Jew. His two letters to Theophilus – our Gospel of Luke and Acts – give us not only a unique glimpse of Christ's nativity and earliest years, but also the beginnings of the Church, in the years immediately following Christ's Ascension. Acts ends with tantalizing abruptness, Paul having reached Rome and being allowed rented accommodation while awaiting trial. What happened next? Did Luke die at that point? Was there a third letter, which still may come to light? These are intriguing questions: but today we give thanks for all we do know of this Greek physician, who was quite probably a friend of the Blessed Virgin Mary, as well as of St Paul; for who else could have described with such poignancy and intimacy the Christmas stories as found in Luke 1 and 2?

The wideness of God's mercy

Throughout Luke's writings shines an interest in Jesus' attitude to non-Jews, the under-privileged and the sick. Human relationships also fascinate this observant, analytical author. It's Luke who tells us that, in all the trauma of the first 'Good Friday', Pilate and Herod settled their differences and 'became friends with each other' (Luke 23:12).

How do we relate to those of other cultures, different outlooks? Have we ever, for example, tried to see Christ through the eyes of a Chinese, a Barbadian, an Indian? Jesus was a Jew, an Oriental. Does this realization impact on our faith, our prayers?

Different gifts

From their writings, Luke and Paul were very different. Paul had one over-riding mission – to preach: 'Woe betide me if I do not proclaim the gospel!' (1 Corinthians 9:16). He would preach to Jews or non-Jews, of any country or none. Luke's mission was simply to record as much as possible of the life and purpose of Jesus and the Church he had come to found – and then to present the record to an educated official, for presumable circulation in the high circles of his day.

Two men, with ultimately the same ambition: to spread the Word. Can we, as Jesus told the lawyer at the conclusion of his parable of the Good Samaritan, 'Go and do likewise'?

226

1 November   *Feast of All Saints*   To be like God

Revelation 7:9–17, 1 John 3:1–3, Matthew 5:1–12

Translated to glory

St John tells us: 'What we will be has not yet been revealed ... when he [God] is revealed, we will be like him' (1 John 3:2). As St Paul tells us, we shall 'comprehend with all the saints' the compass of Christ's love (Ephesians 3:18). Now the anguish, then the glory; now the struggle, then the peace; now the doubt and unknowing, then the certainty and knowledge in all its fullness.

So, can we go forward to meet death with equanimity – even with longing – when we have done all the good we can, in all the ways we can, to all the people we can? It is not easy to accept that God may call us to the company of the saints, before our long-range plans have been accomplished. 'Lord, let me have time to do more for you, to found this Bible College, to get involved with this new mission. Give me time, Lord . . . !'

Time enough

In the Russian Orthodox Church there is a saying: 'Do not worry about time to do everything. If you live, you will have time to do it. If you die, you will not need to do it.' We need to live as those who will one day die. A compliment which could be paid to practically all the saints we remember today would be: 'They were always ready to go.' In the depths of their souls they had already met their God. A deep, inner peace was theirs, even though circumstances and nations might be against them, and martyrdom – when it came – brutal in the extreme.

Saintly company

Do you long to meet these saints? To speak of preaching with John Chrysostom, the 'golden-tongued'? To hear how Lawrence braved the grid-iron? To talk with Our Lady, whose *Fiat* brought to birth the Saviour of the world? Does it thrill you to contemplate listening to Ambrose of Milan, Augustine of Hippo, Basil of Caesarea? To ask them why, and how, and where their faith grew and blossomed?

On this Festival Day, let us stretch our minds to wonder at the great communion of saints: holy men and women – struggling sinners like ourselves while on earth, but translated to glory when their harvest was gathered in.

May these contemplations encourage us to press ever onward, forward, in our sowing and reaping, that one day we indeed may converse with those whom we honour today.

All Souls' Day   2 November   *Commemoration of the Faithful Departed*   Life

'I am the resurrection and I am the life; whosoever lives and believes will never die.' John 11:25,26

Our friends

That once well-known hymn, so often sung at one period on public occasions, 'O God our help in ages past', has a couple of lines that express what the majority of ordinary people most likely feel about death, and their friends and relatives:

> *Time, like an ever-rolling stream,*
> * bears all its sons away;*
> *They fly forgotten, as a dream*
> * dies at the opening day.*

> *E.H. 417; A&M 165*

Is this really Christian teaching? Are we all borne away at death, on that rolling tide of time, to be forgotten like the illusions of a dream-world?

The Christian hope

Although this hymn appears in many hymnbooks, it does not express the Christian hope. What *do* we hope for, after this life? First, let us be clear about what Our Lord Jesus has said. For example, it is clear that Jesus taught that there was a life after death – in Mark 12:18–27, we find that he produces a 'proof text' – 'God is not God of the dead, but of the living – the God of Abraham, the God of Isaac, the God of Jacob.'

This is not mere juggling with words, but serious argument

228

from the unity of religious experience. If God revealed himself to these patriarchs, gave them promises, made with them covenants, then it is wholly out of character that he should have let them just be annihilated at death.

In other words, those who know anything of communion with God in this life cannot believe that this communion will be destroyed for ever at death. The God whom we have come to know, to respect and to love, in the Old Testament and in the New Testament alike, is not that sort of God. He does not have dealings with the living, only in order to let them die eternally!

The condition of the departed

The Bible gives us various insights into the state of the faithful departed. Some New Testament passages speak of 'falling asleep', or 'being at rest'; in Hebrews the impression is that the old saints and heroes remained in an intermediate state until Christ came to permit them to be perfected, with us; the Revelation shows us the blessed dead constantly engaged in worship and intercession. The note of glory recurs again and again.

In the earliest ages of the Church, the blessed dead were thought of as having rest and refreshment, but gradually an element of purging obtruded itself, ending in the crude medieval abuses of 'Purgatory'. Today most would accept the idea of some kind of purification, through the mercy of the Divine Will continuing to act upon us, when this visible life is ended. But to sweep away everything was too drastic, and discouraging or even forbidding prayer for the dead has not worked – the terrible human losses in the First World War broke down such restrictions, and a more reasonable and truly Christian doctrine has gradually taken over.

Our prayers

Nor is this thinking confined to Anglicans and Roman Catholics. The Quaker William Penn, founder of Pennsylvania, wrote three hundred years ago these fine words:

'They that love beyond the world cannot be separated by it. Death cannot kill what never dies; nor can spirits ever be divided by that love and live in the same divine principle – the root and record of their friendship. Death is but crossing the worlds as friends do the seas; they live in one another still. But there must be present that Love which is omnipresent.

'In that divine glass they see face to face; and their converse is free and pure. This is the comfort, that though they may be said to die, yet their friendship and society are, in the best sense, ever present because immortal.'

Remembrance Sunday   14 November

'Peace, peace, to the far and to the near, says the Lord' (Isaiah 57:19) or, *'The harvest of righteousness is sown in peace by those who make peace'* (James 3:18) or *'Greater love has no man than this, that a man lay down his life for his friends.'* (John 15:13) (All from The Christian Year – The Peace of the World)
'The leaves of the tree are for the healing of the nations' - (Revelation 22:2)

Meaning
Why do we meet here today? For what is Remembrance Sunday kept? Our first answer is surely, 'We remember the many who died for their country, and all who suffered' in two great wars; and in the many smaller but none the less violent and brutal battles and conflicts; in attempts to keep the peace, and trying to save innocent inhabitants from extirpation by those of other races or religion, with brutalities and excesses unheard of since medieval days. We can therefore keep this day with pride – pride in the bravery of our forces, in their professional outlook, in the lack of senseless cruelty, a mark we may well note, in contrast, with some others. And praise also in the fact that their cause – our cause – has been a true and right one; an attempt to make peace, a try to defend the right and the innocent, a stand for truth and fairness, and for freedom.

Peace
And we believe we keep Remembrance Sunday for peace.
   In praying for peace, as we all do, we should remember that not all 'peace' is good peace. 'You make a desert, and call it peace,' was the bitter comment on the brutality that formed the Roman Empire; too many opponents of other peoples, other religions, other convictions, try to make 'peace' by brutality, by slaughter, by oppression, by fear.

We should always pray for peace – yes, indeed! – but for a just peace, a fair peace, a right peace, and the bringing of freedom. How wonderful has been the 'Good Friday' settlement in Ireland, and what an example to other nations and places. A peace based on surrender to evil, by contrast, is hateful to God and humanity alike, and will never bring a lasting result.

Inward peace

Jesus Christ spoke of 'peace' to his followers, meaning inward peace, the peace that is not disturbed by outward events, that can carry the holder through fire and torture, evil happenings, through sorrow and distress.

That inward peace comes from centring our thoughts and lives on Jesus, and from really trying to follow his teaching and example day by day. If we can place our final trust and confidence in God, we will gain that inward peace. If all people, if all nations, could only do the same, there would indeed be no problem left about possessing outward peace also.

> *Grant us grace, Lord, to take to our hearts your judgements which overtake us when we set brother against brother and nation against nation. Give us wisdom and strength to fashion better instruments for our common life, so that we may dwell in concord under your providence; and may your Kingdom come among us, through Jesus Christ Our Lord.*
>
> *Reinhold Niebuhr*

Mothering Sunday   *(Fourth Sunday of Lent)*
14 March   Our Mothers

'His father and his mother marvelled at what was said about him; and Simeon blessed them and said to Mary his mother, "Behold this child is set for the fall and rising of many in Israel, and for a sign that is spoken against and a sword will pierce through your own soul also, that the thoughts out of many hearts may be revealed." ' Luke 2:33–35 or, 'Jerusalem which is above is free, which is the mother of us all' Galatians 4:26 (BCP)

Our mothers

It's Mothers' Day today. (There are flowers for the children to bring to their mothers in the congregation, a token of love and respect.) Mothering Sunday is the old name for today; a day for thinking about mothers, our own mothers, what we owe to them.

Let us remember with love their care, their patience, their examples, and above all their love for us. It is a good time to recall also how we have behaved towards them – do we – did we – really show them the love and affection they deserve? Do we understand something at least of their concerns and their problems, their difficulties, and the often immense effort needed to overcome those difficulties?

Jesus' mother

It will help if for a moment or so we consider the mother who is probably the best-known mother of them all: Mary the mother of Jesus, and her care and her love and her example. She is brought before us in Lent by the Church's commemoration of two events. One is the week after next, when Mary is brought before us on 25 March, the festival of the Annunciation, overshadowed this year by the closeness of Palm Sunday (Mary would be the last to complain, in her meekness and modesty).

An example

What an example of faith and trust she shows us, as she is given God's message – that she, of all people, has been chosen by him to play such an important part in his plan of salvation for the world.

'Behold the handmaid of the Lord.' Without that reply, without her acceptance, without her decision, freely made, God's special plan for the redemption of the world would have been frustrated.

Like mother, like child, we might well say; mothers and children, children and parents – reflect each other, for good or for error. In our children do we not see so much of ourselves reflected – our attitudes, our characters, our ideas, our ideals and hopes? If we ourselves tend to be weak, not honest, insecure, we may be certain that these qualities will show up in our children.

Contrariwise, let us be loving, faithful, honest, true – then these qualities, indeed all our qualities, will show up in our young people.

So, what a responsibility lies upon the mothers – oh yes, and

the fathers too, parenthood is a joint concern, let us remember –
in the wider meaning, of course, taking in teachers, clergy, all who
set examples, all who have the power and the opportunity to guide
and develop the young. Pray for all these, give them, Lord, courage
and faith, trust and love, and let them find these qualities in us
too. May these qualities grow in them, and may they want and
care to reflect them in themselves.

> *Heavenly Father, whose blessed Son shared at Nazareth*
> *the life of an earthly home:*
> *help us to live as the holy family,*
> *united in love and obedience,*
> *and bring us at last to our home in heaven;*
> *through Jesus Christ our Lord.*

PHG 60 p. 353

Harvest Festival

'Fear not, O land; be glad and rejoice, for the Lord has done great things!'
Joel 2:21

Thanksgiving

Our theme today, at our Harvest Festival, must be 'Thanksgiving'.
We give thanks to God for the material provision for all the needs
that we have, under the gift of God; and for the work of all other
human beings who contribute to the harvest in the fields and in
the seas, to the delivery of the goods in our shops and markets,
and all that we take home for satisfying our necessities and replen-
ishing our physical needs.

Harvest is a co-operative effort, we should always remember.
In the first place, of course, without the created earth and its fruits
and riches, we should not be able to exist. And without the labours
and skills of human minds and hands, assisted with the remarkable machinery and equipment of both land and sea, we would
not be able to have and enjoy those fruits and riches as we do.

Working together

Think of the farmer's labours, with grain and stock day in and out, in good weather and in bad, suffering from infections and disease in the animals that we now know so much about. Think too of the fishermen who venture out in good weather and bad, in spite of restrictions on the quantities of fish that may be caught, as laid down by politicians under pressures from other countries. Think too of the shippers and dockers and carriers by rail and road who contrive to bring the varied harvests to our towns and villages. And of the preparers, canners and freezers, packers, butchers and bakers, shopkeepers and supermarkets, who make all these good things available to us. Nor should we forget the electricians, the gas men, the water men and all the others concerned with keeping our lights and heating going, and those who meet our many other needs.

Inter-dependent

What a vast and inter-dependent network it all adds up to. Indeed, it is only when things go wrong, when there is a sudden frost spell, when roads and rail are iced up, or when there is a strike by some essential workers, that we realize just how many people and how much effort and skill is involved in provision for our daily lives and daily needs.

Let us therefore give thanks, in a free and generous spirit, for all these good things, and for all the effort and equipment, skill and knowledge, that go into providing what we need for our daily lives.

The Eucharist

So we give thanks for these things and for those people who contribute to our lives and our living – but not for these alone, nor only upon this one day in the year.

For let us remember that every Eucharist is indeed a 'harvest festival'. Do we not, at every celebration, bring bread and wine, creatures of God's gifts and the work of human hands, to be offered? And is not every Eucharist also a thanksgiving for our redemption, for God's provision for our spiritual growth and welfare, as well as for materialistic needs?

Indeed, surely the beginning of the true harvest is Our Lord Jesus Christ himself, for he is really and truly the first-fruits of mankind.

The final harvest

And let us remember also the 'final harvest', the harvest of our immortal souls. We, if we are good corn, useful and of good quality, will indeed be gathered into the Lord's barn, the barn which is his own body.

And so, in hope and in trust, and with thanks, we bring ourselves, our souls and bodies, to be a reasonable, holy and living sacrifice. And in this thanksgiving and in our grateful dependence, as we receive back the gifts offered, the bread and wine that become to us his Body and his Blood, so we are again renewed by his Cross, his Resurrection, his Triumph, so that we can take our places at the Harvest Supper of the Family of God.

Special Occasions (1)   A Sermon preached to the Worshipful Society of Apothecaries of London, in the Church of St Andrew-by-the-Wardrobe upon Master's Day, 12 October 1997, at 12 noon, by the Chaplain, the Revd Joanna Yates, MA.

'The Lord went before them, by day in the form of a pillar of cloud, to show them the way, and by night in the form of a pillar of fire, to give them light.' Exodus 13:22.
In the name of the Father, and of the Son, and of the Holy Ghost. Amen.

A visit to the zoo

I thought the best preparation for this service would be a visit to the zoo. I would prefer it if the animals, who share this world with us, were not locked up; but a well-run zoo, like London's, does perform functions in the preservation of species, in re-introduction to the wild, and in education – there is nothing like coming face to face, even at a discreet distance, with God's other creatures. Virtual reality is no substitute for a living, breathing animal!

And so it was. There were many of my favourites – like the sand cats, the penguins, and Josephine the hornbill, who is older than many of us here in church this morning. And of course the rhinos – normally one sees the less remarkable African rhinos, white or black, at the zoo, but I was in luck! For just passing through, in quarantine on their way to Whipsnade, there they were, tucked away next to the giraffes, two young Greater One-Horned Indian Rhinoceroses – rare creatures, exotic in their armour-plating, but with placid bovine expressions on their faces. They looked beautiful – at least in rhino terms – they were indeed fearfully and wonderfully made. Rare creatures indeed, since there are not many more than two thousand of them left in the wild. Their numbers have been seriously reduced by poaching for their horns, used, alas, in traditional oriental medicine.

Our rhinoceros

Once upon a time powdered rhino-bone was prized in Western medicine, too; and thus the rhinoceros became the symbol of the Worshipful Society of Apothecaries. You can see him at Apothecaries' Hall on many items – on the badges which some of us are privileged to wear, modelled in silver, and in that splendid engraving by Albrecht Durer. Durer had never seen Gomda, the rhino in the picture, but his portrait is almost completely accurate, and the texture of his armour-plating is just right. It's a superb work of art, just as the original animal is a superb work of the Creator's art. To quote Psalm 104:

'O Lord, how manifold are thy works: in wisdom hast thou made them all; the earth is full of thy riches.'

Medical knowledge has come a long way since our Society adopted the greater one-horned Indian Rhino as our emblem – and so have attitudes to the created world, and to the stewardship which humanity is called upon to exercise. We are on a journey which is corporate as well as collective and individual, a journey of discovery, knowledge and understanding; scholars, scientists and saints have contributed to that knowledge down the centuries, and are contributing now, as we travel along.

God's people

The journey of God's people – the pilgrim people – has a long history. Our First Lesson today came from the book Exodus, the story of deliverance which resonates through Jewish and Christian tradition. The people of Israel are travelling, with much difficulty, from captivity in Egypt to freedom in the Land of Promise. They are not struggling alone, but are constantly led and supported by God – represented in the daytime by a pillar of cloud (which is a sign of God's presence in the Gospels, as well as in the Hebrew Bible), and a pillar of fire at night, standing for light and life. Our first hymn echoed that – 'Guide me, O thou great Redeemer'. This is one of those stirring Welsh hymns, to be included on Master's Day – when the new Master is of Welsh origin!

The link
Whether the words are Welsh or English, the link with Exodus is clear:

'Let the fiery cloudy pillar lead me all my journey through.'

God is their leader, and ours, on the journey through life; he is both leader and supporter, giving the pilgrims the bread of heaven – the manna which the people of Israel found in the wilderness. Christians see in this a reference to the Eucharist; but for all who believe in God the 'Bread of Heaven' has a wider application, standing for everything which spiritually sustains us.

That is not only for Christians, not just for a particular set of people, though we are taking part in a Christian service, in a Christian setting, today. Other faiths are represented here, but there is no need for any individual faith to be watered down in a misguided attempt to placate those whose beliefs are different, or who have no religious belief. An important discovery has been made in recent years on our journey – say, during the last twenty years – as people have begun to come to terms with a multi-cultural society.

It is that, trying to find a lowest common denominator of faith does not work, and pleases no one. 'No apology for theology' is a good motto to have; it comes from the world of religious education and church schools, where I have some experience.

Welcome
The Christian ethos, combined with respect for all faiths, makes everyone feel welcome and valued – and both children and adults on their journey are sustained. Inclusiveness of spirit is vital – St Peter discovered that, as was reported in our second lesson today, from the Acts of the Apostles, traditionally the work of the doctor-evangelist, St Luke. Peter came to realize (and it may have been a painful journey of discovery) that 'his' God is the universal God for all people:

'Of a truth I perceive that God is no respecter of persons [has no partiality] but in every nation anyone who fears him and worketh righteousness [does what is right] is accepted with him [acceptable to him]' (Acts 10:34).

Working righteousness – doing what is right – is to be our occupation on the journey, if we accept the challenge. In our second lesson, doing good is bracketed with healing. 'Jesus of Nazareth went about doing good and healing all that were oppressed of the devil' (Acts 10:38).

That is a way of describing psychological disturbance, and it reminds us that there is healing of body, mind and spirit to be done. This is not a new idea at all – Aristotle, in the fourth century BC, wrote of the need for psychological integration – but it has been given more publicity in recent years – in the hospice movement, for instance. My other chaplaincy is a part-time post as one of a multi-faith team of ten at the North London Hospice. This is run on the principles of multi-disciplinary care for the physical, psychological, social and spiritual well-being of the patients and their families, and the staff. I'm sure this is not unusual.

'Beloved physician'

We are not quite in St Luke's Tide yet – his feast day is on Saturday (18 October) – but it is the time of year when the Church remembers the 'beloved physician', as St Paul calls him. St Luke was indeed something of a multi-disciplinary man himself, if tradition is correct and he was an artist, a painter, as well as a doctor and a writer. There is in London a hospital named after him, where clergy, their families, and church workers are treated; consultants give their services free. This is just one example of working righteousness, though there are many more in the daily lives of members of the medical profession.

I am not being starry-eyed; I realize that for anyone in the medical profession, the personal journey often seems to be a trek 'through the night of doubt and sorrow', in the words of a hymn which we have not sung today, for the theme of our service is rightly praise, thanksgiving and celebration. We know that all is not perfect; the visionary William Blake reminded us of that in our second hymn: the heavenly Jerusalem has not yet been built in this or any other land. All is not perfect yet, but much good has been done, and there has been much healing of all kinds on our journey, in our pilgrimage, so far – and there is more to come.

May all creation – not forgetting the Greater One-Horned Indian Rhinoceros, and all our fellow creatures – join in the great hymn of praise, Psalm 150: 'Let everything that hath breath praise the Lord!'

Special Occasions (2)   A Sermon preached by Dr Joyce Critchlow, member of Buxton Team Ministry

'If you are able!' Mark 9:23

Able and willing?

'You *can* do it, if you really *want* to!' Time and again, our parents say this when we are children. Standing between us and success, so often, is that little thing we call 'will'. It isn't really a little thing: sometimes it's so big, it takes a lot of motivating; a tremendous 'plus of determination', as the psychologists phrase it, to get it up and doing: a real effort of will, to get the wheels rolling.

Mañana

At times, we are more willing to 'prioritize' than to go full steam ahead at a task. Well, we call it prioritizing, but usually it is sheer procrastinating – doing what we'd rather do, before tackling a less welcome, or more difficult task. Many Southern Europeans and Latin Americans have a good word for it: 'Mañana' (tomorrow). Mañana, Mañana – and, if Mañana doesn't come, so be it.

On the spot

In this Markan pericope, we find Jesus being 'put on the spot'. From the nerve-tingling drama of the Transfiguration, He comes down to the plain and right into the real world. His disciples are jerked out of their dreamy wonderment, by the man with the epileptic son. 'If you are able,' says the distracted man. What a thing to say to God! But Jesus, loving Saviour that he is, doesn't slate the man for his ham-fisted approach. In good Jewish tradition, he meets challenge with challenge: 'If *you* can believe . . .'

It's a challenge God is forever asking us.

All things are possible

Consistency compels us to take these words of Jesus into our lives. We accept him, we accept his saving grace, his blood of atonement. We accept what he tells us about a God of love. So, in fairness if nothing else, we have to accept that when he says '*all* things are possible' to those who believe, *all* things really *are* possible.

Making mountains?

Have we not all, at times, implied with our actions, our resistance, if not in actual words: 'Look here, I've got a mix-up that even GOD can't sort out!'? Perhaps we have not even rolled the problem over on to him. Perhaps we think it's so mundane, it's for us to sort it out. Perhaps we think we've done something bad, and that the problem in question is only just and fair retribution or reprimand. Perhaps we think God is not a fairy godfather, and there would be no 'magic' solution, anyway. And so we have times – heart-wrenching, traumatic times – when we seem to walk alone: when God appears not to answer: times when we can empathize with Jesus' anguished: 'My God, why have you forsaken me?'

The way ahead

It has been said that although sometimes God may seem slow in coming to our rescue, he never comes too late. The father had struggled with his epileptic son for years. Yet one day a man came down the mountain, and his son was healed. There comes a time, sooner or later, when we *need* the Lord more than anything else: more than all our reasoning and strivings and logic. And he is there.

Let us 'do parley'

A precious bit of Scripture tells us, no matter how small or large our problem is, God wants to hear about it: not just a desperate, last-minute: 'Lord, help!' (though we'll have a lot of those arrow-prayers sprinkled along our spiritual journey), but a really businesslike commitment: 'Come, now,' says the Lord, 'let us reason together' (Isaiah 1:18). You have a problem? *Get yourself prepared to talk God into solving it*. Marshall your arguments, weigh your pros and cons, get all your data into some semblance of order – and do business with God as thoroughly and carefully as you'd prepare for a job interview, or even a Church Council meeting

where you're going to have to get a point across despite opposition.

God is reasonable!
God is a reasonable God, and he has not created automatons. He
invites us to plead with him, to show real dedication, fervour,
interest and stickability in our prayers – whatever it takes.
St Augustine's mother, Monica, prayed for the conversion of her
pagan husband, for nearly twenty years, and for Augustine's
conversion for twenty-two years. How the Christian world has
benefited from her fervour and dedication!

God can change his mind
We must remember God himself is not an automaton. He reserves
the right to change his mind. He is open to persuasion, and can
be moved by his people's pleas. Remember Abraham, and how
he interceded for the inhabitants of Sodom; Moses, and how he
pleaded against the annihilation of the carping, sinning Israelites
in the wilderness.
   'If you are able . . .'
   God can do anything and everything.

Special Occasions (3)   Sermon at the Chrism
Eucharist for the Edmonton Area, Diocese of London,
on Maundy Thursday, 27 March 1997. Preacher: The
Right Reverend Brian Masters M.A., Area Bishop.
Preached in the Parish Church of All Hallows, Gospel
Oak.
'The Spirit of the Lord is upon me, because the Lord has anointed me.'
Isaiah 61:1

There can be no doubt that the office and work of a priest in
today's Church is something very hard to get right in a balanced
way. Going the rounds recently, I am told, has been this somewhat
depressing account of 'The Priest in the Parish:'

*'If the priest preaches for more than ten minutes, he's too
    long-winded.*

*If his sermon is short, he's too easy-going and lazy in his
    preparation.*

If his parish funds are low, he's financially inept.

*If he keeps mentioning money, he's too grasping, and concerned for
    wrong things.*

If he visits his parishioners, he's never at home.

If he doesn't, he's stand-offish.

If he runs bazaars and fund-raising events, he's bleeding his people.

If he doesn't, his parish is lacking social life.

If he starts a service on time, his watch must be fast.

If he's a bit late, he's holding up the congregation.

If he decorates the church, he's spending too much.

If he doesn't, he's letting everything run down.

If he's young, he's inexperienced.

If he's old, he should have retired.

*If he dies, well, he was a potential Archbishop! And we'll never see
    his like!'*

Well, as we look at our priestly ministries year by year, doubtless
many of us wonder whether we might more profitably have learnt
at college basic plumbing, say, or electrical or carpentry skills, or
basic accountancy, rather than church history, liturgy or hermen-
eutics. We are all tempted, from time to time, to see the true role
of the priest as the 'great all-rounder' who gets everything done;
and maybe the greatest besetting sin of any priest is that of a
constant busy-ness.

Reflection

However, each year as we come together on Maundy Thursday
at the Eucharist for the blessing of the oils and the renewal of our
priestly vows, we are given an opportunity to reflect more deeply
on our understanding of priesthood, both in relation to God and
in our service to Church and World. Let us be brought back into
touch with that initial, fresh, sense of vocation which first inspired
us to offer ourselves, in response to the call of God, to serve him
in the sacred ministry. It can be easy in the cut and thrust of parish
life to lose touch with that exciting and insistent call, which for
some of us came many years ago; yet to serve our God in the

priesthood, and to be a steward of his mysteries, is indeed a great privilege and a great joy.

In today's liturgy, we come together to consecrate the oil of Chrism, the oil which is closely associated with the consecration of the whole of life to God, and specifically with priesthood. Let us reflect for a few moments on how our lives are consecrated to God, and how we receive the anointing of his Holy Spirit to give us power in all that we undertake in his name.

Rediscovery

In recent decades the ancient use of oils in the Church has been rediscovered, and is now a valued part of the mainstream life of the Church of England. Through the outward act of anointing with oil in Old Testament times, so were set apart prophets, priests and kings by God – the God who had a special purpose for their lives in the service of his people. The oil was a 'sacramental sign' of the grace of God, freely bestowed upon those called to serve him and follow him in an entire consecration of life.

With such a rich background in the anointing of prophets, priests and kings, it is little surprise that Our Lord Jesus Christ, as the long-awaited Messiah and King of Israel, should see his ministry as anointed by the spirit and power of God. In the synagogue at Nazareth he claimed that ancient prophesy of Isaiah to himself, and announced to all his hearers that the acceptable Day of the Lord had come – the dawn of our salvation. 'The Spirit of the Lord is upon me, because God has anointed me ... today in your very hearing, this text has come true.' The anointed One then embarked on his ministry – preaching good news to the poor, release for prisoners, sight to the blind, freedom to broken victims. That ministry, graced by the anointing power of God, was yet one which was to lead to Calvary, the destiny and destination of his life's work. There as he hung outstretched upon the wood of the Cross (the only throne he had on earth) his whole life of service and sacrifice was crowned by the supreme sacrifice – the shedding of his blood, by which the salvation of the world was obtained.

Fire of Love

Truly, anointing and sacrifice were bound closely together in the life of Our Lord and Saviour: he who inflames our hearts with the fire of his love, and who gives us power through the ministry of Word and Sacrament, to draw others to his sublime love.

How appropriate, then, that the Blessing of the oils should take place in Holy Week, on the day that he shared the Last Supper with his disciples, and on the day before his death upon the Cross, when his whole life was crowned as the anointed One of Israel, who would lead his people back to their God. Anointing and sacrifice, then, are two great marks of our Saviour's life and of his death.

As priests of the Church of God, our own lives must surely be characterized by anointing and sacrifice. Anointing as a sign of the inward anointing and empowering by God, and the outward 'setting apart' to serve him by Word and Sacrament – to enable the whole People of God to be the people that he intends us to be. And sacrifice – our lives as priests must be lived in such a way that the love of God shines through us, and that we always point beyond ourselves, to Calvary and salvation.

Service and Sacrifice

The Cross is the ultimate symbol of sacrifice, of God's power in human weakness, which puts to shame ambitious quest for power and influence in our Church and in our world. Our priestly lives, then, must be lives of service and sacrifice, that enable people to walk the Way of the Cross, so that they may rise with the Lord in his Resurrection of Light and Joy.

So my friends, as today you return to the busy and even hectic lives of your parishes, remember that initial and exciting sense of vocation that made you seek ordination to the priesthood. And remember always the two marks of our Saviour's life – crucified Redeemer and anointed King – **sacrifice** and **the power of God**, and allow your priesthood to be renewed so that we might indeed rejoice in our Saviour, the Saviour of the whole world

B.M.

The Rt Revd Brian Masters died on 23 September 1998
(Born 17 October 1932)
May he rest in peace.